WINGS
OVER
ITALY

To Dennis 'Gus' Varey 1922–2007

A brave RAF pilot and beloved uncle. Thank you for the handmade wooden toys at Christmas, being whisked away to model railway shows, visits to Duxford and the Yorkshire Air Museum.

WINGS OVER ITALY

THE STORY OF FLIGHT SERGEANT DENNIS VAREY and 260 SQUADRON FROM EL ALAMEIN TO THE LIBERATION OF EUROPE

PAUL DAWSON

AIR WORLD

AIR WORLD

WINGS OVER ITALY
The Story of Flight Sergeant Dennis Varey and 260 Squadron from
El Alamein to the Liberation of Europe

First published in Great Britain in 2025 by
Air World
An imprint of
Pen & Sword Books Ltd
Yorkshire – Philadelphia

ISBN 978 1 03613 578 2

Typeset by SJmagic DESIGN SERVICES, India.

Printed and bound in the UK by CPI Group (UK) Ltd.

The Publisher's authorised representative in the EU for product safety is Authorised Rep Compliance Ltd., Ground Floor, 71 Lower Baggot Street, Dublin D02 P593, Ireland. www.arccompliance.com

For a complete list of Pen & Sword titles please contact

PEN & SWORD BOOKS LIMITED
George House, Units 12 & 13, Beevor Street, Off Pontefract Road,
Barnsley, South Yorkshire, S71 1HN, England
E-mail: enquiries@pen-and-sword.co.uk
Website: www.pen-and-sword.co.uk

or

PEN AND SWORD BOOKS
1950 Lawrence Rd, Havertown, PA 19083, USA
E-mail: uspen-and-sword@casematepublishers.com
Website: www.penandswordbooks.com

MIX
Paper | Supporting
responsible forestry
FSC® C013604

CONTENTS

ACKNOWLEDGEMENTS

SITTING AT DUXFORD, 14 September 2024, a pair of Mustangs dance across the azure blue sky, criss-crossed by white mares' tails. The Mustangs hang in the air, zoom, roll and dive. I've known about P-51 Mustangs all my life. Needless to say, the P-51 features large in this book.

This book explores the story of 260 Squadron RAF. Never heard of it? It should be one of the most famous RAF outfits of the Second World War. Why? For film fans, this was the squadron Christopher Lee served with for the majority of his wartime service. Secondly, 260 was one of the 'crack' fighter-bomber squadrons of the war in any theatre. Thirdly, its men had both an avaricious appetite for beer and good food, as much as bravery in the face of the Germans. As this book shows, half a dozen pilots, when forced to bail out or crash-land, escaped from German custody and made a bid for freedom. Fourthly, among the pilots were a clutch of aces, notably James Francis Edwards DFC DFM, Canada's highest scoring ace of the war, and Australian ace Ron Cundy DFC DCM: 260 was a cosmopolitan squadron, its pilots and ground crew came from all corners of the globe, counting Welsh, Scottish, English, South African, New Zealand and Americans on its muster list. Its Pilots' Mess was famed for its good food, cold beer and egalitarian nature.

I have known of 260 Squadron for nearly all my adult life. My uncle Dennis had flown with the squadron. This book charts his war, and of the pilots and ground crew of that squadron from El Alamein to victory in 1945.

I am indebted to Gillian and Martyn Marley for making Dennis's archive papers available to me, and for their support of this project. It has given me an opportunity to get to know my uncle again. It has been an emotional rollercoaster: seeing the name of a family member in historical records is a strange feeling.

Dilip Sarkar MBE is to be thanked for his advice and help in locating archive material. A friend of over forty summers, Dr P. Judkins, an internationally recognised Second World War specialist, has to be thanked for his moral support and answering seemingly endless, banal questions. Sally Fairweather must be thanked for her patience, support, research assistance and love in all my endeavours. James Oglethorpe of 3 Squadron Royal Australian Air Force is to be thanked for allowing me to quote material from that squadron's archives https://www.3sqnraafasn.net.

So too the good people at the 112 Squadron website. I am also indebted to guides at RAF Museum Hendon and the Imperial War Museum, Duxford, for answering queries and provision of notes about aircraft and items in their care.

Disclaimer

I have relied heavily on material obtained by electronic communication and written letter on or before 31 March 2004 and 12 May 2005 – the dates of the first and second draft of the text 'Wakefield Memories' and 'Wakefield's Military Heritage' – with Lionel Shepphard, Mervyn Talbot, William Cundy, James Edwards, directly with them or via third party, as well as seeking their permission to reproduce published material. I have endeavoured, as far as possible, to contact families/agents of the above about the project. I hope their representatives are supportive of their loved one's words appearing in print after being collated twenty years ago or more. I have used my own transcript of publicly available and digital interviews of veterans from the squadron.

INTRODUCTION

THE DOORBELL RINGS. It is early Easter 2004. A white BMW has driven past. At the door, I am greeted by the familiar shape of my uncle Dennis. Tall, brown hair turned grey, pipe clenched in his teeth 'which one are you, Paul or Anthony?' 'It's Paul uncle Dennis,' I replied. A standard question being an identical twin. The family got together several times a year for 'cousins tea parties', but this meeting was special. I had spoken with Dennis and the family about their wartime memories – both on the front and in action – on two occasions in the second half of 2003, for what would be my second book, *Wakefield Memories*, published in August 2005. The family all met together several times during the course of 2004 to 'put finishing touches' to what would be a written testimony of my family. In preparing this book, it planted the germ of an idea about writing a book about wartime memories, and I asked my uncle Dennis if I could talk to him specifically about his war. We met several times. Prior to my grandmother's last illness, he would call once a month to see her: Dennis was my grandmother's oldest friend, after her sister Shirley of course. He was both family and a friend.

Forty-eight books later, I return to my notes and collated material from over twenty summers ago. Dennis was a man with a zest for life, a twinkle in his eye and a store of saucy jokes. Here was a fighter pilot. My grandfather, Rex, had volunteered in 1943 as a boy sailor of fifteen, but by the time he had completed his basic training and fitting out of his ship, R68 HMS *Ocean* – which became operational in August 1945 – the war was over. Uncles Eric and Jim, had both served, one with the Indian Army, a Major of the Staff in Bombay, his brother in Burma, a POW since Singapore, like a cousin by marriage, Lister Simpson. None of them talked about their war.

As the first grandchildren in the family, we became the centre of attention for a collective of aunts, uncles and cousins you could reckon up in dozens. As a child growing up, my twin and I were raised by our grandparents Rex and Jeane, to allow our mother, a single mum who escaped an abusive marriage, to earn a living. We were often 'farmed out' to family to give our grandparents and very aged great-grandmother Lily some respite. On one occasion we were farmed out to Dennis.

Often it was to our aunt Shirley, so going to Dennis was an event, one that became engraved in my twin and I's collective memory.

My uncle lived close to Normanton brick works. An electrician cum engineer at the local hospital, after he retired he volunteered at the hospital where he had worked with my aunt Shirley taking library books around the wards. The quarry and his home were full of cats. He and his wife Mary were animal lovers, and Dennis worked hard to find homes for the cats and kittens. My own first cat came from Dennis, as did my aunt Rachel's cat. Dennis was a beloved family member, as my aunt Rachel remembers, 'with a wicked sense of humour.' I can't remember how old we were, but Anthony – my twin – and I were left with Dennis for a day. It may have been for a school project. After playing trains, we were nestled on his lap – or at least perched either side on the settee – by the art deco fireplace in his sitting room. Loading his pipe – which he was invariably never far from – he took from a bookcase a large, almost A4 landscape book, and a similar sized photograph album. 'If your bad boys,' he grinned, 'don't forget I flew in the same squadron in the war as Dracula.' He then showed us his photographs and told us of his story: for avid readers of Biggles, this was a young chaps very own personal and direct encounter with Biggles. This was better than any book. We went home with our aunt Rachel – she lived at home with us, grandparents and great-grandmother – filled with wonders of dogfights and tales of daring and bravery. Now aircraft obsessed, Dennis and another uncle – also an RAF veteran – took us to Duxford and local air museums like Elvington. I remember visiting Duxford for either the 50th Anniversary of D-Day or VE Day: in the workshop hanger was a Kittyhawk under repair. My twin and I were entertained to a personal discussion of the aircraft and its 'terrible engine'. I think words like 'couldn't pull the skin of a rice pudding' was used in referring to the Allison engines lack of power. Of course, for fancy dress at school for red nose day, it was a tussle who would go as Dennis. I won, and was allowed to borrow Dennis's wings. My twin wore my grandfather's navy 'flat top' sailors cap from HMS *Ocean*. The aircraft obsession lingered and was encouraged by the father of my twin and I's best friend at school, Dr P. Judkins. We went to Elvington with him and his father who flew as RCAF at RAF Holme, where I was to discover my uncle Dennis also flew from at almost the same time. Happenstance?

I have one apology to make with this book. It appears at a time when 260 Squadron has slipped from memory into history. A career in archaeology, researching and writing extensively on Napoleonic subjects, as well as the thing called 'life', transpired to delay completion of this book. It was further delayed when I suffered a Severe Traumatic Brain Injury, the complications of which linger after nearly a decade. It was not until July 2023, on the way back from a research trip at The National Archives, that my twin, his partner and I, decided to call in at RAF Museum Hendon. I was stopped in my tracks by a Kittyhawk with a shark mouth. It 'rang alarm bells' in my head. I could hear my uncles voice telling me about the lads from 112 Squadron who painted shark mouths on their kites. I had promised to write a book on 260 Squadron. Better late than never! I need to thank John Grehan at Frontline for supporting my research endeavours over the past decade and, more importantly, supporting the publication of this book in homage to my uncle, but also to all those who served in the Italian theatre. I hope it is a fitting tribute to those who died with 260 Squadron, and their names 'liveth for ever more.'

I hope the reader craves my indulgence, and that the story of 260 is interesting, and its exploits ask more questions than answers.

Celer et Fortis

(strong and swift, the motto of 26 Squadron)

Paul L. Dawson, Wakefield, Battle of Britain day, 15 September 2024

REMEMBERING'S

HOW DOES ONE start a book like this? Why am I compelled to write? For many the Second World War is Dunkirk, the Battle of Britain and D-Day: all important milestones in the war and worthy of commemoration. But these episodes are just a small part of a global conflict. However, without the Battle of Britain, no further battles would have been fought. Its importance cannot be understated. Indeed, on 19 September 1944, 260 Squadron received the following dispatch which acknowledged:

> On 15 September 1940, the Royal Air Force shot down 185 enemy aircraft over Great Britain. It was the crucial day of the Battle of Britain and the feat made certain of subsequent victory. Now four years later, in the flood tide of total victory, let us remember those who fought and triumphed against odds and who gave to us and to our Allies time to create and marshal the great forces of the United Nations which are now sweeping forward all over the world.

As contemporaries at the time acknowledged, the Battle of Britain was the turning point of the war. The story of the battle has been excellently told by Dilip Sarkar in his multiple volumes that chart the battle day by day. Yet, as we noted earlier, the other theatres in this global conflict have slipped from public consciousness.

D-Day would not have happened had it not been for the North African Campaign and lessons learned in Italy. The Italian campaign is 'the poor relation', especially the air war, when compared to the Battle of Britain, 617 Squadron and Bomber command.

The story of the air war in Italy, as my introduction said, is something I have known about since an early age. But what was the campaign really like? How were pilots trained? How did it feel to fly in flak day after day? I hope this homage – a love story in a way – to my uncle and his colleagues goes some way to answering those questions, and brings this episode of the war to life for the reader. Dennis's experience of war on the home front was similar to many millions. His wartime service was, like for countless tens of thousands of others, unexceptional: not a hero in the traditional sense, 'he got on with the job'; he was 'an everyday hero' although he would deny the last part. His active participation was cut short through being wounded in action. His story, however, is important; not just to me. His experience of the air war in Italy and of his comrades in arms is a compelling story of triumph in adversity; in some cases of incredible bravery. The story of these 'D-Day Dodgers', brings to the fore the importance of the air campaign in Italy, and how that campaign shaped future air operations to the present time.

Wakefield

Dennis Varey was born on 5 March 1922, son of John Frederick Varey. His mother, Nellie, was the eldest daughter of James Harvey (1866-1950), a native of Swadlincote, Derbyshire, and his wife Alice Pollitt (1867-1964). 'Grandpa Jim' was manager of Wakefield businessman John Archer's cocoa matting manufacturer at Westgate Common. Archer had married Elizabeth Harvey, 'Grandpa Jims' older sister. A gifted musician, James Harvey had been choirmaster at Westgate End Wesleyan Chapel, where the Harvey family, as well as the Archers, worshipped for over 100 years. Nellie was one of five daughters. Her brother Joseph had died soon after birth. She was born in 1893, sister Lilly followed in 1895, Mary in 1897, Clarice in 1900 and Ruth in 1905. Dennis's cousins, Jeane (the authors grandmother) and Shirley, daughters of Lilly (1895-1984) and her husband Charles Henry Drake (1894-1964), local businessman and entrepreneur, were close friends from childhood; so too cousins Jim and Eric Bradley, sons of his aunt Mary and Clement Bradley a First World War veteran who lost a leg at Gallipoli. Chapel dominated family life: women's league outings, Sunday School trips to Buxton and elsewhere, tennis, and a myriad of other activities. The family lived at School Crescent in a house completed in 1924, part of what was considered to be the Lupset Garden Village of council houses. This was a semi-detached house, with a large garden to front and rear, just off Broadway Avenue, the main road through the estate. Described as a 'Parlour House type A' it had a living room and scullery downstairs, and three bedrooms upstairs, rented from the council for 10s 0d a week. The bath was under the scullery work table, the toilet was outside next to the coal store. Dennis had been educated at Thornes House School in Wakefield till the age of fourteen. Another cousin by marriage, Wilfred J. Emery (1904-1964), had taught Dennis music and mathematics at Thornes House: 'Uncle Wilf' also played the organ at Chapel and with Eric Bradley at Christmas conducted community carol singing. 'Uncle Wilf' later became a Unitarian, and organist at Mill Hill Chapel, in Leeds, much to family murmerings. Dennis completed his education at Silcoates school for two years, after which he took an apprenticeship with the Prudential in nearby Ossett.

In August 1939 Hitler had signed a non-aggression pact with the USSR. In reply, an Agreement of Mutual Assistance was signed with Poland. On Friday,

1 September, the Luftwaffe bombed the city of Wielun in Poland claiming 127 lives. As my grandmother, Jeane Cresswell nee Drake (1927-2005) recalled:

'August for an 11-year-old appears to have been a string of hot days spent cycling to Coxley Valley for picnics, swimming and playing tennis.

'Parents spent much time, as many would later, listening to the news bulletins and talking about the German invasion of Poland and the Baltic area – Danzig and the corridor were a major worry. All at school were advised by Miss Maris to carry on quietly in school and with their own business in as normal a way as possible. The Friday night (1 September), was spent lying with her sister and friends on the lawn of the family home watching a lone single engine plane fly over, which had to be a Spitfire even then! The last minutes of peace ticking away. From then on, the excitement rose, but parents became sadder and more resolute, they remembered and had fought in the Great War, the War to end all Wars, and their memories were horrendous and now it was happening again 'twenty years' was repeated again and again. The family had no sons, but I had older cousins who were of an age to go, indeed one, Eric [Bradley – ed], had been called up with the militia twelve months earlier.

'The Saturday passed and nothing. No Chapel on the Sunday morning added to the gloomy atmosphere of suspension.

'The wireless was turned on about 1050 and all sat down to wait out the last few minutes, an experience that many do not want to repeat. Then Neville Chamberlains serious voice came on the wireless to tell us and the world that the last hour of the ultimatum had passed and that we were therefore at war with Germany and her allies. Life for many seemed to stop that day, as though no one knew what to do next. In a way the news was a relief.

'The war began less with a bang than a whimper of apprehension.'

Thereafter, a sense of unreality took over with the sudden closure of cinemas and theatres, the cancellation of sporting events, and any event with a large crowd. Further publication information followed about air raid warnings, and the wearing of gas masks. My grandmother again:

'That night the air raid siren sounded nearly all over Britain, but it did not last long. My elderly grandmother, Alice Harvey, lived alone on Dewsbury Road, and during the raid one of her neighbours went to see that she was alright, to be very startled by just her head appearing round the door in its gas mask!'

Almost as soon as Chamberlain's speech ended, a Blenheim light bomber was the first aircraft of the RAF to fly over Germany, taking seventy-five reconnaissance photographs of German warships at Wilhelmshaven, west of Hamburg. The crew of the Blenheim returned home safe and sound; many of those who followed in their wake, were not so lucky. About the early wartime period Dennis remembered:

'1938-9 were tense times for all as Britain lurched from one crisis to another during Chamberlains efforts to appease Mussolini and Hitler, and soon the young men of the chapel were being registered for National Service. Initially, Douglas Wright, Eric and Jim Bradley were mobilised. When war broke out there was a succession of young people and teachers being called to the forces. Once the initial excitement had died down, blackout and other precautions became routine. I was seventeen when war broke out.

'The fear of mass bombing meant that most homes by 1940 had bomb shelters. The shelters were very sturdy, made from corrugated steel, and sunk into the earth. Some of the shelters on Lupset were concreted in by the council, so they were dry. Not every house had one; I think it was a personal choice. Some houses which did not have gardens, or the occupiers were elderly, had Morrison shelters. They were like a large metal box with a thick steel top, strong legs at each corner and mesh sides. One neighbour had hers in the front room and disguised it with a table cloth. People who lived in the city centre terraces with literally one or two rooms on each floor, in a back-to-back, used the cupboard under the stairs, there being no cellar or communal shelter. One of these was under Westgate Railway station: the sign is still painted on what remains of the old station. You sheltered in the arches underneath the station, assuming that it was not hit by a bomb: the station and goods yard made a perfect target. Next to the shelters was an old burial ground: I suppose if the shelter had been hit, it made it easier to bury the dead [laughter], nice and convenient.

'Some Anderson shelters were built on land towards Snapethorpe Hospital, off Gissing Road. Our Anderson shelter was very wet, but our neighbours wasn't. You either died from pneumonia sitting in the shelter, had the possibility of drowning if a bomb landed nearby and you fell in the muddy water, or you took the risk and stayed indoors, or more often than not we went to next doors and used our neighbours. The corrugated steel was good stuff. If you could get some flat sheets, and a couple of Anderson shelters, you could make a very sturdy garage in an afternoon, all you needed was some bolts and basic tools. Some folk of course kept theirs after the war and made them into potting sheds to keep their lawn mower and other bits and bobs.

'Blackout was enforced by the local copper. Ours was PC Fisk 'Fiskey', if he had been in the police all his life, he would never have risen above the rank of constable. He was good for doing odd jobs, or fetching groceries mam had forgotten.'

Jeane Cresswell again:

'The blackout had come, and we were told that in the event of an air raid we must go under the table, a large sturdy oak affair, or under the piano, a boudoir grand with enormous legs. Later, the cellar was emptied out and the marble slabs were equipped with blankets and pillows, reminiscent of a morgue!

'That night the air raid siren sounded nearly all over Britain, but it did not last long. An elderly aunt, Ruth Harvey, lived alone on Dewsbury Road, and during the raid one of her neighbours went to see that she was alright – to be very startled by just her head appearing round the door in its gas mask!

'Autumn Term at school started again in the second week of September, on the fourteenth, to find that the greatest sin on the calendar was not having your gas mask with you at all times. For a while every lesson began with a gas mask check. Later, it became a registration ceremony which lasted until the last days of the war. If you had forgotten it you were sent home to retrieve it. Gas Mask drills, putting them on, chin first and the straps over your head, staff in theirs checking straps. They smelt horrible, puffing and blowing to see that you had a good seal, moving around a little to get used to wearing them, became part of the timetable. Miss Frampton was always meticulous. Sticky white paper criss-crossed the windows to prevent flying glass. Life settled down to normal, for an 11-year-old sitting in class and daily watching the flags move around a map of Europe the war virtually died until Dunkirk came and the Battle of Britain started. After Dunkirk, Wakefield rapidly filled with battered wrecks of men, all highly nervous, and it was not advisable to come up behind them quietly. Pemberton House and Vincent House, on Westgate near the station, were full of men often leaning from windows and calling out.

'The Lupset estate, and certainly others, all had men billeted on them and the hospital blue pyjamas of the wounded men from Pinderfields became a common sight around the town. About 180 evacuees arrived from the Channel Islands and Miss Maris put them up in the Jubilee Hall, pending the finding of permanent homes. The only difficulty was, where would they go in case of an air raid or emergency.'

Dennis Varey continues:

'When Dunkirk took place, trains had to be used to ferry thousands of troops from the south coast to holding camps further north. Railwaymen were called upon to work excessive hours to transport all those men from the beaches of Dunkirk. There were special Red Cross trains to transport those who were injured.

'The southern railwaymen were the ones who bore the brunt of the work and worked for days on end without a break. They then handed the trains over to the London North Eastern Railway and London Midland and Scottish Railway to take the men to the hospitals and reception camps.

'Railwaymen were the only workers who didn't receive danger money and were our unsung heroes during the Second World War. There was no organisation of the evacuated men and no order or system to it.

'I thought it would have been better to try and group men by regiment rather than splitting them all up all over the country. Trains pulled into Westgate and Kirkgate stations, and men would be put into groups, and then distributed all over Wakefield by the police in Lupset. Fiskey, or another copper, would come round and knock on the door, and say these men were billeted on you. We never had anyone billeted on us. It was a rather piecemeal affair.

'The first air attack on Wakefield was by a single German bomber on 28 August 1940. At 1.30 am the sirens sounded. I remember sitting on top of our Anderson shelter watching the bombs drop. If they had hit the council oil and petrol stores, half of Porto Bello would have gone with it; if the bomb aimer had dropped the 'eggs' five seconds either way, then the result would have been cataclysmic. The city had a lucky escape: just four houses in Norton Street, Belle Vue, were destroyed and the blast damaged many more. In one of the raids, Aunt Clarice was visiting with her daughter Joyce; as the sirens went both my mother and aunt tried to get through the shelter door at the same time, which was quite impossible. I came out of the house to see two bums wedged in the door. I found it hysterically funny.

'By now, the battle of Britain had been won, and was followed by the bombing of London, Birmingham, Coventry, Manchester, Liverpool, Hull, and of course the all-embracing South Coast.

I remember coming home from work in the early evening of 16 September 1940 when the sirens sounded. The war had come to Wakefield. That evening ten high explosive and forty incendiary bombs fell over the area from Clarence Park through Thornes Wharf to Barnsley Road, but most landed in open ground. One house, near Busy Corner on Barnsley Road, was demolished; one fireman was injured, the only death was the family's pet parrot! December 1940, three high explosive and twenty incendiary bombs fell on Wakefield. Probably these were dropped by bombers that had overshot their target. Amidst this came the Sheffield Blitz, when for several hours for two nights, I could see the reflection of the burning city in the sky, and could hear the bombers circling, and the local searchlights, one being at Snapethorpe School, quartered the sky looking for them. The skies would dull, the flashes of bombs exploding would be seen and the dull crump, crump crump, of the explosions heard and the sky flare up again.

'I celebrated my nineteenth birthday on Saturday, 5 March 1941, the day before Hitler tried to ensure I would not reach that milestone by sending his bombers to Wakefield. The explosions killed six, one of whom worked for Uncle Charlie at the works in the drawing office, the youngest was a 2-year-old child, the oldest an 80-year-old man, fifteen were injured, five seriously. Ten days later, on the night of 14/15 March 1941, Sheffield was once again the target for a significant part of the German bomber force. However, unlike the raids in December 1940, the Sheffield attack was not this time led by the expert German 'Pathfinder' crews (who used radio beams to navigate accurately). As a result, many of the German aircraft lost their way and attacked Leeds, Castleford and Wakefield among other places. Two large high-explosive bombs fell on Thornes Road, killing five. What had seemed distant and exciting was now literally on our door step. Mam, Uncle Charlie and your grandmother, were all in the firing line.'

About the March raid Jeane Cresswell recalls:

'Drake & Warters, builders and shop fitters, part-owned by my daddy [Charles Henry Drake – ed, 'uncle Charlie' in Dennis's reminiscences] had men working in Sheffield, and they told stories of going into the shelters at night and coming out in the morning to find the town around them literally gone; just piles and piles of smouldering rubble and worn-out air raid wardens, firemen and ambulance drivers coping as best they could. Within three weeks

I went to Sheffield and saw the unbelievable devastation, piles of rubbish with narrow roads cleared between them, and the smell of fire still everywhere.

'Leeds and Wakefield were very lucky. The chief designer of Drake & Warters, Hayden Suthill, was not frightened, but terrified of being called up, and as he was an essential member of staff, Daddy moved heaven and earth to have him reserved. He was only to die some weeks later outside his own gate in the raid on Thornes Road on the night of Friday, 4 March 1941. The bombs landed about 500 yards from The Golden Hind, the family home: we had a lucky escape, but not Mr Suthill: fate is far more important than fear or planning. One of the girl's homes in my class at the High School was damaged but not destroyed. I was tending my pony at Lupset farm when the raid started.

With the war coming to the streets he knew, Dennis volunteered into the RAF. The desire to 'do one's bit' led hundreds of thousands of men and women to volunteer into the services.

TO THE SKIES

FOR MANY IN 2024, military service offers a career, a chance to learn a trade that can be applied in 'Civvy Street'; my uncle joined up because the war had come to his home city:

> 'The call up age for the armed forces was twenty-one, however, they would take volunteers at the age of eighteen years. On reaching nineteen I decided to volunteer. I was the last of the Harvey boys to go: Eric and Jim had gone in 1939. I was told to report to the RAF volunteer reserve station in Huddersfield with about a dozen other lads, where we were given a test in English and Maths. I then had an interview with a warrant officer and was told that I would be accepted to be trained as aircrew. I officially joined the RAF on 27 November 1941. At the end of December 1941, I was passed as Air Observer and co-pilot. I was aircraftsman 2nd class.
>
> 'Then we were taken to the station to catch a train to the RAF training camp at Padgate near Warrington, Lancashire. I was one member of an intake of raw recruits, completing induction forms, followed by a thorough medical examination and intelligence testing. We were immediately issued with our kit and uniform, and then had to march to our billets carrying our civilian suitcase, two kitbags, backpack, side pack and gas mask case, allocated a bed and locker, about thirty of us sharing a Nissen hut, and introduced to the sergeant instructor who was to become our "God and Mentor". His word was law!
>
> 'We were not prepared for the degree of physical fitness we were expected to achieve. At the end of the ten-week training course, I felt fitter than at any time in my life, either before or since. The foot drill, known as "square bashing", turned us into a well-disciplined company acting on orders with split second timing for no one dared to be out of step or sync. I did not mind the foot drill but the forced route marching with rifle and full pack was definitely not my "cup of tea."'

Another who passed through Padgate, albeit in early 1940, was Lionel James Sheppard. Born in 1921 and hailing from Newport in South Wales, he remembers:

'I had applied to join the RAF as air crew in 1940 – one hoped as a pilot – and was called to attend Padgate in the September of that year. Arriving on a Monday evening, I was informed I had to attend an Aircrew Board at 9a.m. the following morning. In the Board waiting room, I found two University graduates ahead of me, both a little older and obviously very much better educated. The interviewers were two civil servants and a group captain who acted as chairman.'

Shep, as he became known, recalled that he underwent intelligence testing and primarily mental arithmetic. Passing the board he had to submit to a medical, and then he would be joining an Initial Training Wing, with plenty of PT and square bashing. Asked if he could ride a horse, he replied no. Flying relies heavily on balance, and a horse rider, it was believed, had already developed the innate sense of balance needed to fly. Shep was accepted to be a pilot. Dennis recalled that a notice about pilot training was posted in March, and he was accepted on 27 April 1942. About initial training and pilot acceptance Dennis remembers:

'After the passing-out parade at the end of the course at Padgate I was told to report to the Aircrew Receiving Centre in St. John's Wood, London. We were marched here and there for inoculations, physical examinations, dental checks and the like. I was surprised that the ARC was located in London when one bomb could have wiped out hundreds of aircrew. The accommodation was in luxury flats in St. Johns Wood. They had been stripped of all their luxuries, but at least we had decent bathrooms and toilets and sheets on our beds. On the second day we all had a compulsory haircut. No comb and scissors affair, electric clippers straight over the top whether or not you gave the hairdresser a sixpenny tip. One airman was processed every ninety seconds.

'We were subjected to large doses of square bashing.

'Everyone had to try and swim a length of the baths and those who couldn't, received a crash course. Numerous tests were used to confirm our fitness to fly, including a night vision assessment. In this you were seated in a dark room on a chair with a restraining collar round your neck. You had to name the objects or shapes which appeared momentarily on a small screen in front of you.

'The food was good, but the discipline irksome and at times farcical.

'The interviews lasted for two days but I can't remember very much about them. I know we were given thorough medical and intelligence tests. We also had colour blindness and eye examinations. Only two out of every five recruits were selected for pilot training, so I considered myself fortunate to have passed the recruiting board, I was pleased to be accepted on 4 July 1942. Being accepted gave me the rank of leading aircraftsman.

'I was immediately posted to Aircrew Disposal Wing Brighton. We were housed in the Metropole Hotel. After a week, I was on the move again to Personnel Despatch Centre which was located at West Kirby, just outside Liverpool. I sailed from a war devastated Liverpool for Southern Rhodesia on HMV *Rangitki*, I think on 26 July.'

RMS *Rangitiki* was a passenger liner owned by the New Zealand Shipping Company. She was one of three sister ships (the other sisters were *Rangitata* and *Rangitane*) delivered to the company in 1929 for the route between Britain and New Zealand. *Rangitiki* was built by John Brown & Company at Clydebank, Scotland and launched on 27 August 1928. At the start of the Second World War the ship was used for transporting children from Britain to Australia before being converted into a troopship. In November 1940 *Rangitiki* was the largest ship in Convoy HX 84 when the convoy was attacked by the German cruiser *Admiral Scheer*. *Rangitiki* and most other ships in the convoy escaped due to the actions of escort Captain Edward Fegen, commander of HMS *Jervis Bay*, who sacrificed himself and his ship to give the merchant ships the time to get away. The following month the *Rangitiki* had another close shave when sailing as part of Convoy WS 5, the convoy was attacked by German cruiser *Admiral Hipper*. Sailing out of Liverpool made her vulnerable to air attack, and once at sea to U-boats.

Another who volunteered rather than be called up, was Mervyn Talbot:

'I was seventeen years eight months old when war was declared against Germany on 3 September 1939 and the call up age for the armed forces was twenty-one, however, volunteers were accepted at the age of eighteen years. As my brother, who was two years older than me, had joined the Royal Air Force on a long-term contract I was anxious to join the same service for the duration of the war. Therefore, as soon as I was eighteen, I volunteered and was accepted in March 1940.

'Initial training consisted of intelligence testing and square bashing of course, at Uxbridge, followed by a further spell at RAF Catfoss in east Yorkshire.

'Of the options available at this time, I elected to take the flight mechanics course at the School of Technical Training in Blackpool.

This lasted from May until October 1940 which was followed by a posting to 44 Maintenance Unit, Angus, in Scotland, but in December I was posted to RAF Khormaksar in Aden.

'This involved a month-long journey on HM troopship *Duchess of Richmond*, accompanied by a naval escort. Amid several alarms caused by enemy submarine activity, we went via Freetown, the Cape and Durban. Aden was a featureless place with much sand, a salt works and a few camels. These so-called "Ships of the desert" were used by local natives to level the landing ground by pulling huge baulks of timber behind them. Whilst there I worked on engine maintenance of Bristol Blenheim's and we were accommodated in comfortable blocks and slept on charpoys whose legs had to be set in tins of paraffin to deter the bugs! Incidentally, one was put on a charge in the event of becoming sunburned or suffering from sunstroke so suitable headgear had to be worn, "the Bombay Bowler" as the topees were called.

'I have press pictures of a camel at work, a worker shovelling salt and a photograph of the interior of a barrack block showing a line of charpoys.

'A year later Daily Routine Orders asked for volunteers for pilot training and I was pleased to be accepted so left Aden for Southern Rhodesia in February 1942 aboard HM troopship *Highland Monarch*.'

To Africa

But why were new pilots being sent to Africa? The exponential expansion of the RAF meant that insufficient training bases existed in the UK, the numbers ultimately required being beyond the means of training units in the UK to provide. The Empire Air Training Scheme was one of the largest defence training initiatives of the Second World War, taking place in Australia, Canada, New Zealand, Southern Rhodesia and South Africa. The voyage to Rhodesia was rather longer for Dennis Varey. He sailed from a bomb-ravaged Liverpool in a troopship:

'This ship had been converted to wartime service so we did not have cabins. It was my first experience of an ocean-going ship so I was enjoying life.

'Eventually we sailed out of Liverpool, headed north around Ireland and joined up with a large number of other ships in a huge convoy, this travelled at a speed to suit the slowest ship, so we trickled along at about ten knots which was all right while we were in sheltered waters, but as soon as we got out into the Atlantic, we hit a storm. I was hit by the worst bout of seasickness ever.

'I stayed in my hammock for a fortnight, with only occasional trips to the toilet. To me the voyage seemed endless, especially as we still didn't know for certain where we were going. We all slept below decks, if you were unlucky on a pile of life vests on a table, the lack of light, ventilation, and the smell of the fuel oil made for uncomfortable living conditions.

'We arrived at Freetown; it was very hot and very humid and we were due to stay there several days as it was rumoured that there was a U-boat pack waiting for us outside the harbour. We heard the depth charges going off but didn't see anything. Rumours of troopship sinkings added to our discomfort.

'Crossing the line ceremony added some joy to the journey. Most of us got lathered with sea water and soap and were unceremoniously chucked in the small pool on the top deck. We had picked up new supplies of food at Freetown, so we had better food than before, and certainly better than what was being endured at home.

'The famous Table Mountain came into view, so we knew our destination was Cape Town. We had been about six weeks at sea. After forty-eight hours, ashore we were all crammed onto a troop train. Destination unknown. We slept in bunks and walked along the corridor in shifts to the buffet car for our meals. It took us two days and two nights to arrive at Bulawayo.'

Mervyn recalls:

'I left Aden for Southern Rhodesia in February 1942 aboard HM troopship *Highland Monarch*. Stopping at Durban, we were welcomed at the quayside by the famous "Lady in White", who sang us ashore and arranged for us to visit local homes before going to Clairwood Camp to await orders for the next stage.

'I arrived at Hillside Initial Training Wing in Bulawayo on 1 March and whilst there was able to visit the Livingstone Game Park to see lots of wild animals including zebras, giraffes, warthogs, monkeys and wildebeest, all of which wandered quite happily alongside us as we drove through.

'After this we saw the Victoria Falls – what a stupendous sight – together with the smaller Rainbow Fall and Devil's Cataract nearby. Then, finally, a canoe trip on the river Zambezi with a South African friend and a visit to Rhodes' grave at Matopos.'

As the war progressed in favour of the Germans during the dark days of 1940, the RAF desperately needed new pilots to replace those lost in combat. A training network was in place in Britain, but due to the lack of resources to train thousands of pilots, the Air Ministry, therefore, turned to the Commonwealth and asked for help in turning fledgling airmen into fully qualified flyers.

The RAF established a presence in the then self-governing British colony of Rhodesia (now Zimbabwe) as part of the Empire Air Training Scheme in May 1940. Named the Rhodesian Air Training Group (RATG), it was activated for the instruction of RAF and RAF Volunteer Reserve (RAFVR) pilot cadets, navigators, air observers and air gunners. Elementary flying was in de Havilland Tiger Moth trainers, shipped from Britain, by RAF instructors, with a high percentage of them being RAFVR sergeants. The Rhodesian Air Training Group operated from 1940 until 1954, training mainly pilots, but also navigators, bomb aimers and gunners up to April 1945.

Learning to fly

Mervyn and Dennis, along with thousands of other young men arrived in Rhodesia to learn to fly: another of those other young men was Shep Sheppard. Rhodesia may have been the last of the Commonwealth countries to enter the Empire Air Training Scheme, but was the first to turn out fully qualified pilots. No. 25 Elementary Flying Training School at Belvedere, Salisbury, opened on 24 May 1940. The original programme of an initial training wing and six schools was increased to ten flying training schools as well as specialist schools for bombing, navigation and air gunnery and a school for the training of flying instructors with stations at Cranbourne (Salisbury), Norton, Gwelo and Heany (near Bulawayo). Over 37,000 members of the Royal Australian Air Force were trained as part of the scheme. Of which 7,600 pilots and 2,300 navigators were trained in Rhodesia.

The Reception Depot and Initial Training Wing (ITW) were situated at Hillside Camp, where students would undergo a primary and a secondary course, each of a six-week duration. This included basic military training such as drill instruction. Dennis Varey again:

> 'I arrived at Initial Training Wing at Bulawayo at the start of September 42, where I remained till January 1943. Something like 700 of us arrived. Decked out in tropical gear including topees we did a lot of square bashing. Hillside camp consisted of two rows of straw huts built by the natives which were being replaced with corrugated tin huts. The climate was perfect. In the day we wore shorts and short sleeves shirts, bush jackets in the evening. The food was great, with lots of exotic fruit like guavas. The canteen was run by white Rhodesians who advised us to drink lime and

lemonade rather than milk. Our huts were cleaned by coloured Rhodesians: the society was strictly segregated, and whites were the masters here.

'At Hillside we began to learn the laws, rules and customs of the RAF. We were taught how to fill in the necessary forms showing next of kin. We learnt how to strip a machine gun, and dig latrine pits. We also learnt to speak in dots and dashes, as well as study navigation, the theory of flight, meteorology, aircraft design and construction. Days began early, at 0600 we had the chance to swim, then breakfast at 0700 before lessons at 0800.

'I got friendly with local farmers, and after completing the course spent a week or maybe ten days with them. Marvellous growing country. Salisbury was like any European city.'

After passing his exams, Dennis was sent to an Elementary Flying Training School. The intake comprised 320 pupils: fifty from Post Initial Training Wing Pool and 270 directly from the ITW secondary course. Dennis continues:

'Now for the serious stuff: I arrived at Induna, home of 27 EFTS [Elementary Flying Training School – ed], on 14 January 1943.

'The next day was my first ever flight. My first flying lessons were on Tiger Moths. The instructor was gentle and helpful. It was thrilling to lift off and float gently across the Rhodesian sky.

'Slowly the training and flying experience stepped up. Training included all the relevant safety rules plus various manoeuvres including aerobatics, spinning, flying under a hood on instruments and emergency landings, etc. It's easy to fly it around while you're up there, but the most difficult part of flying is getting it back on the ground. Particularly in a Tiger Moth because it's of such light construction that a little gust of wind will throw it off balance. But I can honestly say there was some apprehension when I came in to do my first landing. It wasn't until we had finished our course on Tiger Moths that we were categorised as to single engine or multi-engined flying. I was categorised for single engine flying, a fighter pilot, and was ordered to move a few miles away to another airfield in the same general locality. At the end of our course on Tiger Moths we were promoted to Acting Sergeants Unpaid, or ASU's, as we were called. This gave us an entry into the Sergeants' Mess which was an immediate improvement in our living standards. We now had rooms between two of us instead of living in barracks, and eating and living in the Sergeants' Mess was quite splendid after the Airmans' Mess we had become accustomed to. The food was better and we could spend our bit of leisure in relative comfort.'

'What do you think makes for a good pilot?' I asked Dennis:

'I think it's someone who has a natural instinct for flying. That is, I think the most fundamental thing for a fighter pilot anyway is to feel part of the aircraft. To feel the aircraft is part of you. You're one with it, you do things automatically. You don't even think about it. You learn to fly from feel and balance, it becomes instinctive, but you only get that instinct with getting in flying hours.

'Early, I think in the first two weeks, we had to learn how to bail out. We had a parachute and none of us ever thought we would have to use them. We flew up to height and were told by the instructor to bail out. We had been briefed in the morning on what to do, but this was the real thing. climbing out of the Tiger Moth, dropping into the void, counting to six, pulling the cord: as the chute filled, the sudden deceleration was quite something. The feel for freedom as we gently floated down was exhilarating. Would I do it again? No. Unless I had no choice. Some of the boys on the trip got very twitchy about all of this. One simply refused; on landing he was told to pack his bags and was posted away.

'When not flying we had lectures and had to study; no parties, no visits out, just learning to fly. I did not like night flying. But we had to do it. Solo flying was wonderful. The only clouds were the odd fluffy cumulous which were a joy to fly around, above and into. What bliss!

'When we had finished our elementary flying training, we were given a week's leave. It wasn't long enough to go back to Durban so a group of us decided to go to Victoria Falls. We had been told that there were cheap rates available to servicemen so we booked up and set off.

'The journey proved to be quite an experience in itself. The only way to get there was by rail, so we set off from Bulawayo station. The line was a single track and went through bush and semi jungle. We had to stop regularly for water and timber which was used to fire the engine. The trip was to take just over a day and there was no restaurant on board so we bought food from locals who met the train whenever we stopped. At about seven in the evening the train stopped again and all the passengers were invited to get off the train and get on to a series of jeeps parked along the track. We then set off through the bush for what seemed several miles, accompanied by the night noise of the animals in the jungle which sounded quite scary to us.

'We eventually arrived at a building totally surrounded by bush in which a generator was humming away, and were served a very good meal during which the generator packed up twice, the jungle seemed to close in and the animal noises seemed to get louder. We retraced our journey back to the train and started off again.

'The group of us finally arrived at Victoria the next day and soon found that our journey was well worthwhile. The hotel was superb, we later found that it was reputed to be the best hotel in the Southern Hemisphere. Presumably because of the war the place wasn't very busy and we were looked after marvellously. The hotel was about half a mile from the Falls, and in beautiful grounds, baboons would come out of the bush and scrounge titbits from the hotel guests.

'The hotel was some five hundred feet above the Falls and guests got there in a most unusual way. There was a narrow-gauge rail line and a couple of small open coaches with canvas canopies, but no engine. We were a bit mystified by this but got on the coaches and to our surprise a local lad put his shoulder to the coach and off we went downhill with the lad applying a touch of brake when necessary. We enjoyed the ride down but wondered if we would have to walk back up. Having had our trip around the falls we soon found out that we didn't have to walk back up we just sat in the coach and two local lads pushed us back up, which was quite an effort and we felt like getting out and helping.

'The Victoria Falls were absolutely spectacular; no words can describe the awesome sight or the huge noise of the falling water. We went back again and again whilst we were there and were sorry when our week was up and we had to return to our flying.'

The Rhodesian Air Training Group set a target of eighty hours flying time at EFTS level per phase, and 160 hours at a Service Flying School. After completing their eighty hours, the new pilots were promoted to fly the substantially more sophisticated Harvard trainers. These modern monoplanes had a variable-pitch propeller, a greater range of instruments, retractable undercarriage and flaps. Lecture content intensified, with subjects ranging from the physical dynamics of falling bombs to the air recognition of enemy and Allied aircraft. Considerable time was dedicated to 'blind' flying, relying entirely on two points on a map and instruments. Night-time sorties became more frequent and longer in duration. Dual-control Air-Speed Oxfords were employed to train bomber aircrew members such as navigators, bomb aimers, radio operators and air gunners. Dennis recalls:

'We were to report to Thornhill, an airfield near to the local town of Gwelo where 22 SFTS [Service Flying Training School – ed] was based, by 26 March. There was much excitement about our change to the American Harvard aircraft. We also had English Masters. It was great to be in a modern aircraft with a closed in cockpit and electric earphones to talk to the instructor. In the Tiger Moths we had gadgets called Gosport Tubes which consisted of a length of rubber tubing down which were shouted instructions. The Harvard had a bit of a fearsome reputation regarding its landing capabilities. It had a tailwheel which, if you applied too much rudder achieved a caster action, and if you were too heavy on the rudder just after landing caused the aircraft to swing violently and usually to dig a wing-tip into the ground. This in fact didn't seem to be a problem to any of our course and was probably a rumour set up by previous courses to unnerve us.

'We set about learning to handle the aircraft and we had to get altogether a hundred and sixty hours in before we left. These were split up into two halves. The first half was spent learning to handle the aircraft and to put into practice what we had been taught in our classes. We couldn't wait to start the second half because this was concerned with the operational aspects of flying. This consisted of formation flying, dog fighting, air-to-air and air-to-ground firing, and bombing, together with some long-distance navigation exercises. Practically all of this was done flying solo, and was all very enjoyable.

'An odd thing about the course on Harvard's was that when we were halfway through the course we qualified for our wings but were not presented with them until the course was ended. This was of course a very proud moment, we were presented with them by the Station Commander, but the occasion was rather spoilt by being asked to sign for them immediately afterwards. This would have been August 1943. I was now a pilot and full sergeant. To make sure we did not think we knew it all, we had another seventy hours to do before we completed. We were now learning combat techniques, including formation flying, air-to-ground firing, low flying, dive-bombing with smoke bombs, floodlight landings, photography with a camera gun, low-level formation bombing, fighter-bomber tactics as well as a lot of instrument flying. Air-to-ground gunnery was firing at splash targets in a lake. We all flew with long sleeves and trousers: we were told it would protect us from burns if our kite copped a packet. My last solo trip was formation flying. I was determined to get a photo of a flying Master: I secreted my camera in the cockpit. I thought it very skilful to hold the stick with my knees and take the snap.'

The Harvard was one of the first American aircraft ordered by the RAF when a contract for two-hundred was placed in June 1938. The Mk I was powered by the 600hp Pratt & Whitney R-1340-S3H1 engine giving the aircraft a top speed of 180 mph, range of 850 miles and a service ceiling of 24,000ft. No armament was installed. British purchasing contracts reached 1100 before American Lend Lease arrangements began. The MK IIA that Dennis was to fly at Abu Sueir was powered by a 550hp Pratt & Whitney Wasp engine, with a similar speed, range and ceiling. Harvard's were gradually withdrawn from Royal Air Force service in the 1950s.

As well as Harvard's, Thornhill had, as Dennis remembers, a compliment of Masters and Wirraways. The latter was a training and general-purpose military aircraft manufactured in Australia by the Commonwealth Aircraft Corporation (CAC) between 1939 and 1946. It was an Australian development of the North American NA-16 training aircraft. The Wirraway has been credited as being the foundation of Australian aircraft manufacturing. The Miles Master was developed in the late 1930's and first flew in 1939. Those that Dennis flew were powered by an air-cooled Bristol Mercury XX radial engine, capable of producing 870hp and a maximum speed of 296 mph.

Dennis's logbook notes that he also learned Beam Approach and the Instrument Landing System. The principle was generally that, when heading in the right direction the pilot heard a steady note on the radio transmitter. If he veered to the left, he heard a series of dit-dit-dits, and if he went right, he heard dah-dah-dah. Coming into land there were two radio beacons on approach making a rapid series of dah or dits as they were flown over. There was a correct height to be at as the pilots passed over them coming into land. 'An expert pilot could feel gently with the wheels until he touched down on the landing strip' Dennis remembers, 'I enjoyed blind flying and the sense of achievement it gave me; taking off and flying around Rhodesia on the beams, and coming into land at another air strip with ILS. I got average + in my logbook.'

About his experience of pilot training Mervyn Talbot recalls:

> 'The serious effort began at 26 Elementary Flying Training School Guinea Fowl for the first flying lessons on Tiger Moths. This included all the relevant safety rules plus various manoeuvres including aerobatics, spinning, flying under a hood on instruments and emergency landings, etc. There is a list of twenty-nine requirements for the complete training programme on page 3. You were expected to go solo on the Tiger Moth at around eight hours, certainly not more than ten. Otherwise, you would be "scrubbed" and posted to a navigator's course, or air gunner, or bomb aimer and the likes. One after another, fellows around me came in joyously saying they had gone solo and then there were those with long faces that said one word "scrubbed" and then were gone the next day. My first solo

flight came after 8.45 hours of dual instruction and I completed the course after eighty flying hours (thirty-two hours solo).

'Then on to 22 SFTS at Thornhill to fly Harvard's with a similar programme as before, but with a faster service type aircraft. On one occasion I managed to get lost on a cross-country exercise when I was supposed to locate a small building out in the wilds of the savannah; I missed it! When fuel began to get low, I had to look for somewhere to make an emergency landing. Fortunately, I spotted a small native village in the scrub part of the savannah and after making several circuits to select a possible landing area managed to get down safely on a slope amidst some small bushes. By this time several excited tribesmen had gathered around and I asked them to act as guards on the plane.

'As it happened, a colonial officer was resident in the village and he arranged for me to telephone my base and then invited me to share lunch with him and his wife whilst petrol was driven to where I was.

'Pilot's wings were awarded to me on 9 January 1943 after logging 170 hours flying (seventy-seven hours solo).'

Not everyone completed their pilot training. Christopher Lee, who would go on to join 260 Squadron takes up his story about his days in Rhodesia:

'At Hillside, at Bulawayo in Southern Rhodesia, I began training, but suffered from headaches and blurred vision which has cleared up over the years thank God. I was not allowed to fly, at least officially. They didn't quite know what to do with me and then someone decided to put me in administrative and special duties, so with a lowly rank, still not commissioned, I worked for intelligence units, in Egypt and all sorts of different places, some near our lines, some not. During that period, I think I'm right in saying, I was posted to 37, then 70. Then I was commissioned and sent to 260 Squadron as Intelligence officer.'

Egypt and Palestine

Once rewarded with their wings, most of the now fully-fledged pilots were posted to the Middle East and the North African theatre to learn to fly Spitfires or Hurricanes. Having completed all three stages of basic training, as Lee headed to Tunisia, Mervyn Talbot was posted to Almaza in the dusty suburbs of Cairo:

'As a qualified pilot, it was now time to tackle the rigours of flying warplanes in preparation for combat service.

'From Thornhill in February, could have been early March, I travelled northwards by rail on a posting to Cairo and on the way swam in Lake Tanganyika before crossing it from Albertville to Kigoma. Then a brief stop at Tabora station where natives were carving ebony gifts, so I bought two. At Mwanza we boarded a boat for the journey across Lake Victoria to Kisumu where we were due to two weeks' leave at a transit camp. My friend knew a family who lived there and owned the local hotel so we were made most welcome. Then, by way of Khartoum, to the Kasfareet transit camp in Cairo where I met an old school friend serving in the Royal Engineers, whose address had been sent to me from home, and we spent a couple of hours chatting together. Whilst awaiting the move to 73 Operational Training Unit at Abu Sueir I joined a group of thirty servicemen for a guided tour of Ismailia, Jerusalem and Bethlehem.'

'I arrived at Abu Sueir in May where we were to fly Tomahawks, which had a bad reputation for tending to swing on landing. After four hours I proved it by making a slightly heavy landing and it did indeed swing off the metal strip into soft sand and, of course, up on to its nose! As a result of this I had an eye check and it was found that there had been some sight deterioration from living in very hot climates for three and a half years. As I had progressed so far to this stage, corrected flying goggles were ordered for me to resume training and whilst waiting for them to be made up I acted as Link Trainer instructor. Eventually, training continued, but now flying Kittyhawk's, which was the aircraft I would be expected to fly on the squadron.'

Mervyn found that the next stage of his training was delayed whilst his specialist goggles were made. A further delay was encountered when a group of Australian pilots had taken precedent, and he had to wait for the next six-week slot to come available. He would not return to 73 OTU until September 1943, having been based at Heliopolis, near Cairo since the start of June.

Dennis Varey again:

'After getting our wings in August, we had another two weeks leave. On returning to Thornhill from our leave we were put on a train heading north to Kenya: I had been posted to RAF Kisuma, where I arrived at the end of August. On the way north, I took the chance to swim in Lake Tanganyika. We stopped at Albertville, where we crossed the lake on an old ferry and landed at Kigoma. Then followed a brief stop at Tabora station. At Mwanza we boarded a boat for the journey across Lake Victoria to Kisumu. We stopped here for five days.

'It was here I and other lads climbed into a white flying boat: I think it was the civilian Sunderland, or similar to it. We left Kisumu to Khartoum. We spent a night where General Gordon had met his end, before flying into Cairo, to 22 PTC [Personnel Transit Camp – ed] at Almaza Cairo. We flew in up the Nile, and over the pyramids. I think we joined the camp in middle September. It was as a result of his delay travelling to Abu Sueir that I met a fellow pilot who proved to be a long-term friend and who, eventually, I was to be the best man at his wedding, Merve Talbot.

'Landing outside the city, we had a week in the city to see the sites, we explored the pyramids, especially the Cairo Museum. After this it was onto a C-47 and a flight out to Gaza, in Palestine. Compared to Rhodesia, the heat was unbearable. Dust, sand, no shade, just the odd palm tree. It was like living in an oven. If this was the promised land, forget it. It was all scrub; hard ground with lots of little bushes and lots of stones.

'An unexpected feature in Tel Aviv was the YMCA Tower. From the top of this building the views were amazing; features in the surrounding countryside could be identified from panoramic maps etched on metal plates set on the sills of the viewing windows. We were in a hotel; I slept in a comfortable bed and we overlooked the Mediterranean. There were nightclubs and bars and one thing and another, notably the cinema. We had a glorious few days' leave here. We could buy ourselves nice meals. You'd never know that young men were killing each other only a couple of hundred miles away in the Western Desert.

'We spent about three weeks at 28 PTC in Gaza, then onto the Aircrew Rest Camp in Jerusalem. A group of us went on a guided tour of Ismailia, Nazareth, Jerusalem and Bethlehem. In Jerusalem we saw parts of the city, the Wailing Wall, Garden of Gethsemane and the Church of the Holy Sepulchre, where I was given a certificate of pilgrimage, signed by the Archimandrite Kyriakos, Guardian and Superior of the Church. After that, we had a group photograph taken on Mount Scopus overlooking Jerusalem. At Bethlehem we were shown into Rachel's Tomb and also entered the Church of the Nativity through the very low entrance where "Even a King may bow his head" and saw the shrine over the site where Jesus was born.

'From The Holy City, we went to back to Abu Sueir Air Base at the end of October, close to the Sinai Desert where Mosses had crossed with the children of Israel, where I remained till just before Christmas. We were here not to part the waves but to learn to fly American Kittyhawks.'

It was here at 73 Operational Training Unit (OTU for short) Dennis met a South African pilot, Lieutenant 'Larry' Johnson, who he would meet again in Italy. Another who became part of Dennis and Merve's lives was fellow sergeant pilot D. H. Kent, who was rapidly christened 'Duke'; all three becoming close friends.

Mervyn, Dennis, and 'Duke' Kent began training at Abu Sueir on 29 October, flying in the Harvard IIA. On that first day, an hour was spent on reconnaissance and familiarisation. In total three hours were spent in the air. The following day was landings, the 31 October, cross-country flying and formation flying. Aerobatic training took up two hours on 1 November, more of the same happened on the following day. Dog fights and forced landings were the syllabus of 4 November. The next week was occupied with 'more of the same', including flying by compass with a blacked-out hood. After a course of instruction in the classroom about the Kittyhawk, dealing with its design, performance, engine etc, Dennis completed his first solo trip in the P-40 on 9 November. Dennis's note books are full of detailed self-drawn engineering diagrams of the Kittyhawk, engine components, wing design: everything that was considered essential for a pilot to know. So, what exactly is a Kittyhawk?

Kittyhawk's

I had encountered a P-40, the Kittyhawk, on a visit to Duxford with my uncle: a decade later I was keen to ask him about the Kittyhawk, about what it was like to fly, and to answer questions the teenage me failed to ask, such as how do you start it? He had a lot to say about the P-40 and its failings.

Firstly, some history. A 'crib sheet' provided by a room guide at Hendon tells me that American fighters had been traditionally powered by air-cooled rotary engines. Rugged and simple, the Pratt & Whitney epitomised the type, used on the B-17, C-47 and others. The apparent advantages of the high-performance, water-cooled inline engines that had been developed for the ME 109, as well as the Hurricane and Spitfire, encouraged some US firms to adopt the same engine design philosophy. With its P-36 fighter already in production, Curtiss began to look at developments with an inline engine. After experimenting with a 12-cylinder Allison V-1710 during 1938, Curtiss fitted the same type of engine to the P-36A, becoming the P-40 which flew for the first time on 14 October 1938. The new type was ordered in quantity for the USAAC the following year under the Curtiss model designation Hawk 81A. An export model (the H-81A-1) was ordered by France but, was taken over by Britain, who designated the type the Tomahawk. The RAF eventually took delivery of 140 Tomahawk Is (equivalent to the H-81A-1/P-40A), 110 Tomahawk IIAs (H-81A-2/P-40B) and 635 Tomahawk IIBs (H-81A-3/P-40C).

The first Tomahawk Is arrived in the UK in September 1940, devoid of bullet-proof windscreens, protective armour and self-sealing fuel tanks – all items that were specified in subsequent batches. Some of these aircraft were dispatched to Takoradi in West Africa to be flown to Egypt for service in the Middle East. The armament was eventually standardised at six machine guns – four 0.303-inch Browning's in the wings and two 0.5-inch or 0.303-inch guns in the forward fuselage synchronised to fire through the propeller arc. British testing of the Tomahawk soon showed that it would be no match for the Messerschmitt Bf 109E/F in air-to-air combat. This was mainly due to its low-altitude rated Allison engine which performed best at heights up to 15,000ft.

Some of the design defects were overcome with the P-87, which became known as the Kittyhawk during 1942. Although the Kittyhawk looked generally similar to the earlier Tomahawk. The armament comprised wing-mounted guns only (the nose guns having been deleted). The first twenty-two aircraft delivered to the RAF were fitted with four 0.50-inch machine guns, but all subsequent aircraft were fitted with six 0.50-inch guns. The Kittyhawk still had the Allison engine, but used the improved 'F' model, which could deliver 1470hp for combat, but for no more than a maximum of five minutes. The inadequacies of the Allison engine at altitude were recognised by Curtiss at an early stage in the development of the P-40. Yet with no other engine in production, Curtiss had to keep relying on the troublesome Allison.

Dennis flew both the Kittyhawk and the later Warhawk remembering that:

'Entering the Kittyhawk was an art form. If you're about six foot like I am, the most dignified way, was to get on the undercarriage wheel, and then step on to the wing, then walk up to the cockpit. The cockpit was spacious, but compared to the Harvard or Master it was a more complex machine. Once strapped in, you turned on the petrol, then the A/S master switch and the A/S control switch, then battery and generator switches, then the electric boost pumps. All the technical references to the Allison engine are in reverse as the engine is the opposite way round to English ones.

'With all the fuel cocks and pumps in the right place, you then primed the engine *very carefully*; too much and it could start a fire. You then fired the one-shot flywheel starter. Once set up, it was heel down in the clutch until the terrible racket had reached a crescendo, which you could only judge with experience, then toe down on top of the pedal; the prop slams round and fingers crossed, the engine fires. How many "primes" the engine had depended on oil temperature. Once it started you have to move the mixture lever back to "idle" from "Rich", whilst black smoke clouds the canopy and the entire kite is shaking itself slowly to pieces. We were told to never let the engine idle at anything under 1000revs. It runs best at 1200. You then run the engine up, test the magnetos and throttle back. Check out temperature; we always took off with the radiator shutters closed or almost closed. You had to open the throttle *carefully, smoothly* and *slowly.* This minimised the gyroscopic effect and to ensure you did not over boost the engine. If we used the boost over forty-five, we had to report it to the ground crew. Before you took off, you gave the engine a burst to clear plugs, and before switching off. It won't "pop off" the ground, and needs to be doing about 100mph that means 37" pressure in the boost manifold and 3,000 revs. Temperature is ideally between 110 and 120 degrees. You have two warnings if it overheats, the temp gauge and a yellow warning light. We were told to never run less than eighty and danger point at 125. The Allison oil system only has one oil filter, one pressure pump and two gearing pumps.

As soon as your up, its gear up, which took probably half a minute, could be more, which seemed an age. The system to raise or lower the gear was overcomplex: you had to push forward a snib on the gear lever, pull up and then depress the hydraulic trigger on the stick until the indicator showed UP, then you had to change hands and give half a dozen pumps on the hand pump to ensure the gear is up and locked. If you got dropped on by the Luftwaffe whilst dealing with your gear, you were dead.

'Once the gear was up, you could ease back to 35" manifold pressure and 2500 revs for the climb, about 150mph. In the cruise, ease back to 2400 revs and 25"-28" in the manifold. Mixture can be shifted to Auto. The petrol is then switched to the fuselage tank, and the radiator, if open, is closed as well as the air filter. Once at height, the Kittyhawk was superb on the ailerons, and the roll made a Mustangs control in the roll feel horrible. However, the elevators were heavy, more so than the Mustang and desperately heavier than a Spitfire or Hurricane. The rudder is light at cruise speed, above that it becomes heavy: as you reach higher speeds, you are literally jamming the left rudder pedal into the floor to keep it straight. With the lack of an automatic boost, manifold pressure dropped alarmingly quickly in the climb: if you start a loop at 40" you'd come out with 37". The Mustang had a two-stage supercharger: without it, at medium or high altitude the Kittyhawk was out performed by most German types. When we were taught dog fighting, provided you maintain impulsion and convert speed to height, you would be ok. The Kittyhawk excelled in diving rolling manoeuvres: a 109 could not keep up with the roll rate. But on coming out, it would have you as it could turn inside. Worse, the 109 could fly the Immelmann turn, the Kittyhawk would fly into the deck if you tried it. The Kittyhawk was a challenging plane to fly. It was a good airframe let down by a terrible engine.'

When we remember the RAF started the war with aircraft like the Gladiator in front line squadrons against the ME 109, is it any wonder that despite its defects the P-40 was welcomed by the RAF? With the exponential increase in the RAF, beyond UK production capacity, as with France in 1939, American aircraft were a 'lifeline'.

Learning to fight

Turning back to 1943: it was here at 73 OTU that new pilots were taught to fly in combat. Mervyn remembers that at Abu Sueir:

> 'All the preparations for squadron tactics were taught here, including the main tasks of battle formation, dive-bombing, ground attack and also the "Cab rank" system which gave two-way communication between air and ground forces who would identify targets of importance to them. Here there was a ground syllabus of sixty-eight items ending with exams in four subjects. We had half a dozen Spits based at Abeu Sueir which took part in the dog fighting with us. Of course, we were not allowed to fly them, as we had to learn how to fly the Kittyhawk, which we could instantly tell was an inferior airplane. The Kitty was totally outclassed by the Spits.'

Judging from Dennis' note books kept at the time, Armistice Day 1943 was marked with an oxygen climb to 18,000ft. Thereafter close formation and battle formation training occupied the next four or five days, with a special course on spinning and low flying. Dog fighting was the primary agenda on 20 November, along with dive-bombing. Many of the flying exercises were conducted with a cine gun which filmed the plane in flight so that the lesson could be evaluated on the ground by pilot and instructor. Air-to-ground strafing, with 200 rounds, was carried out twice on 26 November, then again on the following day and 600 rounds were allocated for ground strafing on 30 November. The 1 December was occupied with shooting at flying targets in air-to-air gunnery practice. The course completed on 3 December. At Abu Sueir, Dennis had flown thirty-seven hours twenty-five minutes in the Harvard solo and forty-four hours thirty minutes in the Kittyhawk. He passed the course as 'Average', but so had Shep Sheppard, who went on to be one of the best pilots 260 Squadron ever had.

On completion, the group of Merve, Dennis and 'Duke' were given a week's leave. They were back in Cairo by 12 December. Dennis Varey again:

> 'Passing the exam, it was Back to Almaza at the start of December. We went back in Baltimore bombers, I think. I know I flew in one, but I can't say when. I'd now amassed almost 300 hours. Certainly,

the Baltimore's were the target tugs which towed this large cloth targets behind them, that we used for air-to-air gunner practice at Abu Sueir. The targets were called drogues. You'd be firing live ammunition and what we had to learn to do was to make attacks from a quarter, not from directly behind, so you had to lay off deflection, and you had to learn how much deflection to lay off. We were sent out to aerobatics on our own and you could please yourself what you did…you did rolls and one thing and another. Part of our training was aircraft recognition. They concentrated on that quite a bit, so I felt confident that I could recognise an enemy aircraft from one of ours'.

'It was a dusty tented camp and landing ground. When sandstorms blew up, it was difficult to see the tent next door.

'Once back at Almaza, having barely had time to get settled in, it was off to 2nd Base Personal Depot. We flew in the DC-3, the Dakota, or C-47. I was 2nd pilot for these runs and amassed something like thirteen hours on the type. We went from Cairo on 12 December.

'We flew along Egypt and the North African coast, landing at Tripoli to refuel and then on to Tunis on the same day. Housed in an old Italian fort on the coast, we were under canvas for a week. Then on the twenty-first it was a short flight from Tunis to Palermo, and then from Palermo to Naples. It was here we spent Christmas, my first of two in Italy.'

Dennis, 'Duke' and Mervyn had arrived in the theatre in which they were expected to fight in.

CHAPTER

3 SORRENTO AND PORTICI

HAVING ACCRUED OVER 300 hours flying time, Dennis found himself posted to a hastily commandeered villa in the suburbs of Naples. Temporarily grounded, he and the graduates from Abu Sueir found themselves 'at a loose end'. Assigned to No. 2 Aircrew Rest Camp, he arrived on 22 December:

'When we arrived and joined 3 BPD (Base Personnel Depot – ed). This was a holding area for aircrew waiting to be posted. Merve and I were sent to a large villa in Portici and almost as soon as we had dropped our gear in the billet and allocated beds amongst ourselves we were straight off to the showers. For blokes brought up with a bath under the kitchen table, or washing as best we could in the desert, this was for me, a real luxury. Months in the desert with no proper washing facilities made us ever more appreciative of the showers. I think the RAF had put these in, as the villa had been a private house, not intended to house twenty-five or so lads. The showers either froze you or steam cleaned you. We had sprung beds, several to a room. No kitchen. Some of the civilian furniture was left in. It felt a real luxury to have four walls and not a tent.

'We were allowed out in the evening rather than suffer meat and two from the canteen a few blocks away. We'd never seen pasta before, let alone know how to eat it. We all crowded into this little restaurant, it looked like someone's front room, it could have been for all I knew, we were the only service blokes in the place. We ordered spaghetti Napolitano. That's a dish with a fresh egg fried on top. Of course, when it came, we all set out cutting it up with knives and forks, Mervyn dangled his into his mouth with appreciative comments of lovely grub. The voluble momma who had served us, her bust measurement must have been bigger than her height, showed us how we should eat the spaghetti with a fork and spoon. It was all very different to what we had at home. All this food seemed evil given the rationing we had endured at home.'

28

Dennis, in the service, was experiencing a way of life that was totally alien to the home front, and the majority of the Italian population at the time. As service personnel he was 'living the high life'. Being paid, well fed, and most of all 'out of harms way' from the German army and ever-present risk of death that being posted to the front meant. It was, I guess, a total escape from reality, in a cosseted existence only possible through being overseas in the armed forces. As he acknowledged, the life Dennis was living, was in contrast to the one his cousin Jeane lived through:

'Private cars had a small "basic" allocation of petrol and eventually you had to prove your need for that, there were greater rations for essential work, but woe betide you if you were found outside your immediate area or latterly running on Red petrol, which was regarded as a crime. Most cars were "mothballed" for the duration. The blackout of course affected everybody, and "turn that light out!" became a regular yell from Air Raid Wardens. Fines were heavy for people not maintaining a strict blackout. This applied to cars whose headlamps had to be masked with just three slits on each light, and of course after 1940 all sign posts, and in some cases street names, town boundary signs and anything that could give you an idea of where you were, were removed in case of invasion from the air. With only a torch covered with a mask to help you find your way about, life became, to say the least, difficult. "Got your tin hat? Got your gasmask? Got your torch? Goodnight!" became a ritual saying and was heard virtually everywhere.

'Fuel of all sorts was valuable and every effort was made to save it. Coal was rationed, but gas – except for reduction of pressure – and electricity could not be, so in came the rule if possible one bath a week, and only 5 inches of water, that did not mean 5 inches of boiling water to cool off with cold, 5 inches maximum. Many people measured a five-inch mark, and painted it on their baths. So "Save Fuel, Save Lives" became a slogan. The war was full of slogans.

'Food of course was rationed and difficult to come by, all queued for everything from onions, fish, sausage, liver and even nylons. Anything that was not rationed had to be queued for. The smallness of rations did not affect everybody, as you ate what you were given. Fat ration was 4oz a week, as was sugar. Meat was 1/- worth (1 shilling = 5p), half an egg a week. Some things like dried fruit, dried milk, dried eggs and certain tinned foods were on "points". Each item was allocated a number of points and everybody was allocated so many a week, which could be used as you wished, always providing that anything was available, queues depending. Life was very difficult and very unfair for many, anyone who had anything to exchange could usually have a barter system somewhere, and the black market was always there for anyone who had money. At and before the beginning of the war, people were encouraged to stock up on food as far as they could because shops could not carry very large stocks. Butter was preserved in crocks of saline solution, eggs in water glass, tinned stuffs bought along with many other essentials. The older people who had been through the previous war were of course keener to do so than the "war will be over by Christmas" people.

'The real unfairness came when what had been a patriotic duty became regarded later as unfair and unpatriotic, and hoarding became almost criminal. It affected the middle classes more than the working class, many of whom did not have the resources to stock up, "why should we go without when they have something" became a mind set for a lot of people.

'The diet may have been restricted, but it was a healthy one, there were very few overweight children, and in some cases improved the diet of some families, and the children of the real poor were better fed than they would have been without the war, except in the cases, of which there was a number, in Wakefield, where mothers sold their ration books.'

As Dennis commented, quite a difference being in Italy, to being at home in West Yorkshire. Hot baths, showers, good food, no blackout, 'I don't remember going hungry' Dennis remembers 'the shops in Portici in Naples were like those we had at home, and once you got used to the currency change, quite affordable. It was a carefree existence.' It was also a world away from the grinding poverty and starvation experienced by most Neapolitans and graphically recounted by James Holland's excellent books. Dennis continues:

'Naples was our first European city since we left Liverpool. No blackout it seemed, lights all over. The city never seemed to sleep. Thousands of folk all rushing from somewhere to another.

'We spent forty-eight hours in Naples before we arrived in Sorrento, on the twenty-second I think, which was situated on a cliff overlooking a small beach. Its quaint narrow streets, shops and vino bars gave it an air of antiquity, and we felt as if we had moved back in time to a different age.

'Our billet was the Hotel Minerva: named for the ancient pagan Temple of Minerva which stood nearby, it had sixty-three rooms, of which most had sea views and each was furnished with sprung beds, clean sheets, baths, all quite a luxury, topped off with decent food.

'None of us were heavy drinkers, but we did enjoy ferreting among the bars, sampling the local wines which seemed to appear mysteriously if the price was right. It was amazing how none of the Italian men liked Mussolini or the Germans. They had – all to a man – changed loyalties, particularly when trying to sell you something!

'Christmas: my second away from home. We had turkey, chicken, custard and enough booze to sink a battleship. We all had parcels arrive from home containing presents, letters and cards, but it was not the same really.'

It was a sybaritic life. Housed in what in peacetime was a five-star hotel at Sorrento, the divine coast, Dennis was free from the burden of RAF routine, his days were his own. From the pages of his diary we read that days were spent shopping, playing cards, going to dances and concerts. New Year's celebrations resulted in hangovers:

Saturday, 1 January 1944

Saw in the new year in at a dance at the Corcumello [A hotel used as Offices accommodation nearby – ed] with Merve, George, Don & Keith. Keith passes out just after midnight. Did not get home till 0400hrs so missed breakfast. Got a stack of mail and spent rest of the day reading it. Went to bed early at 2200.

Days followed the same routine: breakfast, shopping, going to the cinema, or paying cards at the hotel occupied the morning, then lunch followed by going to the cinema or concert in the afternoon, an evening meal, followed by cards or back to the cinema. Repetitive, but care free. Due to overcrowding, Dennis and Mervyn found that they were billeted once more in a villa in Portici, and 3 BPD on 14 January. Dennis remembers they were all 'very put out having to move, we had been given two weeks leave, and as senior NCOs were to be billeted here and not with the aircrew'. Even when back on base, life was fairly care free:

Monday, 17 January

Breakfast at 0830. Merve & I went into Pompei for the day. Saw ruins and church and bought two strings of pearls for 2400lira. Caught a lorry back full of tomatoes, arriving at 1530 went to Cinema Roma in evening to see *Girl Trouble* with Merve. Bed at 2200.

Tuesday, 18 January

Breakfast at 0815. Merve and I left for Sorrento at 0915. We were very lucky and caught a staff car ride there and said he would bring us back at 2100hrs. Had our meal at Minerva. There was a dance on and we stayed until 2130hrs. Had a smashing time. Got back to BPD at 2300hrs. Curfew 1900.

Wednesday, 19 January

Breakfast at 0815. No mail yet. Wrote some letters. Nothing unusual happened. Merve performed on Piano all morning.

The following days followed the same routine. On 24 January both Dennis and Mervyn, as the senior NCOs in their villa, were placed in charge of twenty-four new pilots ranking as Air Craftsman 2nd Class who had arrived at the depot. About his relatively carefree time in Portici Dennis remembers:

'Portici is just over the bay from, Naples.

'Like everywhere else in the services, the routine was the same; up at 0700, breakfast at 0800, dinner at 1200, evening meal by 1800, curfew 2100. Lights out by 2200. In the billets we had three options: eat out, make it ourselves, or troop to the canteen or NAAFI. RAF meals were always the same and dreadful. Breakfast was a mug of tea, made drinkable with sugar. Often you could see the bottom of the mug through the tea, but it was wet and warm. To eat, inevitably it would be porridge, two slices of bread with margarine, with jam if we were lucky, two pieces of fried spam, and powdered egg. Midday would be some kind of meat and two, and again the same at night. Of course we had NAAFI, we could get chocolate, fags, whatever we wanted, at a price of course. All very different to the Minerva. The food was not that good, but I don't remember ever being hungry. We tended to eat out or make it ourself towards the end of stay. We could buy our own provisions in town.'

Naples was bombed during his tenure, neatly recorded in his diary on 14 and 27 January, and again at the close of the month during the build-up to Anzio as his diary notes:

Saturday, 29 January

Breakfast at 0800. Parades 0835 and 1335, PT and Football, First parade.
As usual nothing doing all day. Heard guns in the evening, probably be air raid with all ships in harbour. Went to bed at 2100hrs. As I thought, air raid 2200hrs

Naples was bombed twice in March. I asked Dennis how he filled in his spare time:

'After morning parade, we were largely spare wanks. We'd hitch a lift into Naples, as long as we were back for parade, our time was our own.
'We'd go to the pictures and watch Mickey Mouse cartoons in Italian. Why, I don't know. Some of the lads were in hysterics. Most days we would go to the cinema Roma simply as something to

do. We'd watch the same film two or three times. We spent a lot of our time going to ENSA shows, or we went to the Opera in Naples. I went to see *Madame Butterfly* and *La Boheme* amongst others. We smoked, talked, drank, played cards: poker, bridge, gin rummy that sort of thing. We never did much.

'Pompei was something else entirely. We were never taught about it at school. Roman houses still standing, and the touching plaster casts of a family sheltering their child, or the couple banging away as the volcano went [Dennis pauses before breaking into a smile], a real case of coming when you're going, I'd say. The Italian guide, of course, waxed eloquent about this in broken English, saying things like "in thisa room they'd a do it thisa way, not thata way" and added to the scene by contorting his arms and legs this way and that.

'A lot of Americans and American WAAFS were stationed in and around Naples. We would chat them up and take them dancing in Naples.

'Then there were the touts. Men would sidle up to you and ask you if you wanted a pretty signorina. As we were unused to the language, we had difficulty in finding out what they wanted, but we soon began to pick up a word or two of Italian and realised what they wanted to sell. The BPD sergeant told us that if we took a slash against a wall we'd get crabs, and if we looked at a woman, we'd get a dose. VD was ninety per cent or close to it. Many lads ignored these dire warnings. Everywhere were notices asking "Is VD one of you souvenirs of Naples?"

'When in camp, there seemed no planning or purpose to what we were doing. Here we were, hundreds of trained pilots doing nothing. To me, it seemed no one had any idea what to do with us.

'At the end of our stay, Vesuvius went up.

Dennis's diary for this period offers the following remarks:

Monday, 20 March

Parade as usual.

Had easy morning reading. Played bridge all afternoon and Bob and I beat Merve and Red. In evening all went to see '*Rope*' at Cinema Roma. Good, but not as good as first one. Vesuvius still pretty bad.

Monday, 21 March

Vesuvius erupting.

After Parade all went to Cinema Roma to see preview of '*Government Girl*'. Olivia de Havilland. Good. Played bridge all afternoon and evening. Jack and I beat Red and Merve and then Red and Bob. Vesuvius very bad.

San Sebastiano destroyed. NAAFI.

Wednesday, 22 March

Air Chief Marshal Dixon on Parade. Read all morning. Vesuvius bad, big cloud, dust, bags of pumice. Bob and I in charge of fifty men in case of fire. Fitted reading lamp up. In evening all went to Cinema Roma again to see '*The Gentle Sex*'. After supper, Jack and I went on to roof to watch Vesuvius. Marvellous sight.

Thursday, 23 March

Parade and PT.

Was late to go to Cinema, so Red, Merve, Dan and I played crib. In afternoon went to Cinema Roma to see preview of '*His Butler's Sister*', Deanna Durban, Franchot Tone and Pat O'Brien. Good. Played crib again until teatime. Bob and Red went to Cinema, again, to See '*The Gentle Sex*', but rest of us stayed in and nattered. Supper. Vesuvius quieter.

Friday, 24 March

Parade, Dixon & PT

NAAFI and then read all morning. Did crosswords for most of day. Stayed in during evening again. Made supper as usual and went to bed about 1100. Vesuvius smoking.

Mervyn remembers:

'On 21 March I witnessed the remarkable sight of the volcanic eruption of Mount Vesuvius. According to the press reports in the "*Stars and Stripes*" newspaper, which I have, a great wall of fiery lava 90ft deep and up to a quarter of a mile wide threatened the villages of San Sebastiano and Massa di Somma. Three days later clouds of smoke and ash, up to 20000ft, still rose from the crest and it was reported that it had cost the lives of twenty-one persons in Salerno province. At least the devastation could not compare with the deadly eruption in 79AD which buried Pompeii. I was able to visit the ruins of that later. Whilst in Naples I was fortunate to visit the San Carlo Opera House on two occasions.'

After the excitement of Vesuvius, routine drifted back to morning PT followed by an afternoon at the Cinema. This carefree existence had to come to an end, and Mervyn was posted to 239 Training Wing as March came to an end. Dennis's diary again:

Sunday, 26 March

Parade as usual.

Did nothing most of morning except read. Did some square bashing in afternoon. Lights failed in evening but made lamp and gave farewell party to Merve and Jack. Made supper when lights came on again and went to bed about 1000.

Monday, 27 March

Parade and pep talk by Squadron Warrant Officer.

Merve and Jack leave for 239 Alt-Vesto at 1300. Wrote letters. Route March and Naafi. In the evening went to see '*Double Stitch*' ENSA, very good. Two blokes moved in. Supper as usual.

Dennis's diary records four months of almost identical mundanity: visiting the cinema one or twice a day, card games, shopping, the odd day out walking to Torre el Greco. With Merve and Jack posted, and left to his own recognizances, Dennis carried on as normal, waiting to be posted as his diary notes:

Friday 31 March

Parade as usual. Easy morning, not feeling too good. In afternoon went to opera to see '*La Boheme*'. Quite good. Had bit of a session in evening, made supper and went to bed very early, George came in pretty canned and all had discussion on girls.

Saturday, 1 April

After parade had small route march and finished at NAAFI. Got parcel from mum. Did nothing in afternoon as not feeling too well. Cold, I think!

Sunday, 2 April

Weather better.

Parade. Posted to 239 Wing. Don and Red posted South East Asia Air Command.
    Went to cinema, '*Phantom of the Opera*' Nelson Eddy, Susanna Foster, Claude Rains in afternoon and evening. Had farewell party at night. Bob and I pretty well on.

Monday, 3 April

Headache! Packed and cleared. Leaving for Naples by Lorry at 1330.

239 Wing had been formed in 1942. It comprised headquarters, the training wing was part of this, 53 repair and salvage unit, 112, 250 and 260 Squadrons RAF, 3 and 5 Squadrons Royal Australian Air Force (RAAF) and 5 Squadron South African Air Force (SAAF).

Dennis arrived at Vasta and 38 Personnel Transit Camp on 4 April and remained here until the eleventh:

'I had been in the transit camp at Portici just outside Naples for three months, maybe more, waiting for a posting to an operational squadron and couldn't have been keener to start operations. From Portici in April 44, it was off to 38 Personnel Transit Centre at Vasta.

'For the umpteenth time since I had joined, we were humping our gear into the back of an 8-tonner for the endless drive across the width of Italy. Viano overlooked the Adriatic, Portici did not. The 8-tonner had wooden bench seats; after a few hours we would stop, get out, stretch, have a slash and get back on. We had day rations with us. The bench seats gave us gip: our backsides ended up feeling like they were made from wood, cramped under the canvas roof, the drive was hot and dusty. We were glad to get to the coast. We were here for a week. Back under canvas. A shock from the villa we had in Portici. Again, it was a case of hurry up and wait. The day I arrived; I met Merve just as he was shipping out to 239 training Wing.'

Both Mervyn, Jack and Dennis would be posted to the same squadron in 239 Wing: 260 Squadron.

260 SQUADRON

THE SQUADRON MY uncle was sent to join was, by 1944, an elite ground-attack unit. Its tactics and operation had been honed since spring 1943 with the development of close air support for the infantry, known as Cab Rank: they could take out targets otherwise out of reach of artillery.

260 Squadron had been raised in the Great War, and had been reformed at Castletown in November 1940, operating Hurricanes on air defence and coastal patrols around Scotland. Overshadowed by the more famous events of Dunkirk and the Battle of Britain, equally important military developments occurred that year.

On 11 June 1940, Italy's Fascist dictator, Benito Mussolini, declared war on Britain and France. Seeking to expand their imperial possessions in Africa, the Italians invaded Egypt on 13 September from their colony of Libya. Mussolini's forces in Ethiopia attacked neighbouring British possessions. After a limited advance, the Italians halted and set up a series of fortified camps around Sidi Barrani. In December 1940, General Sir Archibald Wavell's Western Desert Force of 36,000 men attacked the Italians.

A mobile armoured force under Lieutenant General Richard O'Connor outflanked the Italians at Beda Fomm and pursued them for 500 miles back to Libya. An offensive led by General Wavell ended at El Agheila during 7 February 1941 with the destruction of nine Italian divisions and the capture of 130,000 men.

Hitler realised that he would have to support the Italians in North Africa. On 11 February 1941, Major General Erwin Rommel's Afrika Korps landed at Tripoli. The British had won some spectacular victories over the Italians, but found the Germans a much tougher nut to crack. The German counter-offensive pushed the British back.

By 13 April, the British had been forced back to the Egyptian frontier, leaving the 9th Australian Division besieged in Tobruk. They held out, but after two attempts to relieve Tobruk failed, Wavell was replaced as Commander-in-Chief Middle East by General Sir Claude Auchinleck.

In what is today Syria, French Vichy troops were attacking into nominally British controlled Iraq. 260 Squadron left Scotland in May 1941 heading to the near east. 260 Squadron sailed to the Mediterranean aboard HMS *Ark Royal*, with 238 Squadron aboard HMS *Victorious*. Launched off the *Ark Royal*, both flights of 260 landed on Malta, before being led into Syria, for a brief period fighting the

Vichy French. The squadron was led by Christopher John Mount: during the Battle of Britain, he served as a flight commander in 602 Squadron. In November 1940 he was given the task of establishing a new squadron, 317 (Polish), but after a month he left to take command of 260 Squadron.

It was during these operations against the Vichy French in Syria that Sergeant George Joseph Black, 'Sparky' to the squadron, comes to attention. He had joined the squadron in Scotland and became a stalwart member of the unit. 'Sparky' became something of a legendary pilot in 260; it was well deserved. Not long after arriving in the theatre of operations, Sparky was shot down by the Vichy French. Undaunted, Sparky escaped from the French POW camp, by literally walking through the front gates passed the guards and made his way back to 260. As we shall see, this was not to be Sparky's last air combat that ended with him having to deploy a parachute. Sometime after Sparky had made it back to his unit, squadron records tell us Mount fell ill: misdiagnosed by a vet, he was admitted to hospital with a ruptured appendix. He returned to active service and took command of 238 Squadron.

Now under the command of Squadron Leader D.R. Walker, 260 Squadron arrived in Egypt in August, undertaking ground attack operations. The arrival of 260 was part of the operational thinking of Air Marshal Sir Arthur Tedder, to achieve closer air-ground co-operation. Tedder oversaw the formation of the Western Desert Air Force (WDAF, DAF hereafter). Its Commander, Air Vice-Marshal Arthur 'Mary' Coningham, developed a mobile, highly effective tactical air force. One of the pilots who joined 260 at the time was William 'Ron' Cundy. Born in 1922, in Australia, Ron Cundy remembers that he first felt a spark of determination to become a pilot after viewing the landing of an aircraft with two pilots at Moonan Flat sixty kilometres north-east of Scone, when he was just six years old. Aged eighteen he persuaded his parents that he should enlist as an aircrew trainee under the Empire Air Training Scheme on 14 October 1940. Initially posted to Bradfield Park and then to Narrandera for Elementary Flying Training on Tiger Moths, he set sail on the liner *Awatea* on his nineteenth birthday bound for Canada with a large contingent of aircrews.

After further training, on North American Harvard's, Ron was awarded his coveted wings and became a sergeant pilot. From there he went to England for operational training on Hurricanes before being posted to 135 Squadron RAF, stationed at Honiley near Coventry. From England he sailed for North Africa and 260 Squadron. Ron arrived in time to participate in Operation Crusader.

This had been launched on 18 November 1941 by Field Marshal Sir Claude Auchinleck, and came as a surprise to Rommel, who was launching an offensive of his own against Tobruk. After several days of confused tank battles around Sidi Rezegh, Rommel advanced towards the Egyptian frontier, hoping to cut off the British. Ron Cundy remembers:

> 'Ultimately, as the British pushed the Germans further back, they got them back somewhere around the Tobruk area. A line running south from

Tobruk, they pushed them back to there. The natural order of things was, the fighter squadrons would move forward with the army and they'd be as close up as possible to the army to provide that kind of protection. And we moved to an aerodrome called Sidi Rezegh, being one of the new pilots on the squadron I went forward by truck. Other more experience fellows of course flew the aircraft on. I was quite amazed, this Sidi Rezegh aerodrome was the greatest shambles you could ever see. There were burnt out aircraft, Italian aircraft and German aircraft. There was all sorts of trucks and armoured personnel carriers and even tanks there burnt out. I was quite amazed. Apparently, Sidi Rezegh had changed hands four times. The New Zealanders had apparently been in the battle when they had forced the Germans off it. We were there for some time while the British Army were still pushing them back. But we kept moving and it was a fairly fluid sort of thing at that time. The Germans weren't able to hold the British. The German lines of communication were much longer and they weren't able to hold them. It was subsequent to that that we'd moved on to a place called Gazala.'

As Ron Cundy notes, the Germans had outrun their fuel supplies and their attack ground to a halt, enabling the British to drive them back. Killed, on 27 November, was Pilot Officer Joh Wyley, aged twenty-four. He is commemorated on Column 241 on the Alamein Memorial. Tobruk was relieved on 7 December and Rommel was forced to fall back on El Agheila. In the ensuing air combat, Flight Lieutenant James Bandinel was killed on 14 December. In January 1942, Rommel attacked again. The British were overextended and had not replaced their earlier losses. Rommel was able to advance beyond Benghazi: as the squadron was based at Benghazi it had to 'beat a hasty retreat' as Ron remembers:

'Sergeant Cartwright, a Canadian in the RAF ground crew, was one of those who stayed behind in charge of a number of men, and a Warrant Officer Rixson also stayed behind with fifty men or so. I think the padre stayed behind with them. What they had to do was not only get the aircraft off, but destroy any valuable equipment that they hadn't been able to take out with them and then head off themselves on the coast road; but they were cut off.

'They joined up with some Ghurkhas and they fought their way through the German line. I don't know how many they lost. Cartwright got through but Rixson didn't. They were reported missing and it was presumed they had been taken prisoner of war. But would you believe it, Rixson and two of the people who were with him, walked three hundred miles across the desert and got back to 260 Squadron.'

Warrant Officer Frederick William Rixon was awarded the Military Medal for his bravery as the *London Gazette* of 18 December 1942 reports:

> During the evacuation from Berka satellite aerodrome to Matuba in January 1942, Warrant Officer Rixon was in charge of the squadron motor transport and left by lorry with six other airmen. Fierce enemy fire was encountered along the Benghazi by-pass and Warrant Officer Rixon and his companions were forced to abandon their transports. He then led the party across a swamp, sometimes waist deep, to the sea. Progress was extremely difficult and the party was continually fired at. Eventually they met four friendly Senusies and some British troops. The party now numbered twenty-two and they continued their journey for six days, although tired, hungry and footsore. Occasionally meals of a kind were obtained from friendly Arabs. On the sixth day, the party was overtaken by two Italian armoured cars. Warrant Officer Rixon and three others of his party managed to evade capture and set off towards Mechili. After walking for two more days, they reached an Arab camp where food and shelter were given. After two more days walking towards Tobruk they were rescued. Warrant Officer Rixon showed leadership, courage and initiative, facing great discomfort and deprivations with resolute determination. Throughout the campaign, he has proved himself invaluable and has maintained the highest state of serviceability among the unit's motor transport.

The squadron found itself at Gazala in February, where it converted from Mk 1 Hurricanes to American Kittyhawks, operating as fighter-bombers supporting the Eighth Army, the famous 'Desert Rats.' Ron remembers:

> 'The Kitty Hawks were American designed and built aircraft, but they were not good. They were too heavy. They weren't manoeuvrable enough. They couldn't reach the necessary height, no matter how high we went in them, and we'd go to say 18,000ft, the Germans would be above us, no matter what height. We'd go to 20,000ft and they would always be above us. And one of the things that annoys me is that, at this time they had developed the Mustang in America, at the behest of the British by the way. Rather than Mustangs we got these Kittyhawks, which were not quite as powerful as the Hurricane and weren't quite as manoeuvrable.
>
> 'As a ground attack aircraft, they were no good. They were not a good fighter. They were only ever any good for dive-bombing.'

Equipped with new aircraft, 260 Squadron operated as both fighters, and now as ground-attack bombers. From early February to late May 1942, Rommel was halted by the heavily mined British defensive line, which ran from Gazala in the north to Bir Hacheim in the south. At the end of May 1942, the Germans launched a fresh offensive and, after two weeks of heavy fighting, broke through. They captured Tobruk and pushed the British back into Egypt. Spring 1942, and summer, had been costly for 260's pilots. Pilot Officer Alfred Saunders was killed on 23 March; Pilot Officer Alec Stephen Morley aged twenty-two, was killed on 2 April; Sergeant John Hannaford Alexander was killed on 7 April; Sergeant John William Wareham was killed, aged twenty-two, on 25 April; Sergeant Edmund Tricky on 27 April; Flight Lieutenant Thomas Hindle was killed on 31 May alongside Flight Sergeant Clarence Perley Veysey; Sergeant Harold Clark was killed on 9 June, aged twenty; Sergeant James Cecile Wrigley was killed on 12 June; Flight Sergeant John Vyvyan Carlile was just twenty years of age when killed in action on 26 June; Flight Lieutenant William Robert McKay was killed in action on 14 July; Pilot Officer John Anderson McLean was killed on 18 August. In total twelve pilots were lost in six months.

The see-saw struggle in the Western Desert continued. The vital port of Tobruk was besieged twice. To make up for losses, new pilots joined during from May.

New Pilots

Any squadron would have a constant through-put of pilots, as men became tour expired. In combtat this rate naturally increased. It was now that one of 260's most notable pilots arrived. James F. 'Stocky' Edwards, born on a Saskatchewan farm on 5 June 1921, joined the Royal Canadian Air Force, graduating as a sergeant pilot in June 1941. Posted to the Middle East in November 1941, he was assigned to No. 94 Squadron RAF in the western desert, Egypt, flying fighter/bomber Curtiss P-40 Kittyhawk aircraft with the Desert Air Force. Promoted to flight sergeant, on his first operational flight in 1942 Stocky shot down a Messerschmitt ME 109 on 9 May, he was transferred to No. 260 Squadron. Another Joining 260 in the Western Desert was Shep Sheppard, who flew his first operation on 31 May 1942, having joined on 24 March. Amidst the bitter fighting Ron Cundy remembers that sometime in June, Sparky Black was shot down south-west of El Adem: forced to bail out of his burning Kittyhawk, he landed in an area occupied by the British Army. Ron continues that despite the battle raging around him, Sparky was picked up by a British captain. He was escorted to a tent occupied by a group of staff officers, one of whom, in a most cultured voice, said: 'Majaah, this is Black, I just found him dangling from a piece of silk. Do you have a little something to steady him?' Whereupon the Major produced a bottle of Scotch, poured Sparky a generous portion and sent him on his way back to the squadron. As Sparky reported later – 'it was all done with such panache that apart from the noise of the artillery, one would have never known that a battle was in progress.'

After flying half a dozen times a day, in June most pilots flew two operations per day: primarily escorting bombers or undertaking standing patrols against the Luftwaffe. Tobruk fell on 21 June 1942, and the squadron, like the Allied forces, fell back. Stocky Edwards, succinctly wrote of that period:

'June 1942 was another difficult period for everyone when the Germans were preparing for their advance, and 260 Squadron was primarily assigned to bomber escort duties over enemy concentrations. The enemy lines were only 25-30 minutes flying time from the Gambut airfields.'

Joining 260 Squadron at this difficult period was Sergeant Douglas England. He was remembered by 'Stocky' Edwards as being 'a nice, quiet, intelligent person. He flew No. 2 on quiet shows.' Stocky recalls that Doug 'had the hardest of time of any pilot I ever knew to fly on ops. At first, he didn't appear to have the fortitude to continue flying but he didn't quit or even suggest it [...] I always felt sorry for him. I tried to give him special attention and gradually he came along – succeeding in shooting two or three enemy aircraft. He became one of the stalwarts at the end.' Indeed, 'Doug' went onto a second tour with 260.

The British and Commonwealth forces fell back on the prepared positions around the tiny junction at El Alamein, about seventy miles west of Alexandria. Barely taking time to rest his exhausted forces, Rommel's offensive to take Egypt began on 1 July. All the DAF Kittyhawk squadrons were fully committed and soon in action. Ron Cundy again:

'We were starting to retreat back to El Alamein and we flew as much as we could through the day to protect our army as much as possible. And so, we moved back down to an aerodrome on the Alexandria-Cairo Road. That was when the British Army were able to establish and hold the Germans on that El Alamein line, and when the powers were convinced that the line would hold, we were sent on leave and that was quite a break. We went up to Palestine and Tel Aviv and had a short break there.'

Despite halting Rommel's advance at the First Battle of El Alamein in July 1942, Auchinleck was replaced by Lieutenant General Sir Harold Alexander as Commander-in-Chief Middle East. At the same time, Lieutenant General Bernard Montgomery took over command of the Eighth Army. In late August 1942, Rommel made a last effort to break through; short of fuel and supplies, he was repulsed at Alam Halfa. Ron Cundy again:

'On about 30 September the Germans attacked in great strength, but they did actually break through the British line, Montgomery had set up his rear defences on what they called the Alam el Halfa Ridge. He had dug in his tanks and he had dug in his aircraft guns to give the Germans a hard time. Let them break through on the southern front and then when they started their mass attack, they could knock them off. And actually, we were very much involved then in escorting our bombers to bomb a big wide column of German armour. So, we harassed them by dive-bombing and escorting our bombers for several days and then withdrew again.'

Unlike his predecessor, Montgomery exuded confidence and rapidly restored the army's flagging morale. For nearly two months, Montgomery continued to train and re-equip his army. 260 Squadron found itself re-equipped with the Warhawk version of the Kittyhawk as Ron Cundy notes:

'It was a superior aircraft to the Hurricane, especially when we were re-equipped later on with Merlin engined Warhawk. The Rolls-Royce Merlin was built in America under licence to Packard, and they called it the Packard Merlin. They were a much better aircraft.'

The lack of a two-speed supercharger for the P-40's Allison V-1710 engines made it inferior to Luftwaffe fighters such as the Messerschmitt Bf 109 or the Focke-Wulf Fw 190 in high-altitude combat and it was rarely used in operations in North-West Europe. As Ron notes, the P-40D was fitted with a more powerful 1,400hp Packard Merlin 28, which became known as the XP-40F. This led to the production of 1311 P-40Fs powered by a Packard-built Merlin V-1650-1 rated at 1300hp for take-off and 1120hp at 18,000ft. These became known as Warhawks in RAF use, although 260 Squadron still called them Kittyhawks. As well as receiving new aircraft, Stocky Edwards recalled: 'Many new pilots had arrived on the squadron and intensive training took place. By mid-September 1942 I was leading the squadron on occasions – as just a sergeant.'

Outside of training and learning to fly new aircraft, the war ground relentlessly on: 3 September, Pilot Officer Joseph Bernier went down in flames. Like Stocky Edwards, a Canadian Pilot, he lies buried in El Alamein War Cemetery. Three days later Flying Officer Richard Dunbar, again a Canadian volunteer, was killed in action. He is commemorated on Column 263 at the Alamein Memorial.

Air Support for Alamein

During the campaign in the Western Desert, a major problem for the British was the lack of co-operation between their armour and infantry, meaning they were fighting almost separate battles. The result was that the infantry did not receive the support it might have done when it needed it, and the armour frequently fell victim to co-ordinated enemy attacks. The Luftwaffe had perfected the interplay of armour, infantry and airborne artillery in 1939. It was a lesson the allies were slow to learn: it needed the right aircraft, reliable radios and a change in operational thinking. By 1943, the RAF at long last was able to put theory into practice. Under Montgomery, better co-ordination between all arms was implemented, and vital lessons were learned that were crucial to the success of D-Day. Amidst this transformation of 260 Squadron, Sparky Black went tour expired on 13 September 1942 and left on the eighteenth. Ron Cundy remembers Sparky was 'always with a happy disposition and unfailing sense of humour – he was one of the most popular members of the squadron [...] after the war he studied law and ultimately became a judge.' Before that career beckoned Sparky was to complete another tour with 260 Squadron, but that all lies in the future.

Sparky was replaced by Battle of Britain veteran, Flight Lieutenant Kenneth 'Hawkeye Lee' on 18 September. Hawkeye had flown with 501 Squadron in the Battle of France where he shot down five German bombers to become an ace. He was posted to 112 Squadron RAF in late 1941, having been a flight commander with Special Duties Flight at Stormy Down, and later at 52 OTU at Crosby-on-Eden in Cumbria. Sparky's departure and Hawkeye's arrival marked the beginning of an intensive period of training, but as Shep Sheppard relates:

> 'The training period that was supposed to last a month ended quite suddenly on 6 October and we were back in business that afternoon as top cover to the bombers who were going to give Daba a basting. Daba and Fuka were the main German Air Force bases and the strategy was to destroy them on the ground and in the air, so when the push did come, the Army would be free from enemy aircraft attack. Although we did not see any aircraft, the landing ground at Daba was very well defended by ack-ack and Jerry knocked four of the bombers down. On 9 October we did a three squadron strafe with our squadron leading, to what had been LG 104 (which was west of El Daba) [...], the following day we did a recce to Daba and Fuka which was followed by a forty-eight Bomber raid. One ME 109 took a crack at me but his shooting was poor.'

This attack was part of the Allied 'preparation of the battlefield' to neutralise enemy air power prior to the coming offensive. Keeping the Luftwaffe grounded, or at least neutralised, was the heavy rain in early October which had turned the German airfield complex at El Daba into a quagmire. It gave DAF the upper hand to attack the Luftwaffe on the ground.

The turning point came at El Alamein on 23 October 1942, when General Montgomery inflicted a decisive defeat on the Axis forces. Once battle had joined, Shep Sheppard flew eight operations over the next seven days:

'The real battle was on, and it appeared that the Jerry Airforce were now intending to have a go – there were more Jerry aircraft about in those seven days than we had seen in nearly two months. Jerry had obviously been saving his resources in an anticipation of a push by us. We did a sweep, then a standing patrol over Daba in the morning […]. In the afternoon we did another patrol over Daba but now the ME 109's and Macchi 202's were up in strength and in amongst us. Everything happens quickly in a dog fight. Turning to face the attack suddenly there is one right in front of me, Macchi 202, so I get after it, get in a good burst and that was the end of him […] I then got after another, an ME 109 this time, but he dived away and I followed. The Kittyhawk was much heavier than the ME 109 and was therefore faster when diving: and as he turned towards the left I was able to cut inside him and give him a good burst. He pulled up with the intention of jumping out but, suddenly, there was a "ping" and I realised I had picked up a bullet from somewhere and oil began leaking over my windscreen […] the engine finally gave up the ghost and I turned in along the coast and made a belly landing on the beach wheels up about eight miles east of El Alamein just as the engine caught fire.'

Shep, unscathed after the 'pancake' landing, was back with 260 Squadron by 2000 the same day. He continues '23 October was a great day because it really was the turning point in the war – we were going forward, and this time there was no coming back.' Killed that day was Warrant Officer 1st Class Eric Tomlinson. A Canadian volunteer, he lies buried in El Alamein War Cemetery.

Three days later, Ron Cundy achieved his fifth victory. It was witnessed by Stocky Edwards:

'Cundy spotted a Ju 88 flying low in a westerly direction and out to sea. Cundy dived on it, and his section followed. Within minutes he watched it career toward the sea. Cundy's shot had hit the 88 in a vital spot. Sprays of water leapt high into the air as it crashed into the sea.'

In the same operation that Ron clocked up his fifth victory, bad luck befell Canadian Sergeant Gordon George Rattle, when he was shot down during the early evening of 26 October. Born in Ontaria Canada in August 1915, he was an optical technician by trade before joining the RCAF in September 1940. Like most pilots with 260, he was promptly christened with a nickname 'Rick'. Taking off at 1615 the flight encountered a group of ME 109's. It was on this trip that Ron Cundy claimed a 109 shot down, as did 'Stocky' Edwards, as did Sergeants Thomas and Rattle. However, during the dogfight 'Rattle was himself shot up,' remembered Ron Cundy. 'Stocky'

Edwards recalled that on seeing pieces flying off Rattle's Kittyhawk, who was flying as his No. 2., he got himself behind the 109 firing at Rattle and opened fire, forcing the German pilot to abort the attack. Despite the timely intervention, the instrument panel of Rattle's Kittyhawk had been totally destroyed, the hood had been totally shattered, Ron Cundy remembered that 'Rick' was wounded to the neck and leg and was losing a lot of blood. Fighting against losing consciousness, Rick remarkably made it back to base, belly landing at 250 mph. His Kittyhawk was a 'write off', but he was alive. He had been very lucky. Rattle would be back with 260 Squadron before too long. In the dog fight in which he nearly lost his life, it seems that Rick was fighting with one of the best German pilots in the theatre of operations: German ace Gustav-Siegfried Rodel.

During the battle of El Alamein, DAF had claimed 150 enemy aircraft shot down: pilots from 260 were responsible for eighteen of these victories. In reply, eight Kittyhawk's had been shot down and six badly damaged. Six pilots had been killed on 239 Wing: from 260 Squadron Pilot Officer Charles Edwin Ody was killed on 26 October and Sergeant Ronald Mockeridge was killed on 1 November. Rattle was the only downed pilot to survive despite his wounds. He was a lucky pilot, and his luck would hold during his time with 260 Squadron. In comparison to the success of DAF, the Luftwaffe shot down 100 Allied planes: slowly but surely DAF was gaining vital air superiority which was to be vital in what Montgomery was planning.

That same day the squadron welcomed back 'Pedro' Hanbury for another tour in command. He had succeeded Walker in March 1942, whose tour expired at the same time as Sparky, and was replaced by Squadron Leader Devenish DFC. Osgood Philip Villiers 'Pedro' Hanbury, had joined the RAF in June 1940. During the Battle of Britain, he had claimed four victories flying with 602 Squadron: in September he claimed DO 17s damaged on the seventh and twelfth, destroyed an ME 110 on the fifteenth, shared a Ju88 on the twenty-first, destroyed a JU 88 on the thirtieth, and in October, damaged a JU 88 on the fifth and destroyed an ME 109 on the thirtieth. In May 1941 he joined 260 Squadron. On 14 December he destroyed a JU 88 and damaged an ME 109. He was given command of the squadron in March 1942. His combat victories continued to mount and he shared an ME 109 on 3 April, destroyed a JU 87 and an MC 202 and probably destroyed another on the twenty-fifth and was then hit himself and made a forced-landing near Gazala for which he was awarded the DFC:

> This officer continued to engage the enemy until his aircraft was so extensively damaged that he was compelled to land. Throughout, he displayed magnificent leadership and courage. Squadron Leader Hanbury has destroyed at least five enemy aircraft.

He destroyed another ME 109 and probably another on 27 June and claimed yet another on 6 July. Pedro was tour expired on 19 July, and formally took back command of 260 Squadron on 4 November 1942. He was considered to be one of the best squadron commanders of the era: brave and charismatic, he led by example. Hanbury went on to claim a damaged ME 109 on 14 December, and on 2 January 1943, claimed another ME 109 destroyed and an ME 110 on 17 April.

In the aftermath of victory, Operation Supercharge began on 2 November. It was the final phase of General Montgomery's great battle at El Alamein. After a costly two-day slogging match to penetrate the German defence lines and minefields, the British tanks finally broke through. Rommel ordered a withdrawal, and his broken formations streamed back westwards. The objective was Tobruk. A member of 260's ground crew was Sergeant William Cartwright, a Canadian, we met him earlier. Without the ground crew of armourers and mechanics, the squadron would have ground to a halt. Stores and spares, as well as munitions, were ferried from landing ground to landing ground by the ground crew. His diary details operations and the laborious process of the ground party getting to Landing Ground 75 to allow 260 to support the attack on Tobruk:

5 Nov. Waiting to move. 'A' Party move out.

6 Nov. Move off two hours before dark. I drive a brand-new Dodge 3-tonner – six wheels. Make twenty-six miles and sleep in blue.

7 Nov. 130 miles in nine hours – good going – ninety before Tiffin – small rations. Dodge running fine. Stop near an abandoned Jerry stores wagon – full of kit and loot it. Passed scores of burned-out tanks, wagons, guns, etc. thousands of prisoners and dead blokes. Jerry going back fast and there's loot all over the place.

8 Nov. Forty-three miles in eight hours. Crawling along nose to tail. Road packed. Terrible going. Met 'A' party. Give them two days rations and off they go again. Forget Blitz [his dog – ed] at petrol filling point and go back three miles for him.

9 Nov. On again. 100 miles and reach LG-75 before dark and take over kites.

260 Squadron did not remain long at LG-75, they were off to Gambut on 12 November, at Gazala on 17 November, and by 19 November they were at Martuba, as Bill Cartwright's diary explains:

13 Nov. Find abandoned Italian Officers' Mess. Crockery – brand new boots, radio and a couple of cases of tinned veal (supper).

14 Nov. Pass Capuzzo and a couple of Army wagons with wheels blown off by mines.

16 Nov. Go to Tobruk. Loot everywhere. Try to fix up a Henshel, but it's too long a job. Plenty of special overhaul tools left in hangers and tents still full of Jerry camp beds. Boxes of brand-new machine guns. Crashed Heinkels all over the drome with their instruments and guns intact. Found 1500 rounds for my luger, a box of lemons and a Renault. Brought back new 5000 litre bowser.

19 Nov. Reach Martuba in dark. Jerries left twelve 109's here. Four Serviceable.

One of the 109's was 'obtained' by 260 as a squadron hack. Christened HS-! It remained with the squadron until late February or early March 1943. The 109 flew alongside 260's more famous capture, HS-? Which we mention later. About the 109, Sergeant Pountain remembers the ground crew were given permission to service the 109 and:

'When the work on the 109 was complete we were surprised to find that B flight commander had already flown a 109 when he had been a test pilot with Aircraft Assembly Unit at Kasafreet. He test ran the engine, and the following day, flew the aircraft. Several squadron pilots then flew it. It was not a popular aeroplane, however, due to its very frightening characteristics on take-off, and even more so, on landing. After a week the CO stopped any of the squadron pilots from flying the 109. Two days later it was collected by a salvage crew and loaded on to a "Queen Mary", and taken to Kasafreet.'

The 109 gave the pilots of 260 first-hand experience of the performance and flying characteristics of their German opposition. This knowledge was to come in very useful over the coming months. In returning to the 'day job' of fighting the Second World War, the squadron on the morning of 18 November arrived at Gazala and:

'...in the afternoon did an immediate sortie [...]. It was a long trip, two hours fifty minutes [...] we strafed Benina aerodrome near Benghazi and I added three aircraft to my tally, albeit on the ground, which I suppose do not count as fighter victories, but is a major factor in wiping out the Hun Air Force, especially as two of the three were fighter aircraft and one a JU52 transport plane. We stayed at Gazala until 8 December [...] we moved up from Martuba to Belander.'

Shep Sheppard adds that on 22 November, 260 Squadron joined 239 Wing, initially comprising 3 and 450 Squadrons RAAF and 250 Squadron RAF. 260 replaced 112 Squadron, which had been sent to support the 57th USAAF Fighter Group. Whilst at Gazala Ron Cundy remembers:

'I said to the CO one night, "I've only got twenty minutes to go to finish my tour." He said, "Well, I'll forgive you the twenty minutes, you can quit now." And I said, "No, I want to get those 200 hours in." And he said, "Well all right you stubborn so and so, we've got a good one tomorrow for you." I said, "What's that?" He said, "We're strafing an aerodrome at Magrun," which was some 200 miles into the desert down in behind the German lines. And of course, if there was one thing we hated above all else, it was strafing German aerodromes, because they were heavily defended. I felt like saying, "No, I won't bother going." And then I thought, no, I'll regret it for the rest of my life if I don't get my 200 hours in. So away we went and as it happened, when we were approaching the aerodrome there was low cloud and very heavy rain, so we couldn't really see our target. And after stooging around for a little while in this low cloud and heavy raid, the CO called it off. So we never got to strafe Magrun and we returned to base. But that was two hours and twenty minutes, so I finished up with 202 hours and 10 minutes operational flying.'

For Ron, the war as a combat pilot was over, but a new adventure was just beginning.

Operation Torch

For those remaining on active service with 260, the action did not 'let up'. For Shep Sheppard things were 'hotting up' as:

'From the 9-23 December, we really got stuck in and I did fifteen sorties, mostly dive-bombing and strafing, but on the seventeenth we patrolled the forward area giving cover to the New Zealand troops and, I believe, that was the longest sortie I ever did – three hours. During that week we only saw two enemy aircraft.'

No. 260 Squadron's sorties were in support of Operation Torch – the Allied invasion of French North Africa – which followed in December 1942, more squadrons arrived to pressurise Axis forces, while in Tunisia, the DAF helped the Eighth Army to outflank enemy defences in south-eastern Tunisia. Rommel retreated into Tunisia. The invasion force was commanded by the American General Dwight D. Eisenhower and included the British 1st Army. Even with the Germans in retreat, pilots were lost. Canadian pilot, Warrant Officer Class II George Hartung was killed on 5 November, Flight Lieutenant Cecil Clement Hood Davis was killed on 20 November.

After their initial resistance, the Vichy French agreed to a ceasefire. The Allies advanced into Tunisia, but the Germans reacted quickly and succeeded in blocking the route to Tunis at Kasserine.

It was at this point that the future commanding officer of 260, Peter Stanley Blomfield, arrived. He had commenced pilot training at No. 19 Elementary Flying Training School, Sealand, in July 1941, first going solo in a Tiger Moth later in the same month. Following further experience gained with Harvard's on another course at Tern Hill, he was assessed as 'above average' and posted to No. 71 Operational Training Unit at Carthago in the Middle East, where he converted to Tomahawks. It was here that Shep Sheppard had undergone fight training from 28 December 1941 to 13 March 1942. For Blomfield, the next stop from 71 OTU came during January 1943 when he attended 239 Training Wing and converted to Kittyhawks, prior to being posted to No. 260 Squadron for the commencement of his first operational tour at the end of the month. At this stage in the war, the squadron was based at Castel Benito. On joining 260, Blomfield was interviewed by the Commanding Officer, Pedro Hanbury, about whom he recalls:

'Didn't suffer fools at all lightly, gave the impression of being as mad as a hatter on the ground; however, a cold, efficient leader and killer in the air. When I was asked to step into his trailer for acceptance/refusal, he glanced through my logbook, grunted something that mercifully didn't sound too disparaging and said, "And how long d'you think you'll last then?" All I could think of at that moment was a stuttering, "Well, sir, at least as long as tomorrow morning, perhaps." I was in. "O.K," he said, "come on and have a drink, there's only bloody awful Iti vermouth!" I flew as his number two for the next two months: what I learned in that short time probably enabled me to stay alive in spite of all the Me 109s could do and to remember for always his oft-repeated adage; "He who fights and runs away lives to fight another day: the fool who stays and takes a chance gets took home in an ambulance!" No wonder that we all loved him.'

Hanbury was a formidable pilot. The *London Gazette*, Tuesday, 30 April 1943 reports:

This officer is an inspiring leader whose courageous example has contributed materially to the high standard of operational efficiency of the squadron he commands. In operations covering the great advance from El Alamein, Squadron Leader Hanbury led formations of aircraft with great skill, attacking and harassing the enemy with destructive effect. In attacks on the enemy's dispositions near Ksar

Rhilane and at El Hamma, Squadron Leader Hanbury exhibited great dash. His fearlessness, efficiency and unswerving devotion to duty have been worthy of the highest praise.

Almost as soon as he arrived Blomfield was put through his paces during the afternoon of 10 February, assessed as competent, Blomfield flew his first operational flight on 11 February. The flight of twelve Kittyhawks led by 'Stocky' Edwards was in the air at 0900 on what was designated an armed recce. The trip was eventful for 'Doug' England: to his dismay, following bombing a column of fifteen German lorries, he found his Kittyhawk had been damaged by flak and small arms fire. With his engine compromised, he was forced to belly land. Unharmed, England walked across eighteen miles of desert and was back flying with 260 twenty-four hours later, and back on operations on 15 February.

As alluded to earlier, pilots were just one part of a larger military machine that constituted a squadron, and enabled it to function. Shep Sheppard notes that:

'Without these chaps [...] one would simply not fly. Engine fitters, airframe fitters, wireless mechanics, electricians, armourers, batmen, parachute packers, storekeepers, cooks and even fatigue wallahs, they lived in and around your aeroplane, in the dispersal area or even outside your mess. There were always two on your aircraft when you went to it, the windows and hood had been polished, your wings had been wiped down, and the last thing to come off would be the engine hood. Your parachute would be put on your seat which they would help you strap on, once you were in the plane, they would strap you in. It was their aeroplane and you had it on to loan to do a job. One of them would signal clear to start up and after the engine start would clear away the chocks on your signal, whilst the other would sit on your wing end and guide you out from dispersal. Whilst you were lining up, he would be off your wing giving you the thumbs up and they would not take their eyes off you until you were airborne. It was a team effort.'

Behind the pilots, as Shep Sheppard tells us, a squadron had 300-350 officers, NCO's and other ranks involved in landing ground defence, maintenance, cooking, parachute packing and a minutia of tasks that made a squadron operational. Robert Henry Maxwell 'Bobby' Gibbes commanding 3 Squadron (RAAF) remembers:

'The comradeship and team spirit between each and every member of No. 3 Squadron was always very real. The squadron pulled together as a team, a magnificent team. When there was a job to be done, they went to it, irrespective of their particular trade. At times a superhuman effort from every member was called for, particularly from the ground personnel, who carried out their onerous tasks silently and cheerfully, often under the most shocking conditions.

'They had to set up and strike camp almost continually. This is in itself a very big job. A little tented city would spring up and then disappear within a period of three hours. They had to travel hundreds of miles in extreme discomfort on open dust-laden lorries, the hot sun drying every drop of moisture from their aching bodies. Occasionally, they had to journey in soaking rain, wet, cold and miserable. More often than not, when they did arrive, tired and hungry, at their destination, aircraft had to be serviced; this, of course, coming before their own personal comfort, just as the horses did in the old cavalry period.

'It is hard to single out any particular section. Every man was a cog in the machinery of the squadron's organisation. While every job might not have been so apparent, yet if one man failed, the organisation would no longer run smoothly […]. It was a common occurrence to hear aircraft engines run-up and tested far into the night; to see armourers cleaning guns, re-arming and bombing-up in the total darkness; working by torchlight, electricians and wireless mechanics carrying out repairs long after the average man is fast asleep.'

What was true for 3 Squadron was true of 260 and all other squadrons in the theatre. One of the armourers with 260 was Corporal, later Sergeant Fitter, Pountain, we met him earlier. Joining the RAF in 1938, serving with 64 Squadron at Church Fenton. He was posted to the newly formed 260 Squadron at the end of 1940. The Imperial War Museum holds Pountain's personal archive, which offers us the story of 260 that is seldom explored, that of 'those who also served.' 260 was stood down from 23 to 30 December.

Delta Lily

No. 260 Squadron, if it is remembered at all, is remembered not for its pilots, but for an aircraft the squadron 'borrowed from Hitler, which was nice of him really to let us do it' quipped Dennis Varey, Delta Lilly, a captured HE III Mk 5. It had been adopted in November 1942 at Gambut, as Shep Sheppard recalls, 'we found a Heinkel III Mk 5 with two new engines beside it, so someone had obviously left in a hurry!' The German's had also left an important technical manual for the aircraft behind. Armed with this information, the potential of getting the Heinkel flying and to use it for squadron transport was not lost on Pedro Hanbury. To that end, aware that he had an experienced pilot off operations in Ron Cundy, Pedro approached Ron saying:

> '"Well, now you've finished your tour I want you to get that Heinkel back here and we want it on the squadron." So, I took some ground staff to it and they were able to change the engine. One of them fortunately could speak German and read German and had a manual, so we were able to do what was necessary. But no one on our squadron had ever flown a twin-engine aircraft, let alone a German one. So, dilemma, what to do? But there was an American squadron which had come and flown with us when they first went into the desert and I knew they were all terribly experienced pilots. So, I went down to their mess and asked if any of them had every flown a twin before and what the story was. A Captain Margolin from Texas said, "Well, I've got five hours on Boston's." Five hours on Boston's, and I thought, hello. He said, "I'll take it off for you if you come with me." So, I really wasn't too impressed with that because I thought I would have liked to have had someone with more twin-engine experience. Anyhow, to cut a long story short, we got the thing organised. The Germans had mined the aerodrome so I had to contact the army and get a Pioneer battalion to clear us a runway down through these mines. Anyhow, Margolin took it off with me sitting beside him. We got it back to the squadron.'

Painted in squadron markings HS-?, Delta Lily was used to take pilots on leave, fetch and carry supplies, and then after a friendly fire episode, she was painted bright yellow in late December 1942. On her nose she carried her own 'badge of honour': a crimson shield in which was painted an overflowing beer glass. Ron Cundy again:

> 'The serious business of keeping the squadron supplied with the good things of life began on 7 December with a 2 hours 20 minute trip to LG-97 at Mariyut on the outskirts of Alexandria. Sergeant Tac Takvor a Canadian, accompanied me as co-pilot. Armed with a ready supply of cash I contacted our old friend and supplier, a Greek gentleman named Agnides [...] he seemed able to get anything we wanted, from pork to turkeys, to fresh vegetables, to tinned food and alcohol of every variety. Nothing was too much trouble for him.'

Ron writes that he went on 'shopping trips' on 8 December, 15 December and on Christmas Eve, on the latter filling the Heinkel with 'with beer, whisky, turkeys and legs of pork packed into the bomb-bay.' Remarkably, the Christmas Eve shopping expedition was captured on film, and can be accessed on YouTube, Shep Sheppard continues, that having filled the Heinkel with beer, and whatever else could be packed into her, 'on its return, we were very generous to the other wing squadrons by letting them have a share of the beer – making a small profit for our mess fund.' Pedro Hanbury estimated it could carry 600 tins of beer. Ron Cundy recalls flying a German bomber was not without its pitfalls:

> 'I used to fly that Heinkel backwards and forwards between the squadron and Alexandria, bringing it up-loaded with goodies.
>
> 'But there was a funny incident... the squadron had moved to Marble Arch, and I was approaching it loaded with all these goodies. Just before that, some German bombers had taken it upon themselves to bomb the local aerodromes and I could see way in front of me an aircraft burning on the ground. And the ack-ack had actually shot down one of these JU88s.
>
> '3 Squadron RAAF had been scrambled to intercept any further incoming raids, and I could see them coming. I heard one of them call up and say, "There's one of the bastards." I knew he was looking at me. Fortunately, I had the radio and made contact with them so I said, "Get away, this bastard's friendly." I thought what a terrible thing it would have been if I had been shot down by our own fellows with all those goodies on board. But the rotten so and so's pulled in around behind me as though they were going to make an attack on me, but they were only trying to frighten me, I think. Anyhow, I landed it safely.'

Thanks to Ron and Delta Lilly, that Christmas, with everyone stood down, Shep remembers:

> 'We were able to give the ground crews on the squadron something of a real Christmas. We "found" boxes, tables and benches and set them all down somehow or other, then fed them a real Christmas dinner of roast turkey and beer. The officers, pilots and senior ground staff NCOs waited on them in the traditional RAF manner and we all enjoyed it immensely – Christmas Day in the desert at Marble Arch 1942 was something to be remembered.
>
> 'Afterwards, our mess was invited to the Sergeants' Mess and, in the evening, we had our own Christmas dinner [...] we were not allowed to hang about, however, and do nothing during the stand down. There was squadron formation, dive-bombing practice and

the odd air test to do, but on 30 December 1942 we got two sorties in, and I believe it was the show of the year.

'A landing strip had been prepared at Gzina which was possibly some ten to fifteen minutes flying from the front line. The Hun started flying again, not in combat, but sneaking in when they thought we were too far back and using the 109's to strafe our troops at the front. The object of the landing strip was that we were able to fly from base, do a fairly long patrol and sweep over the forward area, and then, instead of the long flight back, land at Gzina and refuel and re-arm as necessary and return for a second patrol before going back to base. The whole wing did this on a cover basis, each squadron flying in two sixes. Our squadron did the first stint and having been stood down for a week, we put a fairly strong team on the first flight. As we came off our first patrol, our second flight took off and we went into Gzina to refuel after a very uneventful patrol with no shots fired in anger. The same thing happened with the second flight [...] in the intervening period the Hun sent up ten ME 109's to strafe the troops and we must have taken off about the same time as they did. They obviously thought we had returned to base. We came on the scene, six of us, just as they were lining up to make their strafing run and we bounded them good and proper.

'Before we got back to base after the show, the Army had confirmed five ME 109's shot down on our side of the line and Bobby Brown claimed a sixth, but was only given a damaged because no one actually saw it hit the deck, so Eddie Edwards, Fallows, Doug England, Thornhill and myself each got one. We had arrived on the scene at about 5-6,000ft so with throttles through the gate, mixtures on rich, we were really travelling at a very good speed when we hit the ME 109's. The remaining four broke for home, but from the drive we had the speed and we were quite sure that none of them got away; I got a very good burst in at two more 109's and in all possibility shot them down, but there was really no time to stop and look and then we found ourselves spread all over the sky, we were called to reform, finished our patrol and returned to base.

'None of the other pilots that day had any joy. I think the Hun decided to call it a day [...] I believe six Kittyhawk's wiped out ten ME 109's. It also gave a boost to the squadron because we were still suffering a bit from the bad do we had on 20 December when we had lost Thagard, McClive and Adams.'

Pilot Officer Jack Takbor was killed on 19 December, aged twenty, Victor Joseph Thagard, also a Canadian, aged twenty-one, was killed in action on 20 December.

Killed the same day was Warrant Officer Class II Lloyd Peter McClive, aged twenty-five, from Flint, in Michigan USA. Killed on 30 December was Sergeant Harry Harvey Steele, a Scot from Irving in Ayrshire, he was just 21-years-old when he was killed in action. A sad end to the year.

Having remained on squadron over Christmas, in the New Year of 1943 Ron Cundy remembers:

> 'The group captain in charge of our outfit, who I'd got to know pretty well, said, "I'd like you to stay, you can have your old squadron. When your present CO finishes his tour, you can take over your old squadron." I just wanted to get back to Australia and they agreed and that's what happened. So, I flew to Alexandria in the Heinkel and went into camp at Cairo waiting for the boat for home.'

Whilst in Alexandria, Pedro Hanbury had arranged for the Heinkel to be serviced and painted yellow. Shep Sheppard remembers that on 6 January Pedro tasked him to collect the Heinkel and in a short pep talk about flying a twin-engine aircraft, merely indicated:

> '"It has got two of everything instead of one." What he did not tell me was that everything was in German! However, I went down to Marble Arch in the flight garry [...] the corporal fitter was the one who spoke German and he gave me the gist of what was what. On the morning of the seventh I ran the engines up to test them and was completely dependent on the corporal for translation and interpretation of the instruments. For instance, we flew on miles per hour, the One Eleven on knots; the ASI was in metres, whereas ours were in feet, but eventually I felt I knew what I was about. One great thing about the Heinkel was its nose was completely glass, which enabled you to see everything. I was ready for my first flight on a twin-engined aircraft, which was also my first solo on a twin. The trip time from Marble Arch to Gzina was about forty minutes, but I played it safe.
>
> 'On 8 January we took the One Eleven from Gzina to Marble Arch and then onto Maryut at Alexandria, returning on the twelfth to Gambut 2, then to Gzina and immediately onto Hammeret East to where the squadron had moved. We had been able to find or borrow, I know not from where, a Pilot Officer Carins, who was a twin-engined pilot and I flew as second pilot on these trips, my main function being to fill up again with the necessary goodies we required for the mess, and also to square up our account with our friendly Greek Agnides who supplied us with whatever we needed.'

Corporal Armourer Pountain notes that Cairns came from a nearby Blenheim squadron. Blomfield recalls that on one occasion Delta Lily was used to fetch gallons of Stella larger from Cairo that had been 'found'. Improvisation being the mother of invention, lacking suitable storage or transportation receptacles, the lager was poured into the Heinkel's long-range fuel tanks. Whilst initially a good idea liberating a consignment of free lager, Blomfield opined that even though 'the tanks had not as yet been used for fuel. It might have improved the taste of the beer if they had.' Where and how the Stella was 'found' has never been disclosed: it may be a state secret.

CHAPTER

5 BEGINNING OF THE END

AS 1943 BEGAN, 260 Squadron was based at Marble Arch: they attacked Castle Benito on 21 January, which the Germans evacuated on the following day as they moved back from Tripoli. 260 Squadron attacked Zuara harbour and town during the twenty-third, 'when I led the wing of thirty-six aircraft' remembers Shep. The Wing, 260 included, then moved out to Castle Benito as Bill Cartwrights diary reports:

> 23 Jan. Tripoli entered at 9 o'clock [...] cartridges going up everywhere. 'A' party leave for Castle Benito – due south of Tripolo twelve miles – once Jerries' biggest repair base.

> 24 Jan. Forty-five minutes by air to Benito. See white buildings of Tripoli as we circle to land. Nice place – partly ploughed up. Six hangers in ruins, some filled with Fiat G-50s. Trees and unserviceable Italian aircraft all round drome.

> 25 Jan. Move to billets a mile away. Very comfortable. Pick up a spring bed. Electric light working.

> 26 Jan. Pouring with rain. Lucky to be in such good billets. Well just round the corner, so haul water, heat it and had a hot bath. Glorious, you don't miss one till you have one.

> 27 Jan. Send A party to Tripoli – nothing to eat or drink. Fetch eight gallons of red wine from brewery half mile away. You can smell it from here. Drunks everywhere.

> 28 Jan. Pick up tools from Itie tool store. Bags of aircraft spares and gear left in stores.

> 29 Jan. Fix up two 1,135 litre water tanks on roof for bath. Have a stove and cistern in bathroom. Have hot baths nightly now after work. Swell.

Necessity is the mother of invention goes an old saying, and it was clearly a case of adopt, adapt and improvise to make life comfortable in the North African desert.

As Cartwright notes, as the Germans retreated, they did whatever they could to destroy landing grounds: often literally ploughing the landing strip up.

Cartwright was not alone amongst the veterans of 260 Squadron in having memories of the brewery near Tripoli. The brewery he mentions was in reality an Italian Army wine depot that had been abandoned during the retreat: 260 Squadron's motto should have been 'waste not want not', as by this stage in the campaign they had become experts at 'obtaining' copious amounts of alcohol, often from less than legal means. Canadian Pilot 'Nick' Nichols, described by Blomfield as 'our tame scrounger par excellence', had uncovered the hastily abandoned Italian wine depot, leaving behind huge vats of Chianti. Pilots of 260 were never ones to miss an opportunity as Blom recounts. The long range tanks previously used to transport gallons of Stella came in useful once more:

> 'Nick filled five and brought them home. Shortly after this the Army closed the depot to the RAF. Rumour had it that in the very vat from which Nick had syphoned his haul was found the body of a New Zealand sapper. He was reported as being deep mauve and beautifully preserved! The only too obvious jest about the wine having plenty of body did the rounds.'

Another who remembered the episode was Shep Sheppard who adds some more detail:

> 'To ensure that this supply of red wine remained in our possession we spread the rumour we had found a dead body in it. Looking to increase our comforts, we found a large empty house on the edge of Castle Benito landing ground, close to what had been married quarters, it had a large garden attached to it and we gradually built up a large stock of chickens, cows, pigs and a lamb. I still have photographs of the lamb, which became something of a pet, but which eventually found itself to the dining table.'

The obvious question is, where and how did 260 obtain these animals, and as the squadron advanced across the desert, how did 'the powers that be' not notice the squadron transport producing various farmyard sounds of baa, cluck, oink and moo? Blind eyes were turned no doubt, and would be again, when the squadron tried to invade mainland Italy, complete with menagerie.

Off operations from 24 January to 6 February, the down time provided all ranks of 260 much needed rest, and judging by the stocks of alcohol, a few good parties! February was not the best of months to resume flying as Bill Cartwright notes:

> 8 February. Kites go on patrol in pouring rain.

> 9 February. Drome is waterlogged.

> 10 February. Rainy season has really set in.

If it was not rain that caused issues, it was dust storms as Sergeant Cartwright explains:

> 18 February. Dust storm blowing all afternoon and evening – makes everyone loggy and ill-natured.
>
> 19 February. Dust still hanging around.

Confined to tents, or vehicles, tempers clearly frayed: very understandably. For much of the second part of February, 260 was concerned with local defence of their landing ground, training, or escorting 112 Squadron as 'top cover' to defend the lower flying fighter-bombers from the Luftwaffe. Some offensive flying did happen: Pedro Hanbury led a flight of twelve Kittyhawk Mk2 into the air at 0900 on 26 February. The target was a Luftwaffe airbase at Garbe West, top cover being provided by 112 Squadron. Following the bombing run, a Junkers 88 was observed and strafed. The German landing ground at Bedj Teual was bombed by 112 Squadron with 260 Squadron providing top cover. Both squadrons attacked Bedj the following morning. The Germans knew they were coming this time, and intense flak and ground fire was encountered. Flying Officer Roland Strongman Kent's Kittyhawk was hit: a serious engine fire broke out, the Kittyhawk smothered in flames and streaming black smoke was observed to plummet into the deck: Kent was presumed killed as he was not seen to bail out. A Canadian, he was aged twenty-two when killed in action and is commemorated on Column 271 of the Alamein Memorial. Also killed the same day was New Zealand Pilot, Sergeant Neil Edward Cundy. From Wellington, again he was just twenty-two when he died. He lies in SFAX War Cemetery in Tunisia.

260 Squadron was back at base at 0835, but 'there is no rest for the wicked' and was back in the air at 1225 providing cover for 450 and 112 Squadrons. As the two squadrons began their bombing run, four 109's 'jumped' the flights. At the same time, the German defenders put up intense 88mm flak. A shrapnel splinter wounded Sergeant McParland, yet despite losing a lot of blood and flying a Kittyhawk which had a strong resemblance to a colander, he managed to coax the crippled airplane back to 260's base. Meantime, Sergeant Stohr, 'flew for his life': outnumbered by four or five 109's twisting, turning, trying to be as difficult a target as possible until all his assailants had fired all their ammunition and broke off the attack. As could be reasonably expected his Kittyhawk was badly shot up, loosing hydraulics, he was forced to belly land. Wounded, he was, like McParland, evacuated to a field hospital. Both were lucky to be alive. The Kittyhawk was a remarkably tough and resilient airframe.

During the first days of March, Hanbury trained his men hard, with practice bombing runs and air firing target practice occupying the second and third of the month. After five days bombing strategic targets or 'anything that moved', 260 Squadron were off to a new landing ground on 8 March as Blomfield recalls:

'We were ordered to set up shop in a dust bowl at Neffatia: the 'A' Party left at crack of dawn to ensure that the aircraft detailed for that morning's show would find fuel, ammunition and perhaps tea ready for them on the new advanced landing ground. The 'B' party, bulk of squadron personnel, reserve aircraft, M/T, everybody's kit etc. left the following day. There being a few more pilots than aircraft – for obvious reasons – some of us were transported in the 'tame' Heinkel 111 which had been donated to the squadron at Derna by the New Zealand sappers. Pedro's aircraft was unserviceable at the time so he flew the He111 with all the gash pilots aboard: I recall Geoff Fallows (NZ flight commander), George "Muscles" Tuck (a Yank from Detroit), Oscar Stohr, a Rhodesian Sergeant who was to be killed a week later [...] The flight, a mere fifteen miles was fraught: a sandstorm blew up in the sudden way they do: visibility marginal, port engine coughing occasionally, no option but to put down somewhere. Pedro found a gap in the gloom and put the Heinkel down on another forward air strip. Never had the time-honoured phrase, "Semper in excretum" been more applicable.'

Soon after, someone in officialdom came calling about the Heinkel, and she was taken away to be evaluated.

Operational again on the tenth, Hanbury led a flight of twelve Kittyhawk's as cover for 112 and 250 Squadrons who were on a strafing run against German troops. Attacked by a similar number of 109's, Hanbury led red section against three 109's, whilst Stocky Edward, who led Blue Section, dealt with the others. After breaking off the action the flight headed home, enroute strafing more German motor transports: two lorries had been destroyed but no claims made for the 109's. Flak brought down Flight Sergeant John Colley: badly wounded he was forced to belly land, and died later of his wounds. Colley, son of James Edward and Nellie Colley, of Leytonstone, Essex, was twenty-two when he died. He is buried at SFAX War Cemetery in Tunisia.

Training occupied the 13 to 20 March. Blomfield reports in his logbook: '21 March: Bombing and strafing El Hamma. Wizard target. Many M./T. fires. Destroyed two a./c. on ground and one truck in flames.' Sadly, Sergeant John Hamilton Orr was shot down that day. From New Zealand, he was aged twenty-one when he died. He is commemorated at El Alamein.

A particularly successful attack took place on 22 March when twenty Hurricane HD's of 6 Squadron, escorted by fighters from 239 Wing, attacked a concentration of tanks and vehicles located by tactical reconnaissance. The attack claimed twenty Mark III Panzers hit, with four being set on fire, twelve Mark IV Panzers hit and one set on fire, five lorries and one 88mm anti-tank gun destroyed. However, 260 did not escape the encounter unscathed. Killed in action that day, was Sergeant

Oscar Michael Stohr, aged twenty-two. He is commemorated on Column 272 on the Alamein Memorial. He was the son of Dr F. Stohr and Elsie Stohr of Kapiri Mposhi, Northern Rhodesia. On the twenty-ninth, Canadian Pilot, Warrant Officer class II Weston Blair Stauble was killed in action aged twenty-one. The son of Adam Joseph and Dawsina Lillian Stauble, of Alaska, Saskatchewan, Canada, he is commemorated on column 172 of the Alamein Memorial.

Enter Dracula

March ended as it began, with ground attack, and escort either to 112 Squadron or to flights of Baltimore Bombers. One of those who joined the squadron whilst in the desert theatre, and remained for most of the Italian campaign, was Christopher Lee. The squadron diary records he joined the unit on 2 April 1943, taking up his post two days later. Lee had been commissioned from Leading Aircraftsman at the end of 1942 as a Flying Officer.

The day he joined, the squadron was recovering from being bombed by German Ju 88's. The squadron, based at En Hamma had just arrived at their new landing ground from Medinne. The squadron diary reports that at dusk on 3 April, two Ju 88 enemy were spotted over the landing ground. Local anti-aircraft fire was put up, forcing the bombers off the intended target, bombs instead fell on the road leading to the landing strip. In the morning a sortie of fifteen ME 109's attacked the air field, dropping their bombs from altitude due to the ack-ack put up. Bombs straddled the air field. One 109 was hit by ack-ack, 260 Squadron suffered no losses. Lee arrived during a lull in the enemy attack. In the later afternoon, the airfield came under long-range German artillery fire. During the night, German aircraft were again over the airfield dropping marker flares. As the sun crept over the horizon on 6 April, the German heavy artillery had moved forward and began dropping 120mm shells onto 260 Squadron, hitting dispersal, and damaging aircraft from sister squadrons. Quite a portentous welcome to life in 260!

Lee was a key member of squadron personnel, and would be till the end of November 1944. Lee was he squadron Intelligence Officer, about his duties he recalls:

> 'I had a great deal of authority and also a great deal of responsibility. In my trailer I had to keep all the pilots updated on where the bomb line was, so we didn't go over it and bomb the wrong place, or stay behind it and bomb the wrong place, which would have been us. I kept them up to date with what was going on in Russia and everywhere else. The responsibilities were enormous. I was twenty-one and the responsibility was such that if I made mistakes, people died. [...] my job was to interrogate every single member of the squadron as soon as they got back from a sortie and ask did

you hit the target? Where were you? Was there any anti-aircraft fire? Did you see any enemy trucks or trains? Did you strafe them/ bomb them? What the weather was like, if they'd seen any other aircraft. They answered as best they could, and I forwarded that to the senior intelligence officer of the wing. He'd pass it up to group who'd pass it up to HQ. I'd write it all down in the squadron diary so we had a record of everything, marked top secret.'

Lee's broader duties were to liaise with Wing intelligence to ensure that the squadron undertook and was aware of its duties. Later on, he was the primary contact with Rover Control – more of that later – in co-ordinating bombing strikes with the army. It sounds all very boring, but without Lee, the squadron could not have operated offensively or defensively. All rather mundane compared to the 'myths' of Lee the spy and SAS operative, but an essential role in the squadron.

About Lee's duties Shep Sheppard adds:

'We had a trailer for our operations and intelligence room, used for both briefing and de-briefing and everyone on show dumped their wallets etc. into someone's hat and left these items in the trailer. Hoisted outside the trailer we had fitted, or rather attached to the trailer, a small flagstaff to which we attached one of three flags; a white flag denoted the squadron was on sixty minutes readiness; a green flag denoted thirty minutes readiness and the red flag meant we were on five minutes and everyone was required to get down to ops at once. When the red flag went up, young Harry Curnow would dash into the mess and start to play on the piano – yes, you've guessed it – "the red flag."'

How 260 Squadron had obtained a piano – like the farm yard menagerie! – in the desert and moved it around has never been disclosed by the veterans.

Victory in North Africa

The Tunisian campaign of early 1943 was the final stage of the fighting that had raged back and forth along the North African coast since the first Italian drive into Egypt in 1940. Originally controlled by a Vichy French government, Tunisia had been occupied by German forces following the surrender of Vichy forces in French Morocco and Algeria in November 1942. The combined American and British 1st Army advancing into Tunisia from Algeria hoped to move quickly through Tunisia to meet up with the British and Commonwealth 8th Army advancing across Libya after the victory at El Alamein, thereby crushing the Axis forces between them.

This was prevented, however, by the rapid reinforcement of Tunisia with German troops from Sicily and a series of skilfully executed defensive operations. By February 1943 the Allies had lost the initiative in Tunisia and a command reorganisation followed. Gradually, after much hard fighting, the 1st Army advancing from the west and the 8th Army advancing from the south, pushed the Axis forces into a pocket around Tunis. By the time Christopher Lee joined 260 Squadron, the war in the Western Desert was almost over. Blomfield's logbook reports:

> 8 April: Top cover to 112 Squadron. Diced with six 109s over Sfax. Damaged engine cut, spun from 4000ft. 2 trucks. P./O. Gray and Sgt. Peters killed […] 14 April: Fighter sweep. Jumped 12 109s – Eddie destroyed 2. Got in some good squirts – 2 damaged. 1 confirmed 19.4.43.

Eddie was Canadian ace, 'Stocky' Edwards, who like Shep was one of the veterans of 260 Squadron when Blomfield joined. Once Tunis has fallen, the Germans had their backs to the sea. Their objective was to withdraw to Sicily: either by air or by ship.

The squadron moved to El Djem during the course of 15-17 April. As well as fighter-bomber rolls, the squadron was involved in air combat with the Luftwaffe. These sorties were often intercept patrols. Blomfield again:

> 22 April: Sweep over Tunis Bay. Squadron got 9 Me. 323s. S.A.A.Fs got 24! [personal score] 2 Me. 323s confirmed.

British Intelligence, known as 'Y' Service, had intercepted German messages that the Luftwaffe were using the giant ME 232 transport aircraft to evacuate Cap Bon. These 6-engined leviathans could carry 200 troops at a time. Unarmed, the only defence the aircraft had was from the soldiers inside shooting their rifles through windows. They were almost sitting targets. As 'Y' Service had not intercepted an exact time, 239 Wing was sent to intercept at different times. 5 Squadron SAAF was up first and intercepted the majority just after take-off at Cap Bon. 260 Squadron followed, and by the time 112 Squadron RAF arrived, all the ME 323 had been downed. The interception of the ME 323's resulted in hundreds of German's drowning in the Mediterranean.

With Hawkeye Lee going off squadron, on 23 April an old face returned to 260 Squadron – this time as a Flying Officer – George 'Sparky' Black, to have a second 'bite of the cherry' with 260. Sparky was given command of A Flight with Stocky Edwards heading B Flight.

Two days later, during the course of the 25 April, acting Flight Lieutenant Stocky Edwards shot down two 109's and also damaged a third. In the same operation, Acting Flight Lieutenant J.E. Stewart shot down a 109, two more 109s being destroyed by Flight Sergeant Parlee and Sergeant Rattle. Acting Squadron Commander 'Pedro' Hanbury destroyed a fourth 109. The same day, 27 April, Blomfield was on 'Top cover to 3 and 450 Squadrons. Bombed three Italian cruisers – 2 hits – such flak!! Shot down. bailed out. Picked up 2 hours later.'

Anti-shipping operations off Cap Bon were assigned to 260 on 5 May. Whilst dropping their bombs, the flight was jumped by four ME109's and Sergeant Carver was shot down. He bailed out and got back to the unit forty-eight hours later. He had been picked up by a German motor launch, which was itself intercepted by a British destroyer. He and the Germans were then taken to Malta, from where he flew back to join 260 Squadron. The goal of the operations was to sink German troopships.

On 7 May 1943, the British 7th Armoured Division captured Tunis, the capital of Tunisia, and the US II Army Corps captured Bizerte, the last remaining port in Axis hands. The strong and intimate air support provided to the Eighth Army by 239 Wing made a critical contribution to the success of its operations. Cut off from supplies of rations, ammunition and fuel by an Allied naval blockade, the fate of the Axis forces around Tunis was inevitable; the last pocket of resistance surrendered on 13 May 1943. Some 250,000 Germans and Italians are taken prisoner.

Shep Sheppard again:

> 'Our squadron decided that now the show as over, we would have a celebration party and we invited everyone who was anyone in the Desert.
>
> 'What a party if turned out to be. We had our cow sent up from Castel Benito, ready slaughtered, and we roasted a whole side of beef. We also had one of our pigs killed and roasted that. Booze flowed freely and if you survived till 4.20 AM the following morning, you were served with breakfast of bacon and eggs.'

As Shep notes, 260 had become adept at being adhoc farmers, rearing cows and pigs to supplement the meat ration as well as geese and chickens for eggs, and meat. Somehow, in addition to the piano the squadron's pilots had obtained for their mess – how and from where in the middle of the desert? – a radio and a gramophone. Shep remembers:

> 'One record that was continually played on the squadron had the Andrews Sisters on one side singing *Apple Blossom Time* and the on the other side *Perfidia*. That record was part of the squadron and must have been played, two, three or perhaps four hundred times.'

Almost as soon as the party was over, Pedro, once more tour expired, was posted to Air Headquarters with DAF on the seventeenth. A day later, a future Commanding

Officer arrived, Leonard 'Leo' A. Malins. He had been posted from 145 Squadron with the rank of Flight Lieutenant and immediately as Flight Commander, replacing Stocky Edwards whose tour had expired. Pedro never returned to 260. His flight returning to North Africa was shot down on 3 June 1943 and he was killed. Major E.C. Saville, a South African, replaced Hanbury as CO.

With no operations, time was spent playing cricket, swimming in the med, as well indulging in inter squadron football and soft ball matches. For many of the veterans of the Desert campaign, thoughts turned to the future. Shep Sheppard remembers:

'Fifteen months on the squadron had turned me from a boy into a man. During that period, I had learnt that as you progress so your responsibilities become greater. I had my "Wings" for a year and ten months, but to me it seemed a decade.

'What had I achieved? Officially, one hundred and forty-five operational sorties, of which some sixty were strafing jobs, undoubtedly the most dangerous of all flying sorties, and accounting for the most stress on pilots, and the most deaths. Officially, three enemy aircraft destroyed in the air, one probably destroyed and three damaged, plus three destroyed on the ground, plus a small merchant vessel and Siebal ferry, and numerous vehicle and men […] the Doc told me straight – you are getting tired and it is time you took a rest. So, I did, going on leave officially from 21 June to 12 July, after which I was instructed to report to HQ Middle East Air Force in Cairo.'

Whilst 260 Squadron was getting some much-needed rest and relaxation, and new pilots trained, the Allies had turned their thoughts to what next: The invasion of the 'soft under belly.'

HELLO ITALY

6

HAVING PUSHED THE Germans out of Africa, thereafter, British policy in the War can be considered to be opportunist: the victory begged the question of what next.

At a conference in Casablanca in January 1943, four reasons for invading Sicily were given: firstly, to knock Italy out of the war. Secondly, to open up the Mediterranean – with its shipping routes and access to the Suez Canal – and possibly even further. Thirdly, with victory in North Africa considerable numbers of Allied forces were in the Mediterranean, some use needed to made for them in the theatre due to the lack of transport back to England. Fourthly, Britain and America needed to do everything they could to help the Russians and open a second front – to meet all objectives, in 1943, the Mediterranean was the only place the Allies could realistically bring Germany to battle.

The argument went – and quite logically – that if Italy could be knocked out of the war as an Axis power, the German army would have to divert considerable amounts of war materiel and troops to the Mediterranean. If the allies landed in Italy, it meant the Germans would have to occupy the entire Italian landmass, and secondly, and as importantly, the Germans would have to replace perhaps half a million Italian troops in Greece and the Balkans. By 1943, Germany was already severely stretched both in North-West Europe, and on the Russian front: a third front was something they could ill afford to fight on. Operation Pointblank, the Allied heavy bombing of Germany, was slowly but surely destroying German industrial capacity. By this stage in the war, thinking had already turned to what would be Operation Overlord, and Churchill argued persuasively, that the cross-Channel invasion of France needed as a pre-requisite the dispersal of German forces away from the Channel coast, which is what the Italian campaign offered. Moreover, many in Whitehall felt that getting boots on the ground in Italy, was the best way to encourage the growing resistance to Germany: resistance to German occupation was developing in the Balkans, which was a crucial centre of oil production. No fuel for tanks or aircraft, and the German army would be neutralised. In addition, by capturing southern Italy, especially the large airfield at Foggia, the Allies would be able to bomb aircraft production centres in Southern Germany out of reach to bombers flying from southern England and further denude industrial capacity. We should not forget, that having defeated the Italian forces in the Mediterranean, capturing Rome could be seen as a culmination of the campaign, and be a consequential moral boost for the Allies: the first occupied capital to be liberated. On paper therefore, the invasion of Italy looked to offer the Allies huge benefits.

To lead the forthcoming offensive, the victorious general in North Africa was named as Commander-in-Chief of the Allied Armies in Italy: General Sir Harold Alexander. Under his command were two Armies, the predominantly British Eighth Army under General Bernard Montgomery, and the predominantly American Fifth Army under General Mark Clark. Despite some reservations, the invasion of Sicily 'was on.'

Invasion preparations

As part of the build-up of forces for what was to be the invasion of Sicily, it was important that adequate air cover was provided: in preparation of this 239 Wing was to move to a secret destination. Getting ready for the invasion of Sicily all took time and organisation. A wartime squadron had thirty or so pilots and perhaps 300 ground crew. Moving fifteen aircraft, dozens of lorries, fuel tankers and tonnes of munitions fell to the squadron's staff and highly capable NCO's. The key to all of this, as Bill Shoesmith of 3 Squadron RAAF explained, was:

> 'Comradeship... This we all learned a lot about... How to pull together as a team – and this is from the highest to the lowest. And this is something that I feel that we really came out ahead in ... because for the length of time we were away together (and that, for most of us, was over 3½ years) there was very little friction between us... Although, naturally, a few minor little disagreements, but nothing of any major proportions. And even allowing for this, the bond of teamwork was always there.'

239 Wing Operations Record Book tells us on 1 July Group Captain 'Jackie' Darwen, commanding the wing, held a meeting with the squadron commanders from the wing 'accompanied by their respected Adjutants, Engineer Officers, Equipment Officers and Intelligence Officers' to inform them of the move and coming invasion. The squadron diary tell us, 260 moved from Zuara Landing Ground to 38 Personnel Transit Centre on 2 July. Sergeant Armourer Pountain remembers that on this occasion he was placed in charge of sixteen armourers as part of an advanced party. Assigned two lorries, the vehicles were to carry two re-arms of ammunition for the squadron's Kittyhawk's. A third lorry carried more ammunition. The party were allowed to carry with them their webbing equipment and a bedroll and a tool kit. They and everyone else in the squadron had been issued mosquito nets and commenced taking Mepacrine tablets to guard against Malaria. In charge of the detachment was the squadrons adjutant and Flight Sergeant Pugsley as senior NCO.

Moving out at 0900, the squadron arrived at 1300 after which 'tiffin (lunch) was served and afterwards instructions were given to "standby" for any special orders that may come through.' Moving an entire squadron was no easy task. As no orders came through the squadron diary records:

> It was extremely hot and great difficulty was experienced to find a shady spot; swimming was arranged in the sea. The bathing party returned after an hour's bathing [...] The whole night was spent at No. 38 PTC and it was not until the afternoon that orders were given to proceed to Tirpoli Docks. The parties embarked at approximately 1630 hours, by now the men were keen to be getting on with the job. The convoy left at about 1700 hours, the voyage was quite uneventful, the sea was very calm, and the L.S.T (American Type) on which we were traveling ploughed its way smoothly.

About these, Pountain adds that the Landing Ship Tanks (LST) were moored with bows to the jetty, with the bow ramps resting on the jetty itself. Once the lorry had driven onto the ramp, they had to drive down a sloping internal ramp onto the base of the ship. All men, other than the driver and co-driver had to board the LST as foot passengers. Once the squadrons lorries had been reversed into the hold of the LST, each wheel had to be chained down. Once secure the driver and co-driver joined their mates on deck. Early the following day the squadron diary reports:

> We discovered that Malta was our destination, at 1700 hours [4 July – ed] we arrived in Valetta where the troops disembarked. The troops left the ship quietly and made their way in small parties to the vehicles which were to convey them to Camp 6 Saint Paul's Bay. The journey through the town was quite exciting, as it was Sunday evening, it appears as though the whole inhabitants were out to enjoy the cool of the evening. Many people cheered as we went through. Camp 6 was reached by 2100 hours, by then it was quite dark, but a mug of tea, which was most welcome, was ready us, bully and biscuits were eaten and then all personnel retired.

The men had slept overnight in the open, and were issued tents on the morning of 5 July. Arrangements were made for "Liberty Runs" into Valetta where 'wines and spirits were plentiful but extremely expensive' lamented the squadron diary.

Operation Husky

Thanks to the greatest deception of intelligence in the Second World War – Operation Mincemeat, on 9 July 1943 – Operation Husky, the Allied invasion of Sicily, had begun under the overall command of General Dwight D. Eisenhower. US General

George S. Patton's Seventh Army landed on the southern coast of Sicily and British General Bernard Montgomery's Eighth Army on the south-eastern coast. Their two armies comprised the Fifteenth Army Group, led by British General Harold Alexander. Husky was to be one of the largest amphibious operations of the entire war, with more than 3,000 ships (under the command of British Admiral Andrew Cunningham, Commander-in-Chief, Mediterranean Fleet) transporting more than 150,000 Allied troops (eight divisions by sea plus two airborne divisions) over the next three days. It was a crucial learning experience for Operation Overlord. Vital air cover was provided by more than 4,000 airplanes (from the Royal Air Force and the US Twelfth Air Force under the overall command of British Air Chief Marshal Arthur Tedder).

239 Wing Operations Record Book reports:

> July 9. Group Captain J. Darwen led twelve aircraft of No. 112 Squadron to Malta. Twelve aircraft from each No. 3 RAAF and No. 250 Squadrons also arrived.

> July 10. The attack on Sicily commenced in the early hours of this morning and the first news received was of a satisfactory nature. Everything is reported to be proceeding according to plan.

> July 11. The Wing came into action for the first time today since the cessation of hostilities in Tunisia. The following squadrons flew to Sicily to bomb targets on the Catania-Siracuse Road, No. 3 RAAF, No. 112 and No. 250.

> July 13. Aircraft of No. 260 and 450 Squadrons flew from Zuara to Luqa (Malta). Two squadrons carried out a bombing and strafing raid in the St Michele- Grammichele area. During an attack by 112 Squadron, No. 450 (RAAF) and 260 Squadron were bombing and strafing the Catania area, S/Ldr G. Norton, the squadron commander, was seen to 'go in' with smoke pouring from his aircraft. Total sorties for the day – 66.

As the invasion got under way, the pilots of 260 Squadron were still at Zura, training hard for what was to come. Formation flying, air gunnery, and dive-bombing practice being carried out over ten days. At 0510 on the morning of 13 July, Major Saville, commanding 260 Squadron, led fourteen Kittyhawks to Malta, landing at 0740 at Luqa aerodrome. Pilot officers were billeted in the Modern Imperial Hotel, senior NCOs were billeted in the poor house.

In order to move to Sicily, the ground party of 260 Squadron left on 14 July, again embarking on an American LST which docked on the eighteenth. Shortly before landing Pountain recalls an announcement was given that they were about to land on Sicily. As the LST approached the coast, drivers and co-drivers and other personnel were ordered into the hold to unsecure their vehicles and get ready to disembark, and to ensure that reverse gear was engaged. Pountain recalls a loud grinding noise followed by a sudden jolt as the LST made contact with Sicily. Thereafter the bow ramp dropped, at Portapolo beach. Once the ramp was down, it was followed by the 'Start Engines' sign being illuminated, a green warning light followed and then red, and 260 drove onto Sicily led by the adjutant. The ground party arrived at Pachino No. 2 Landing Ground to prepare for the aircraft to arrive. Blomfield remembers that the landing ground at Pachino had been:

> 'Carved out of a vineyard! The weather was hot, the devil thirst was upon us; there were dusty grapes in abundance. We partook copiously. No one told us that the season for picking was still some weeks away. The following day Montezuma had no small degree of vengeance: most of the wing were relieved in both senses.'

Due to the airstrip being close to a reclaimed marsh, Blomfield relates, 'the mosquitoes could not be counted in any cubic foot of airspace. Anyone outside his net after 7 pm could have been lifted and carried away.' Sergeant Armourer Pountain agrees: he remembered that at dusk everyone retired to their 'bivies' or changed into long trousers and long-sleeved shirts, sleeves rolled down and fastened at the wrist to provide a mosquito-proof veil. He remembers the noise from the wings of millions of mosquitos was quite frightening. So bad was the situation that on the morning of 19 July, 87 Octane Petrol was liberally sprayed into ditches, on bushes and into foliage around the camp site. The petrol was ignited with a tremendous roar and sheet of flames, which eased the mosquito situation somewhat, but not entirely, as after a further twenty-four hour's, tented accommodation was established on a hillside nearby well away from the ditches and ponds of stagnant water which was home to the mosquitos.

Having established a secure beach head on Sicily, 'what next' was uppermost in allied thinking despite the fact the the island was still controlled by the German army. Churchill argued persuasively and correctly, that the 'what next' was to invade Italy, and to land near Rome. It was not to be. The lack of landing craft, and from November, infantry and heavy bombers which were to be withdrawn to support Operation Overlord, meant that rather than invading around Rome and 'the knee of Italy', it was to be the 'toe and ankle' that was to be the landing point. This was a strategic error on the part of the allies: it represented the allies opportunistic and naïve thinking about the campaign. The intention had to be to take Rome and establish strategic air force bases around Foggia to bomb German armament production in Austria. Sound thinking. Landing in southern Italy was the best that could be hoped for given the logistical resources available. Rather than a short campaign to take Rome, it meant a war of attrition which could have reasonably been predicted if anyone had actually looked at a map of Italy. Once the allies were on Siciliy, Italy had to be next in an inevitable chain of events that lead to the maelstrom of Cassino.

On 18 July, despite Churchill's severe misgivings, General Dwight D. Eisenhower won support from the Combined Chiefs of Staff for a two-part operation, the first part in Calabria (Operation Baytown), led by Montgomery, the second at Salerno (Operation Avalanche): both beaches were importantly within range of Allied fighters based in Sicily. A third subsidiary landing, Operation Slapstick, witnessed elements of the British 1st Airborne Division being transported by sea to seize the port at Taranto. With plans made, all thoughts now turned to the invasion of Italy, and completing the conquest of Sicily. Joining 260 Squadron that day was a new pilot, sergeant Maurice Gordon 'Bill' Nelson.

During 22 July, troops of Patton's Seventh Army took Palermo, the regional capital of Sicily, with Major General Lucien K. Truscott's 3rd Infantry Division at the head of armoured columns covering 100 miles in seventy-two hours. Palermo was the first city liberated by US forces in the Second World War. At the same time, the objective of the Eighth Army, headed by Montgomery, was to seize Messina on the north-eastern tip of Sicily: the advance was slowed by stiff resistance from the German Hermann Göring Parachute Panzer Division. That day 260 Squadron flew two operations, both interdicting German motor transports and attacking anything that moved. Early in the morning, Saville, flying as Red leader and Blomfield as Blue, attacked a convoy of over forty motor transports and strafed three tanks. No claims were made when the twelve Kittyhawks landed at 1045. Marshalling yards at Catania was the target for a Wing bombing operation on the twenty-third. Saville led twelve Kittyhawks from 260 Squadron, joining twelve from 250 Squadron and further twelve from 450 Squadron (RAAF). In the raid, four steam engines were destroyed along with ten wagons, with many others left burning. After strafing the stationary goods trains, Saville ordered that neighbouring goods warehouses, and an ammunition dump were to be attacked: both were destroyed with direct hits from remaining bombs. The squadron diary recorded the smoke from the fires rising to 1,000ft. All landed safely at 1405.

Formation flying practice occupied the 24 July.

Significantly, on the night of 24/25 July a majority of the Fascist Grand Council approved (nineteen for, seven against, one abstention) a motion of no confidence in Benito Mussolini. In the morning King Victor Emmanuel III met with Mussolini, removed him from office, and had him arrested. In his place, Marshal Pietro Badoglio, former chief of the Italian general staff and member of the Fascist Party, was named as prime minister. Badoglio declared on the radio to Italy that, 'The war goes on and Italy remains faithful to its word' in remaining loyal to Hitler. Mussolini was held in multiple locations, before being confined in the Hotel Campo Imperatore on the Gran Sasso d'Italia in the Abruzzo Mountains, one of Italy's tallest peaks. At 1000 the same day, Saville led ten aircraft from 260 Squadron in another Wing operation, joining twelve from 250 Squadron in an Armed Recce, bombing a railway junction. A second joint operation took place in the afternoon. Airborne at 1740, Malins led a flight of eleven, with twelve Kittyhawk's from 250 Squadron: the objective was breaking roads to hinder the German withdrawal.

The 26-27 July was 'more of the same': breaking roads and railways and interdiction of German transport and armour. Blomfield records: '27 July: Bomb and strafe C.S. Andrea. Wizard bombing on railway sidings. Clobbered a motor-cyclist. P/O Payne missing.' That afternoon, 260 Squadron flew for a second time against these railway sidings, both operations being led by Jackie Darwen.

Training, specifically dog fighting, occupied the 28/29 July. A Wing operation took place on 30 July, again interdiction, followed a day later by providing the Eighth Army with close support: strafing and bombing German trenches and lines as well as bombing German gun positions and clearing a path for the infantry.

The 1 August witnessed the hardest fighting yet seen of the entire campaign: the US 1st Infantry Division ('the Big Red One'), under the command of Major General Terry de la Mesa Allen Sr. ('Terrible Terry' Allen, as he was known to his men), battling the Germans for the town of Troina, located in central Sicily. With the Germans on the high ground and US forces under enemy observation for the duration of the battle, US losses were heavy, but the Americans ground forward. It was a portent of things to come.

As the fighting intensified the squadron moved to Agnone landing ground by 3 August. Being close to the front, the aircraft could remain over the operation sector before returning to refuel and re-arm.

Rhubarb, Rhubarb, Rhubarb

Blomfield records: '3 August: Rhubarbs round Etna. Got a "flamer" with Leo. Heavy Breda.'

Leo is of course Leo Malins.

Unsure as to what a Rhubarb was, on a visit to the RAF Museum at Hendon to access material relating to 260 Squadron I asked one of the staff what such an operation was.

The helpful archive room assistant told me that Rhubarbs were defined as patrols over territory occupied by the enemy, to be made by single fighters or formations up to a flight in strength, operating under cloud cover. The patrols were not to be made, however, when the cloud came down below 2,000ft which was later changed to 1,500ft. After ending our conversation, the guide returned and handed me a printed document all about 'Rhubarbs'. From this, I learned that on 'Rhubarb' patrols pilots could legitimately attack the following:

> Enemy military forces, including naval auxiliaries, troop transports and military supply ships could be attacked in any circumstances which did not infringe the Red Cross conventions or involve disproportionate risk to civilians.

Military works, fortifications, aerodromes (whether designated military or civil), and stores and dumps of military supplies could also be attacked on these terms.

Military establishments and depots, including barracks, camps, billets and naval dockyards, could be 'specifically selected for attack' only if they were known to be in use or occupation by Germans or Italians.

Shipyards, factories, and other establishments engaged in the manufacture, assembly or repair of military material, equipment, or supplies, as well as power stations ancillary thereto, and also fuel and oil producing plants, refineries and storage installations, could be attacked, but not if attacking them involved the intentional bombardment of civil populations or undue risk to civilians. They should also be known to be working for the Germans or Italians.

Lines of communication and transportation and means of inter-communication serving military purposes could be attacked if attacking them did not involve the intentional bombardment of civilian populations or undue risk to civilians; but attacks on moving trains and on merchant ships were specifically forbidden.

My guide then added, trains became regarded as a legitimate target from October 1941. Rhubarbs, he concluded, were considered by 'Top Brass' as a waste of time and pilots. As we shall see, this was true for 260 Squadron in Italy. However, for the pilots themselves, Dennis Varey believed they offered a chance to 'let off some steam': free from standard operation procedures by and large, pilots could chose their target and inflict as much damage as they could; 'pay back' for lost friends.

Horrors of War

As we touched on, one of the very legitimate critiques made about Rhubarbs, and by Douglas Barder no less, was that these operations were 'wasteful' of good pilots. Those conducted by 260 Squadron proved his point. On 3 August, the Kittyhawk being flown by Pilot Officer R.S. Brown on a Rhubarb was hit by a 20mm cannon shell. Brown was flying at 'deck level', so at a hundred feet, give or take, and made a very easy target. Perhaps because he was so low, the shell went through the mainplane and wounded Brown. Shrapnel tore into his left thigh. Despite blood loss, he made it back to base. Brown was off operations for four months and was lucky not to loose his leg. The Kittyhawk was so severely damaged as to be considered a 'write off', but the engine was taken into the pool of spares. Brown would do two tours with 260 Squadron. Before his first tour expired, he passed his maps of Italy to Dennis at the end of May 1944 and was back with 260 Squadron on 24 November 1944.

During 4 August, 260 Squadron carried out six strafing runs in groups of four aircraft. The targets were anything that moved. After a successful morning during which Saville and Blomfield claimed a motor transport each and on a second operation Malins, Bruce Page, Blomfield and McParland between them claimed two MK IV tanks damaged, three motor transport damaged and one destroyed. For the third time that day Saville led twelve aircraft up at 1450. The objective was to obliterate two columns, each of over twenty German lorries: on attacking the first column, ten lorries were claimed as destroyed or damaged, with one on fire. The flight then attacked the second column: three lorries were claimed damaged and one destroyed. The pilots of 260 did not have things 'all their own way'. Coming in low to strafe fleeing soldiers who had jumped out of their lorries, Flight Sergeant Rattle came under machine-gun fire from a German tank. His Kittyhawk, belching black smoke, the squadron diary tells, Rick turned away and climbed, presumably so he could jump over the side. Realising he would not make it to a safe height to jump before the stricken aircraft expired or exploded, he ditched into the sea. Sergeant McParland and two other pilots went up on a search party at 1520, but no evidence of the crashed aircraft or inflatable dingy was observed. He was recorded missing, presumed killed.

Flying as Rattles No. 2 was Sergeant Douglas Lory. During that August afternoon, he was in the wrong place at the wrong time: an 88mm shell smashed into the rear half of his Kittyhawk, FR304. The tail unit sheared away, leaving Lory strapped into the cockpit and wing section as it began to tumble and fall to earth. The reserve tank, behind the pilot, had been holed and was leaking high octane petrol. Realising he had to escape or plunge to his death, Lory threw back the hood on its runners and dived over the edge at 7,000ft. As my grandmother adroitly used to comment, 'fate is more important than fear or planning'; never was a truer sentiment expressed than what happened next. As Lory jumped into the void and his petrol-soaked chute blossomed out, the Squadron Operations Record Book reports a spark or other debris from the burning Kittyhawk ignited the fuel vapour coming off the chute. The parachute quickly burned away, dropping burning fabric onto Lory: his fuel-soaked flying attire catching fire. He dropped, burning, to his death. I cannot begin to imagine the fear, pain and sheer terror of those last moments. An appalling way to die. Flight Sergeant Lloyd Douglas Lory, Royal New Zealand Air Force is commemorated on Column 278 at the Alamein Memorial. He was the son of Jacob Henry and Lettia Lory of Takoroa, Aukland. He was aged twenty-five.

A day later Pilot Officer William Herbert Parlee was reported missing, presumed killed. Like Rattle, he was Canadian, hailing from New Brunswick. He enlisted in the RCAF on 25 September 1940. Progressing through the Commonwealth Air Training Plan between autumn 1940 and spring 1941, he arrived in England that summer. Allocated to 416 Squadron RCAF, he was transferred to 260 Squadron in October 1942. During his period with 260, he was promoted to warrant officer and then pilot officer. He was just twenty-one when he died. He is commemorated on column 271 at Alamein Memorial, Egypt. Major Saville wrote the following letter to his mother, Letha E. Parlee:

'Unfortunately, I cannot give you much information on the circumstances of his non return. We had been out strafing motor transport on the coast road north of Mount Etna where a fair amount of light anti-aircraft fire was encountered. Bill was still with us as we turned out to sea on the way home, but when we arrived back, he was missing. He did not call up on the radio, and no one saw him in any difficulties at all. Aircraft were sent out afterwards to search the area where he was last seen, but the pilots returned without any information. Everyone in the squadron joins me in extending to you our deepest sympathy at this time of anguish and uncertainty. Bill's presence will be sorely missed in the squadron, as he was extremely popular with everyone, and also one of our most capable flyers.'

Blomfield and Sergeant Thomson had been sent up at 0745 to look for Parlee as soon as Parlee was noted as missing at 0640. Blomfield recced an area twenty miles square and found nothing. In his report, Blomfield recorded that a Spitfire from a sister squadron was observed to be hit, and the pilot bale out. Blomfield and Thomson landed at 0835.

An investigation carried out after the war, found no conclusive evidence of how he died. Two Kittyhawks were shot down that day, the second flown by RAAF Flight Sergeant Kennet Goulder. The investigation found, they believed, Goulder's wreckage. Parlee was considered to be lost at sea, for unknown reasons.

The war was starting to take a heavy toll on 260 Squadron. As my uncle noted, you had to get used to losing your friends: friendships were superficial so you did not get 'too attached'. In essence you had to live in the moment as you never knew if you would come back from the next sortie. The psychological strain must have been immense. Bobby Gibbes of 3 Squadron (RAAF), a sister unit to 260 in 239 Wing, expressed his own feelings very openly as follows:

'Perhaps you think that the life of a fighter-pilot was somewhat glamorous, but believe the words of one who knows. There's no glamour in this role in warfare. No, none whatsoever. You do not know what it means to live for days, weeks, months, and even years with the fear of violent death gnawing at your very guts [...]. Have you watched that line of dust grow larger until at last it breaks into many minute moving ants, each a truck, or tank, or gun, manned by many men? The enemy in all his powerful might. You steel yourself and give the order to attack. Reflector sight and gun switches checked on. Who knows what lies ahead. Down you dive, a grimly-streaking mass of fighting might. You weave to clear your tail of any surprise attack by enemy fighters, and to fox the flak. No flash of guns and no bursts of flak – down and down. Suddenly a small burst of flak and then hell itself lets loose; but you are now in range – those moving guns and troop-filled trucks can never stop in time.

'You take aim and fire. God, watch those tracers fly. They hit their target. Some draw flames and others only smoke. Those trapped troops are as good as dead and some of those who do jump clear are merely riddled bodies whose contracting nerves and sinews have hurled them clear.

'Your attack is over – you break, weaving madly, diving, zooming climbing out of that hell to safety. You hear the sudden thud of a bursting shell and feel your aircraft leap like a wounded deer. Your heart stops still. You are still climbing, out and away. You examine your instrument panel closely, eagerly, hopefully, in abject fear. God, a thousand times better dead than to be forced down here – a prisoner – better dead. You nurse your engine fondly, that failing, surging, dying oil-smeared motor. Too battered and too low to avoid the front lines and that deadly small-arms fire. Too worried to care. Your lines – safety. Nothing matters now. You are alive. Why the old bus might still hold out. Your drome is in sight – the field is clear. You try your wheels, but no. Your hydraulics fill your cockpit with stinking slippery oil. Too low – too late for the emergency system – straight ahead losing height. Throttle off, switches cut, you hit and slide ahead. Your speed drops off, your nose ploughs in. Sand is spewed for acres. A sudden jar. You've stopped, alive and wildly elated. [...] You breathe again, then bum a lift to the camp, and to look like a man, ask if you'd catch the formation if you took off in another aircraft, conscious as hell of the shaking hand, the ashen face and a voice which can't hide a tremor.

'No, there's no glamour in being a fighter pilot.'

Miracles do happen

Amidst tragedy, miracles do happen. Contrary to expectations, Rick Rattle was not dead. He put to good use his basic training of how to evade capture and how to behave in prison camp. These skills, were part of basic training for all pilots as Dennis's notebook from Abu Sueir relates:

General Intelligence

If after having force landed in enemy territory you manage to make your way to a neutral country, say you are an escaped

POW. This necessitates you have to see the British Consul and once in there you are on British soil and under British jurisdiction. If captured in enemy territory, the best time to escape is in between the time of capture to the time of confinement. The only information you have to give is name. no. rank under the Geneva Convention. On arriving at a Pukka POW camp you will be searched and your clothes taken. Your clothes and any personal belongings will be returned in all probability. There is usually an Allied officer in charge of a batch of POW's who is spokesman. If an attempt at escape is to be made, always inform the officers who may be able to give you valuable information. If an escape is made and a sentry or enemy is killed you cannot be charged and tried for murder. The maximum penalty is 30 days solitary confinement: from information received it appears that Germany, for her own good, is abiding by the Geneva Convection. If, however, in escaping you kill a civilian you are immediately handed over to a civilian court to be tried for murder.

Always keep a portion of your uniform. A uniform under the Geneva Convention constitutes 3 buttons, your wings, stripes etc. Never carry firearms or any written information, this constitutes a spy. Meat is not given in these camps but you are entitled in these camps to the same quantity and quality of food as German soldiers. In addition, POW's receive Red Cross parcels.

Discipline in POW camps

Shaving, keeping yourself clean and saluting officers etc. is requested. This is also for moral and propaganda purposes. Airmen, privates and ratings can be made to work but only on work of non-national importance; gardening, cooking, waiting etc. S/NCO's can only be made to work as supervisors. Officers can not be made to work at all, but usually they organise sport, lectures etc. if the airman is working as a skilled worker, he gets 1/- a day, if unskilled, 6d. S/NCO's get ¼ for supervising skilled work, 8d unskilled. Airmen & NCO's pay is carried on, including allotments, flying pay is lost. It is paid into his account. P/O £6 per week, F/O £8.

Never give your word of honour not to escape, if you do and it comes to the ears of the British Government you are immediately branded a traitor. Your word can be given for a set period however.

If you are not captured never travel in more than pairs. The people to help you are the peasants & poor, oppressed people. Don't approach anyone in a town. All broadcasts, letters & literature are organised solely by the Red Cross.

Aids to Escape

Map printed on thin tissue paper
Double sided maps printed on silk
Brass compass button
Collar stud compass
Magnetic pencil clip
Magnetic fly buttons
Hacksaw blade
£10 in money
Pack of goods: 14 Horlicks tablets, tube of Nestle milk, compass, Stalozone tablets for purifying water, Benzathine stimulant, map, gun, toffee, matches, rubber bottle.

As hinted at, this theory was put into practice by Rick Rattle as documents held in the National Archives at Kew relate:

'I took off from Agnole at 1400hrs on 4 Aug 43 in a Kittyhawk aircraft sortie. About 1540hrs I was hit by flak and had to ditch in the harbour of S. Marie Tecia, south of Riposto. I landed about 300yds off shore, removed my harness, and swam in my Mae West to a rock 100yds from the shore, Here I removed my Mae West, checked to see that I had no papers and swam ashore.

'I arrived on the beach at S. Maria Tecia at about 1550hrs, and was taken into the custody of armed civilians, who searched me and removed my escape money and maps. Later, I was taken over by two Italian naval petty officers. I was taken to a small local headquarters, where an Italian civilian put alcohol on my head wounds and fed me. He asked me the type of aircraft I was flying and the number of the crew. I told him this, as my aircraft was visible in the sea. I was then taken to an Italian barracks, where my head wound was dressed and I was sent to hospital at S Maria D. Malati. Here I was put into a room by myself with guards outside, and my wounds were dressed and stitched. An officer brought a Red Cross form for signature. I refused to sign the false one, and he brought the correct one, which I signed with my name, number and rank only.

'This officer saw me daily, and tried to pump me, but I gave him no information. I was preparing to drop out of the window of the night of 7-8 Aug, and had ripped my sheets for this purpose, intending to hide near Mount Etna. At about 0300hrs on 8 Aug, they warned me they were leaving, and the hospital was evacuated about 0400hrs.

'We moved in lorries to Riposto. The rear lorry was shot up by the RAF en route, causing 16 casualties. No Red Cross was visible.

We arrived about 0700hrs at Riposto, where I was put in the same house as the Italian Officers, with two guards in my room.

'I was here until 10 Aug. I became particularly friendly with a Sargenti Maggiore and an Italian-Austrian private. An Italian major was in command and evidently put off handing me over to the Germans until 10 Aug when the Royal Navy shelled Riposto. I was taken in a truck by the major, a lieutenant, the Sargenti Maggiore and the private to San Cosdio a few miles away. I was brought before the German Commandant (Schmalz Division) He had been told by the Italina major that I was the pilot of a Curtis plane, and tried to interrogate me further. On my refusing to answer, he threatened me and, handling his revolver, said, "I assure you I intend to spend no time whatever with prisoners of war". He then rebuked the Italian major for having kept me for six days without notifying the Germans. Feelings and words ran high. At this moment a despatch was handed to the German officer and he left the room. The Italian major walked over to me and said, "do you think you will like your new friends?" I answered that at any rate they were soldiers and not like the Italians, who allowed the Germans to rape their women, shoot their soldiers and loot their homes, ending, "If I had prisoners of war, I am damned sure I would not let someone else take them from me!"

'This started them all talking nineteen to the dozen and at the suggestion of the Sargenti Maggiore, I was bundled out of the room by another door, and a jacket of an Italian Corporal Maggiore was put on me in place of my bush jacket. I was wearing corduroy trousers and suede shoes. The Italian officers and the private then drove off, and I walked back with the Sargenti Maggiore, passing the German road block to where an Italian lorry stood on the side of the road, full of Italian troops.

'I was told to get in and feign sleep. We remained there for about an hour and then drove back to Riposto, where my bush jacket was returned to me. At about 0900hrs on 11 August I was put into a lorry, one of a convoy of four, with guards and other troops. We drove to Fiumerfreddo. They told me this area was staffed with Germans, and we were dispersed in a large lemon orchard occupied by two German 88mm guns. I was hidden in a stone woodshed, and kept their two days, being fed and cared for by the Italians.

'While I was there, the place was well strafed by my own squadron, who put one gun out of action and caused four German casualties. Later that evening the British started shelling the whole area with 25-pounders, and kept it up until about noon on 12 Aug.

'The Italians had become very panicky by this time, and their officers had left with their transport. They offered me a rifle, which I refused, and gave me a steel helmet and the corporal's jacket. I then walked in a westerly direction on the top of a gorge, where I met the private and a cook, who carried a sack of supplies. We found a clef in the gorge where we sheltered for four hours.

'The private went out to reconnoitre, and came back with a boy who led us to a covered slit trench above the gorge, where we stayed hidden from the Germans until the morning.

'The Italian population of Fiumerfreddo were sheltering just in case further up the gorge and the private did a deal with them on food supplies. The private and I joined them, and the private left us. We stayed there until 15 Aug, when the Germans blew up the bridge over the gorge about 0400hrs.

'News was later brought that the British were near, I picked up the cook and five other Italian soldiers, including one officer, and after climbing out of the gorge, came upon a British machine-gun post, whence I was directed to Advance Headquarters. There I handed over my Italian prisoners and shortly afterwards met General Montgomery and staff officers who questioned me.'

After spending time in hospital, Rattle was promoted from sergeant to flying officer in the General Duties section of the Royal Canadian Air Force on 22 August 1943. For him, combat operations were over. Rattle was not alone in putting theory into practice in escaping from German custody as we shall see.

CHAPTER
7

THE 'MEAT GRINDER'

SECRET NEGOTIATIONS BETWEEN Eisenhower and the Badoglio government took place on 5 August to arrange an Italian surrender to the Allies. This did not mean that the Italian campaign would be a 'walk in the park': rain, mud, and mountainous terrain meant the campaign became a war of attrition, akin to the 'meat grinder' of Verdun in the First World War.

The following day, after the surrender had been agreed, the US 1st Infantry Division took Troina as the Germans evacuated and continued their retreat to the north-east of Sicily. 239 Wing Operations Record Book reports:

> Two pilots, one from each of 112 and 260 Squadrons are missing from today's operations. Total sorties for the day – 69.

The Italian campaign was starting to be one of the hardest 260 Squadron would ever fight.

One of 260 Squadron's pilots had a miraculous escape a day later. On 8 September, Major Saville had led A Flight up at 1145 on an Army Close Support operation. After attacking the primary target, Saville led the flight on a strafing run against a column of over thirty German vehicles. The column included four Mk III tanks, six half-tracks towing 88mm guns, four Kubel waggons and other vehicles. In the attack three lorries were destroyed along with a staff car and a half-track. Two gun trailers were also damaged, along with an 88mm gun, a 75mm gun and a Mk III tank. An electrical substation was strafed, resulting in a huge fire. The German army, well aware of the threat by 'Jabos' were increasingly ever more capable of defending themselves. German ground fire from the tanks and half-tracks crippled the Kittyhawk flown by Flight Sergeant Curno. With smoke pouring from the stricken aircraft, he coaxed the aircraft over what he hoped was Allied lines. Crash-landing, he was rescued by a detachment of Royal Marine Commandos, and returned to 260 Squadron on 10 September. He was posted to General Duties on 13 September, his active combat participation was over.

As well as facing losses in combat, the Germans were still capable of offensive actions to try and ground the RAF. On 11 August the war came to 260 Squadron, as Christopher Lee remembers:

'We were shot up by JU88 bombers at night, which no one thought would ever happen in Sicily. It was unexpected to say the least because we had air superiority.'

The squadron diary provides more information:

The landing ground was illuminated by moonlight. Flares were dropped at 2230, which guided in more JU 88s who dropped bombs and incendiaries which set fire to surrounding stubble fields. Four Kittyhawk's were seriously damaged as were some of the squadron's vehicles. Disaster was averted when wooden ammunition boxes caught fire, but were dragged away from aircraft by ground crew, Corporal Arthur an armourer, and Leading Aircraftsman Dempster, a cook. Both men broke open the boxes and extinguished the flames despite other ammunition boxes exploding as bombs fell around them.

239 Wing Operations Record book reports 'the sun-dried grass burned with considerable ferocity', adding that Wing Commander 'Jackie' Darwen led a party of pilots and ground crew to put out raging grass fires before they burned out of control and incinerated 239 Wing. One man was killed and three wounded.

This night attack was to keep the DAF on the ground: the Germans had begun evacuating their forces that night from Sicily across the Straits of Messina. Thus, it was imperative that the evacuation was not interdicted by the feared 'Jabombers.' Because the RAF was grounded, the bulk of the German force on Sicily escaped during the early morning. Despite the 'early morning wake-up call', or even in spite of it, Darwen was in the air later that day. Darwen had an irrational hatred of the Germans, and was becoming increasingly reckless with his own safety when on operations. During this sortie that day his aircraft was hit twice by ack-ack to the wing, and was hit again to the engine, blowing the spinner cap off the propeller. Seven sorties were flown that day to hinder the evacuation of the German army.

On the morning of the twelfth, 260 Squadron began anti-shipping operations, endeavouring to interdict German transports. Ten barges in the straits of Messina were attacked on the fifteenth. Blomfield recorded, 'Heaviest ack-ack I've ever seen. Flight Sergeant Hamilton missing.' The squadron diary reports Colin George Hamilton, Royal New Zealand Air Force, was seen diving down on his bombing run, and never seen again. His Kittyhawk simply disintegrated from ack-ack fire. He had no chance to get out before the burning wreck plummeted into the sea. The only consolation was that one of the six landing barges ferrying German troops he was attacking was sunk. Hamilton, is commemorated on Column 2478 at Alamein.

The losses for 260 Squadron continued to mount: On 17 August Flying Officer Thornhill was shot down by ack-ack: The Operations Record Book reports 'intense medium and heavy fire crippled a flap causing considerable damage.' He managed to return to base, pancaking close to the strip. Four pilots had been lost in a week. The lottery of life and death, certainly did not favour 260 in those desperate weeks in August. German Anti-aircraft gunners were well trained and deadly accurate at their task at hand.

Despite these losses, the Allies were making headway against the Germans. 17 August also witnessed the Allies enter Messina, ending the conquest of Sicily. American troops of Patton's Seventh Army won the 'race to Messina,' arriving just a few hours ahead of Montgomery's British and Canadian troops. The Germans did everything they could to fend off DAF and deployed perhaps the highest concentration of anti-aircraft guns of the war on Sicily and south Italy. Blomfield records: '25 August: Army co-op. Very hazy. No targets. Heavy A.A. Crashed near Catania.' Blomfield was lucky. His Kittyhawk pancaked, and he escaped before it exploded. With the help of Sicilian civilians, who provided him with shelter, rest and food, he was back with the squadron after forty-eight hours. Shep Sheppard remembers about ack-ack:

> 'Dive-bombing and strafing was probably the most rewarding type of op because you could see what you were doing and, also, you were getting a result on every show. There is no question of course, that in attacking the targets that we did, it was a most hazardous job. There was heavy ack-ack, light Breda, machine gun and ordinary rifle fire to cope with, and if you got hit low down in the attack, you did not have much chance to get out. If you did get down, the guys you had been strafing would not greet with you with a bottle of gin!'

260 Squadron were rested during the twenty-sixth: the following day it provided escort for twelve B-26 Mitchell bombers, which would also be the squadron's duty on the thirty-first.

Four operations were flown that day. The first, a flight of eight, was up at 0920 and back at 1130. Malins led up four Kittyhawks at 0920, all landed at 1130. Blomfield led up another flight of four at 1335, Malins had taken up eight moments before at 1330. Malins was to escort twelve Boston's, attacking a target on the Italian mainland. Heavy cloud meant that the bombs were dropped on pinpoint reference and no results were observed. Ack-ack was fired through the clouds, and as the four Boston's made their turn for home, they were jumped on by four ME 109Gs. The 109s came up through the cloud, and behind the bombers and the Kittyhawks providing cover. Australian Pilot Officer Bruce Page found he had two 109s on his tail, taking damage in the tail unit and mainplane he dived into cloud to escape, coming out at 500ft. Pilot Officer Harvey (RCAF) and Flying Officer Flury engaged the 109s, but made no claims. On approaching home base, Page found his electrical systems had been 'shot to hell' and his landing gear failed to deploy. Page had no option but to belly land. He was unhurt, but the Kittyhawk was severely damaged. This was 260 Squadron's first encounter with the Luftwaffe since April. Air superiority was vital if the invasion of Italy was to succeed.

Operation Baytown

Despite the Allies best efforts, the Germans and Italians had succeeded in evacuating over 60,000 of their troops, as well as much of their equipment, from Sicily to mainland Italy. Their losses, which eventually amounted to 156,000 men, were suffered mostly by Italian units. On 3 September, Montgomery's Eighth Army launched Operation Baytown, an amphibious operation at Reggio di Calabria, the toe of the Italian peninsula. Baytown was to be a diversion for the primary landings at Salerno. The day Baytown began, the Badoglio government secretly signed an armistice with the Allies. Bill Shoesmith a sergeant with the ground crew of 3 Squadron (RAAF) recalls in 1988:

> 'When the Italian Army surrendered, we thought that it'd just be a case of going straight up to the top of Italy to the Swiss Border and continue on from there. But, oh no! Jerry had something to say about that and he was determined to make the Allies fight every inch of the way up the Italian mainland. Little did we know then that it would be another two years before we came back to Taranto on our way home.'

The Germans contested every inch of ground.

The amphibious assault had been preluded by medium bomber strikes over the previous day, with 260 Squadron providing escort. Montgomery's goal was the total destruction of German lines of communication, so railway lines, roads and bridges became key targets to obliterate. The bombing raids continued in advance of the landings. Providing the slower and more vulnerable bombers was 260 Squadron's objective for D-Day. 239 Wing Operations Record Book relates:

> Sept. 3rd. The fourth anniversary of the outbreak of the war heralded the attack by Eighth Army on the Italian mainland [...] Escorts to medium bombers were provided [...] on the last operation of the day, 20 plus MT were bombed near Oppido. Three fires were started. Total sorties for the day – 70.

The Wing was detailed to engage in the interdiction of German transports and railway engines: basically, if it moved it was a legitimate target.

To help the Eighth Army grind its way forward into mainland Italy once it had landed, 239 Wing was detailed to bomb and strafe German gun positions and strongpoints. One such operation was on 5 September, when Major Saville, at the head of A Flight of 260 Squadron was airborne at 1145. They were briefed by Intelligence Officer Lee that the target was gun positions in the Viro Valentia area. The pinpoint was bombed from 1,000ft. After the bombing run, Saville headed north and strafed a column of thirty plus motor transports. The column included four MK III tanks, six half-tracks towing 88mm guns and four Kubel wagons. Three of the lorries were damaged, so was a half-track and a Kubel wagon, an 88mm was shot up, as was a 75mm and a MKIII tank. On the return leg, a power substation was destroyed. Flight Sergeant Cuiro came under enemy fire. His Kittyhawk III was crippled with an oil leak and a glycol fire; he was forced to crash-land. Rendered unconscious in the crash. After coming too, and realising he needed to escape before being burned alive, he managed to leave the aircraft despite being heavily concussed. Taken into the protective custody of Italian partisans, who hid him from German patrols, he was rescued by a patrol of Royal Marine Commandos who 'patched him up.' He was well enough to return to 260 Squadron during 10 September. He had a miraculous escape. Cuiro was transferred to General Duties the following day following a debrief by Christoper Lee; for him the war as an active participant was over.

With Montgomery gaining a toe hold on mainland Italy, on the early morning of 9 September, General Mark Clark, commander of US Fifth Army, initiated Operation Avalanche, the Allied landings on the Italian Peninsula at Salerno. The British 1st Airborne Division captured Taranto without opposition as part of Operation Slapstick. The same day, Eisenhower announced that the Italian government under Badoglio had agreed to an armistice with the Allies (through General Giuseppe Castellano in Cassibile, Sicily) and that Italy would have the status as a 'co-belligerent' against Nazi Germany. In response, German forces carried out Operation Axis (Fall Achse), occupying Italy using troops already in the country in conjunction with forces moved into Italy via the Brenner Pass. Hitler ordered that Italy be treated as an occupied country. Field Marshal Erwin Rommel was given responsibility for the occupation of Italy and also responsibility for disarming the Italian armed forces.

The German commander in southern Italy, Field Marshal Albert Kesselring, led the resistance to the Allied landing at Salerno. German forces moved to disarm Italian garrisons in France, Yugoslavia, Albania, and Greece. Kesselring launched a counter-attack on 10 September with the 16th Panzer Division, which for a time, threatened the integrity of General Clark's beachhead. Admiral Alberto da Zara surrendered the Italian fleet to British Admiral Andrew Cunningham, Commander-in-Chief, Mediterranean Fleet, at Malta.

On 12 September it was decided that 239 and 244 Wings would move to the mainland. During this move Blomfield relates that the last of Nick Nichols menagerie of animals was 'for the chop.' He had 'obtained' a piglet in North Africa, from an old Italian settler, kept it at Castle Benito with the other animals, and somehow had smuggled it first onto Malta and then onto Sicily without the 'powers that be' noticing. The pig, remembers Blomfield, was initially:

'...a small black and white cuddly lump, it moved with us, fed well on bits from everyone's meals, liked the odd draught of vermouth or chianti, and flourished and grew. Word got around and the powers that be said a definite "No" to any further progress of it to the Italian mainland. She had grown into a large and not at all cuddly lump, but was everyone's friend. There was a lot of pork there! Nick had obviously to undertake the task of her demise. I shall never forget the look on his face as he led her away to a quiet corner of the camp with a 0.38 Smith & Wesson in hand. The cooks did a splendid job though.'

On to Italy

Moving fifteen aircraft, dozens of lorries, fuel tankers and tonnes of munitions, fell to the squadron's staff and highly capable NCO's. Sergeant Pountain remembers 260 Squadron flew from new Siracuse:

'In support of the Eighth Army as they started the invasion of southern Italy. Firstly, in the toe of Italy and later following the airborne landing near to Tarranto. I forget how long the early campaign in southern Italy took. Eventually, however, some staff officer at Airforce Headquarters dreamed up a really crackpot scheme for an advance party of 260 Squadron to fly into an Italian airfield at Grotaglie near Taranto. We were to fly in two United States Dakota aircraft with our own aircraft as escort.'

This probably explain the demise of the pig: she could have been 'accommodated' on a lorry out of harm's way and officialdom, but not a Dakota. 239 Wing Operations Record Book reports:

13 Sept 43. Three DC3 Aircraft took off at 1410 hours, escorted by the Group Captain and Squadron Leader OP F. Illingworth (OC No. 112 Squadron), both in their own Kittyhawks. Some two hours later, the pater arrived at Grottaglie airfield. Flak was going up over Taranto as the aircraft landed. The Group Captain introduced himself to Colonello Napoleoni, the Chef d'Aeroporte. Conversations were immediately commenced and it was at once apparent that little or no support could be expected from the Italian Air Force, as the

Germans had taken all the transport, and had destroyed everything that had not already been destroyed by Allied bombers.

In total fifty-two DC3 were used to move 239 Wing to its new landing ground, where 260 Squadron's remaining ground party arrived on the fifteenth in the squadron's transport, some sixteen lorries and other vehicles on a LST. Turning to the pages of Sergeant Pountain's memoires, he tells us that the Dakotas carrying the ground crew kept their engines running once they landed due to the threat from the Luftwaffe, and the armourers, mechanics, et al, were told to get out sharply so the USAAF pilots could make a quick getaway. This 'air-mobile' movement had been a hasty improvisation, due to the lack of LST and to provide much needed reinforcement as quickly as possible given the Allied Salerno invasion had been badly pinned-down and the Germans looked capable of driving the Allies back into the sea. By the time it came to land 260 Squadron in Italy, the Dakota pilots had become well versed in 'air mobile' operations: they had already unloaded 3 Squadron (RAAF) the day before. 3 Squadron thus became the first complete Allied squadron to attack from a mainland Italian base. Within minutes of landing 3 Squadron's Kittyhawks had been refuelled and loaded with bombs. Taking off, their bombing runs surprised the German divisions besieging the Salerno beachhead as a contemporary account reports:

> The men who did that job were to reap the reward of deep satisfaction the same evening, when our pilots returned from their bombing and strafing of German mechanized transport on roads leading down to the beaches near Salerno. The success of that show was summed up by Squadron Leader Brian Eaton, who was at that time in command of the squadron and later received the D.S.O. and D.F.C. When he returned from the mission he said that some 700 vehicles were bunched together into 'beautiful targets.'
>
> It was obvious, he added, that the Hun had been caught by surprise, unaware that the fighter-bombers had moved from their base in Sicily.
>
> A scoreboard hanging in the squadron's operations room made most satisfying reading at the end of three days' flying. Twenty-five mechanized vehicles completely destroyed, eighteen set on fire, and eighty-four otherwise damaged, four motorcycles and their riders wiped out, one goods train shot up and brought to a standstill, numerous enemy troops killed, wounded, or thoroughly frightened...That was the formidable list of successes achieved in only four missions in three days.

Despite the ground being on the mainland, the pilots and aircraft of 260 Squadron were still on Sicily. The last long-range strafing run from Sicily, took off on 16 September, Sergeant McParland was hit by flak, trailing white smoke he was seen to crash-land in a field close to the bombing run target. He escaped from the stricken Kittyhawk moments before it erupted into a sheet of flame. Thankfully, he evaded capture by the Germans and was concealed for four days by Italian civilians. He was handed over to a patrol from the Cameron Highlanders sometime on 19 September and returned to unit twenty-four hours later.

The squadron's serviceable fifteen Kittyhawks landed at the new landing ground at 1630 on the eighteenth. About operations that day, Blomfield reports, 'Bomb M./T. Guardia Lombardi. 2 x 250lbs. George got direct hit. Hit by 40mm. Pranged on our side – a./c. a write-off.' Sparky Black had been posted to 450 Squadron in May, and returned to 260 Squadron on 16 September. On this operation, Sparky was leading Blue Section with Blomfield as his wingman: the pair got separated from the main flight, and instead attacked a column of German lorries, estimated as forty plus. Blue Section attacked the target, despite intense ack-ack, and clearly Blomfield was at the wrong place at the wrong time. He was close enough to 260 Squadron's base to walk back and be back in the air on the following day.

The Allied Military Government (AMG) was announced on 18 September. It had control over the zones of combat in Italy and the Naples region, with its indispensable port. Authority in the liberated provinces of Taranto, Lecce, Brindisi, and Bari was ceded to the Badoglio government, but under the oversight of an Allied Commission, directed by Noel Mason-McFarlane, former British governor of Gibraltar.

On 19 September, tragedy struck 260 Squadron: Major Saville led twelve Kittyhawks up at 1215 on an armed recce along the Benevento Road at Montella. Over thirty German motor transports were observed and bombed from 2,000ft. After strafing the formation, which claimed one lorry destroyed, five damaged and eight German soldiers killed or seriously wounded. Saville, Sergeant Mills, his No. 2, and Sergeant Smith, turned east and flew south along the road from Avellino. Coming in low, flying at 500ft, the three aircraft came under machine-gun fire. Saville's aircraft was hit and side slipped to port, the wing-tip striking the hill side. The Kittyhawk was then seen to explode. Saville was not seen to get clear. Sparky Black took over the formation, all remaining aircraft landed safely.

Saville was reported missing. Major F.W. Venter from 5 Squadron (SAAF) was named as temporary replacement for Saville on 22 September.

Having been rescued by the Germans, on 23 September Mussolini established the Italian Social Republic, a puppet regime often referred to as the Salò Republic because of its location in northern Italy. Marshal Rodolfo Graziani was named Minister of Defence. At the same time the Germans began to organize the first round-up of Italian men born between 1910 and 1925 for forced labour, dragooning some 18,000 men in Campania and Latium.

On the twenty-fifth, the squadron moved to Bari landing ground

> The civil airport at Bari was occupied by the Spitfire wing, so we were housed on a temporary airfield. We had, however, the best

of the bargain. Our airfield was less than a mile from the centre of Bari. We were allowed into town whenever we were off duty. Bari was a really nice little town. In many ways like Tripoli. Lots of Cafes and bars.

Heavy rain at the end of the month curbed operational flying. It was during this lull, that here at Bari, Sergeant Pountain reports that corporal armourer Watkins returned to base rather excited: so important was the news, that he demanded to see Major Venter. In the well-established tradition of 260 in 'sniffing out Alcohol', it transpired that Watkins had met a brewer who had been supplying the Germans with beer, with the German army in retreat, the brewer was naturally enough looking for a new client to buy his beer. Venter duly negotiated with the Italian brewer twopence halfpenny per bottle, with a penny returned for each bottle. Thereafter, 260 Squadron had a regular and cheap supply of beer until 'the powers that be' got wind of the arrangement in early October and the allocation to 260 dropped to a dozen bottles a week, less than a quarter of the former allocation. Much grumbling followed from the squadron.

One of the problems that 260 faced when operating from Perforated Steel Plate landing strips was rain. In one notable occasion on 27 September, Major Venter led Red Section of A Flight up at 1200 to carry out a sweep at Foggia. Low cloud and torrential rain forced Venter back. Venter was first to land at 1340 and encountered no issues. However, the squadron diary reports that as Sergeant Curteis came into land, his wheels locked up: the wet landing strip was a giant 'skid pan' and his Kittyhawk slammed into a stationary Kittyhawk stood at dispersal. Sergeant Duguid, moments later, came in to land and had the same issue: his brakes were ineffective, the wheels locked and his Kittyhawk skidded out of control off the landing strip. Neither pilot was injured. The Squadron Operations Record Book reports: 'Maj Venter landed at base during a rainstorm, three of the section making crash-landings. The remaining section did not attempt to land and proceeded to Gottaglie then returned to Bari after weather conditions had improved.' Blue Section was led by Leo Malins, who landed at 1520.

The same day that Venter slithered off the runway, an uprising known as 'Four Days of Naples' began. It started with the townspeople erecting barricades and attacking German soldiers across the city. In the German counter-attack, more than 660 Neapolitans perished during four days of fighting. Elsewhere, troops of the British Eighth Army captured the airfields near Foggia. A more detailed armistice agreement was reached between the Allies and the Badoglio government, exerting Allied control over the Italian armed forces and pronouncing the aim of eradicating Fascism on 29 September.

During 1 October Allied troops entered Naples. Two days later the squadron began its move to Foggia. During the move, the squadron adjutant received news that Sparky Black had been promoted to the rank of flight lieutenant: someone on 239 Wing was clearly uncomfortable with a flying officer leading a flight. It was also a recognition of his service and leadership. 'Foggia Main', Sergeant Pountain remembers:

> '...was a large airfield which been previously been a main Regio Aeronautical base. Later, many temporary airfields were constructed on the Foggia plain, and the complex became the home of hundreds of American Fortresses and Liberators.'

On 7 October, Group Captain Darwen led twelve Kittyhawks from 260 Squadron on an armed recce, being airborne at 1625. The formation flew from base at 8,500ft as 239 Wing Operations Record Book tells us what happened next:

> It is recorded with profound regret that G/Capt J. Darwen DFC failed to return from an operation which he was leading over an enemy target at 1700hrs today [...] On account of heavy rain which fell all morning, there was no operational flying until late afternoon. The first armed recce was led by G/Capt J. Darwen DFC. Approaching Palata, eight plus MT were sighted. Three were bombed in a dive down to 1000ft. Most of the bombs fell among the MT, and some on the town itself. Intense and very accurate light a/a was encountered. Both G/Capt Darwen and his No. 2 are missing from this operation. One a/c believed to be the G/C's was hit by a/a in its bombing dive, and was seen to crash in flames. The other was also hit, and was last seen with white smoke pouring from his engine over the target area.

Darwen was a career RAF officer and saw active service on the North-West Frontier 1936-40. At the outbreak of the Second World War, he returned to the UK and became squadron leader of 152 Squadron in May 1941 and then 112 Squadron. Darwen's wife, Marjorie, had been seriously injured while dancing with her husband in the Cafe de Paris, Coventry Street, in a London air raid on 8 March 1941: she died in his arms at Charing Cross Hospital. She was 20-years-old. This event infused Darwen with a pathological hatred of the Germans. In early 1942 he was posted to the Middle East and saw active service as Commanding Officer 243 Wing. He was no tent bound commander, rather he flew at every opportunity with his pilots. In early 1943 he became OC 239 Wing and preferred to fly with his old command, 112 Squadron. He was twenty-seven when he was killed and lies in Sangro River War Cemetery. Sergeant Trevelyan, who flew as Darwen's wingman, bailed out of his burning Kittyhawk. His parachute blossomed out, but rather than landing gently and being able to walk away, Trevelyan hit the earth with considerable force and was killed. Five days later, his identity discs were recovered by an officer with the 2nd Battalion Northamptonshire Regiment. Kenneth Trevelyan was from Gloucester, aged twenty-one when he died. He lies buried in the Moro River Canadian War Cemetery.

Elsewhere, 3 Squadron (RAAF) and 450 Squadron were earning an enviable reputation as a contemporary account makes clear:

No. 3 Squadron, for instance, had a real field day early in October, when it broke its record for the number of vehicles destroyed in any one operation. Attacking a convoy which consisted apparently of well-filled petrol lorries, it returned to base with the grand strafing score of twenty-five 'flamers', three 'smokers' and twenty-five damaged, with three destroyed petrol dumps thrown in for good measure. In addition, the squadron destroyed two motor vehicles with bombs, and also scored four direct hits on the road. The leader of the formation was Squadron Leader Murray Nash, (later D.F.C. and Bar, who at that time was an undecorated flying officer). His score for the outing was three petrol dumps and four motor vehicles destroyed, as well as one vehicle damaged. Flying Officer Jack Doyle (who has since been promoted to the rank of squadron leader and awarded the D.F.C. and Bar) bagged five 'flamers' and one damaged on the same show. Every other pilot in the formation returned with something to his credit.

A day or two later the same squadron demonstrated how forcibly the fighter-bomber can affect the trend of battle when employed in close support of the Army. The Germans were known to be mounting a heavy counterattack in the Termoli area. No. 3 Squadron was entrusted with the ticklish task of bombing German troops massing less than a mile from our own forces, and of striking also at road transport bringing enemy reinforcements and supplies into the area.

So effectively did the pilots do their jobs that the Army sent the squadron a message stating that, largely due to its intervention, the counter-attack had been completely stopped. Eaton (by this time Wing Commander) led the show. His bag consisted of one Tiger tank set afire, one armoured car and two motor vehicles destroyed. A fortnight earlier he had fractured a bone in his left hand. But, with the cockpit of his Kittyhawk modified to his own specifications to suit this disability, and with his hand and forearm encased in plaster, he continued to fly.

Meanwhile, No. 450 Squadron was fully living up to the high reputation that it had earned in past campaigns for its skill in harassing the Hun. One October afternoon it had a highly profitable outing in the Pescara area. First it bombed and strafed two motor transports, leaving one on fire and the other smoking. Then eight more mechanized vehicles, partly concealed beneath some trees, were bombed and machine-gunned, five of them being set on fire and the remainder damaged. Next, a petrol dump in the same locality was set ablaze. Then, to round off the afternoon's work, our pilots strafed two stationary motor buses, damaging both of them.

That single mission typifies the Desert Harassers' determination to seek out the enemy in his hiding-places, and exact heavy toll of him whenever and wherever he is found.

What was true of these two squadrons was equally true of all of 239 Wing, 260 Squadron included.

CHAPTER

8

CASSINO

HAVING TAKEN NAPLES, the Allies knew that if they were to break out and gain Rome, they would have to smash the German Gustav Line to open the road to Rome. Italy is perhaps a perfect country to defend: east-west rivers and mountain ranges offered the Germans layer after layer of defence lines to withdraw back. The 'soft under belly' was far from soft: that was becoming all too apparent with the resistance they encountered.

In what would be four great battles (January-May 1944), the Allies attempted to punch a hole through the Gustav Line at Monte Cassino. The town and monastery above it marked the entrance to the strategically pivotal Liri Valley: if the Allies gained the valley, it opened the way to Rome. The Germans fortified the monastery, some 500ft above the town, and had also constructed minefields and fortifications in the surrounding hills and valleys.

In order to minimise casualties, the Allies launched a massive aerial bombardment of the German defences prior to their assault. This laid waste to the historic monastery and surrounding town. However, most of the German defenders survived and were able to exploit the ruins to create an even more formidable set of defences.

It was from Foggia that the squadron began close support operations with the Eighth Army in the opening stages of the combat for Cassino.

The 19 October brought 260 Squadron a new and unique challenge. Recognising 260's skill at bombing, the squadron was chosen by Wing HQ to 'knock out' a heavy calibre German railway gun which was operating at Caprinosa, dropping shells onto the Eighth Army. Blomfield notes rather laconically that the Eight Army rather objected to the large shells falling on them, and thus tasked DAF to resolve the problem. Intelligence reports told Wing HQ that the gun was housed during the day in a railway tunnel. The mission brief was to destroy the gun out in the open, or to block it up in the tunnel. Sparky Black led the first operation against the gun at 1540. Blomfield relates that:

> 'Four aircraft were detailed to liquidate the pest. The pilots were briefed to "skip" the bomb at low-level and place our two

500pounders with delayed action fuses into the tunnel mouth. The hillside about the tunnel was about 150 ft high. The first trip that I led was aborted after ten minutes in the areas, because cloud was down to almost deck level.'

The Squadron Operations Record book confirms that cloud was 10/10, and with no alternative target the flight of twelve retuned to base at 1640. The following morning Sparky Black led A flight, with twelve Kittyhawks, back up at 0810. Blomfield adds:

'Again, low cloud, but this time enough ceiling to be able to see the target. All four aircraft bombed from about 100ft. Some bombs were seen to enter the tunnel mouth, some buried themselves in the embankment alongside. There was intense, but mercifully inaccurate light flak and no one was badly hit. Later, the army sent a message saying that they were having no more sleepless nights. Later still, when the area was overrun, they found that the tunnel mouth was blocked and there was a huge hole in the hill. The gun was there and a small tank loco had been blown off the rails and a large section of the roof had been blown in.'

Blomfield's logbook records: '19 October: Bomb tunnel – Carpinone. Wizard bombing – tunnel mouth blocked. Heavy flak.' For this action, Blomfield was awarded the DFC, the citation in the *London Gazette*, 25 August 1944, states:

Flight Lieutenant Blomfield led his section in a daring attack on the tunnel with delayed action bombs, dropping his bombs at a height of 30ft in the face of intense Breda fire. The attack must have been most effective for the Army was never again worried by that gun.

Sangro river

The Battle of the Sangro River was one of the most important frontal clashes between the Allies and the Nazis during the first phase of the Italian Campaign. It focused on the conquest of the Gustav Line positions. From November 1943 onwards, the British Eighth Army, under the command of Montgomery, after moving up the Trigno area, came up against enemy blockades positioned at the strongholds built along the defensive line from Ortona to Cassino. Due to its characteristics, the Sangro River was identified by the Germans as a stop line. The battle that followed was bloody and costly for both sides.

Amidst this, Christopher Lee had learned of the whereabouts of the body of Major Saville, shot down on 19 September. On 3 November the squadrons adjutant, and the Rev A.T. Clark from 239 Wing Headquarters, set out to find the body. Near to the Posco Tavern in the Tremete valley, the wreckage of a Kittyhawk was found, its number matching that flown by Saville. On questioning the Correlo Carmine family who lived in a house called 'Appito' they related, as they had done to members of Eighth Army a few days earlier, that they had seen an aircraft come down in flames which blew up on impact. The son of the family found the remains of a body in the wreckage and buried it in the edge of the crater. A propelling pencil, the squadron diary tells us, was found in the crater, which was the property of Major Saville. The grave was marked with a ring of stones, hastily white washed. A cross was erected bearing Saville's name and service. Squadron Padre, Reverend Clark then led prayers of commemoration. Eric 'Danny' Saville was born in Eshowe, Natal, on 3 February 1922, attending Durban High School. His first posting was to 2 Squadron (SAAF) in the Western Desert on 15 October 1941. He moved to 112 Squadron in August 1942 as a flight commander. He was awarded the DFC in September 1942 for five confirmed kills, two probable's and three damaged. In May 1943 he was promoted and took command of 260 Squadron in lieu of Pedro Hanbury. He now lies in a military cemetery in Naples.

Rain and low cloud meant that operational flying in November became 'hit and miss.' One of the operations that did take place, on the tenth, was when Sparky Black led A flight, all twelve Mustangs, to attack a German Headquarters complex at Ston in Yugoslavia. Airborne at 1110, Sparky had to turn back early due to engine trouble, handing over the lead to Blomfield. The *London Gazette*, 25 August 1944, reports:

> On 10 November 1943, information was received by the Yugoslav partisans that a German HQ was situated in the town of Ston in the Peljesac Peninsula. Flight Lieutenant Blomfield took the squadron to the town and managed to locate the site. He led the bombing with great accuracy and then carried out several determined strafing attacks, leaving the HQ a smoking ruin. Later reports from the partisan sources confirmed that twenty-five Germans of the HQ were killed, together with the destruction of the horses and motor transport.
>
> This officer's whole operational tour has been characterised by his outstanding dash and determination, both in the air and on the ground. These qualities, together with his cheerfulness, is a never-ending source of inspiration to the other pilots.

Back on the Sangro, between 20 and 27 November, Montgomery's battalions carried out their first operations, establishing a bridgehead that immediately became the target of intense German artillery action. On 28 November, the Allied attack began, developing into an intense action that lasted three days, inflicting heavy losses on the enemy, who were progressively forced to retreat. Besides the hundreds of casualties resulting from the military confrontation, the battle resulted in several problems for civilians. In those November days, the liberation of the towns of Alfedena and Castel di Sangro was counterbalanced by the retaliation, looting and destruction carried out by Wehrmacht soldiers near Roccaraso, Gessopalena and Lettopalena. By December the river had been crossed.

Mud glorious mud

Bill Shoesmith from 3 Squadron (RAAF) again:

> 'We had only been on the [Foggia Main] 'drome a short time (naturally a Fighter 'Drome) when the "Powers That Be", in the shape of the US Air Force Bomber Group, came along and told us, in no uncertain terms, to "get lost" (or words to that effect) as they were going to come onto it, to make it into a Bomber 'Drome.
>
> 'And so off we go, a short way to a place called Mellini. (Later on, called "The Mud of Mellini" – bloody miles of it. Mud, Mud, and more Mud.) Even getting into the place was a hazard; the road in had a very steep "camber" on it. It was very simple to have your truck slide off the track. Everybody was getting in on the act, including myself.'

260 Squadron moved out to Mellini on 30 November, not returning to operations until 3 December. Close Support operations dominated the first day's flying from Mellini: Sparky Black leading operations at 1010 and 1310. Despite attempting to attack targets, bad weather and cloud meant many operations were aborted as targets were totally concealed. Blomfield's logbook reports: '9 December: Bomb and strafe Tollo. Repeat performance. Collected 2 huge holes!' Major Venter led a Close Support Operation on the following day. Venter claimed one motor transport destroyed. Thereafter, 260 Squadron was stood down till 20 December. Lest we imagine Bill Shoesmith exaggerated the Somme-like conditions the pilots and ground crew faced in winter 1943, the Medical Officer of 239 Wing bluntly stated:

> 'The landing ground continues to resemble a snipe bog rather than a Landing Ground. The transport between Wing Headquarters and the Landing Ground frequently become stranded in a sea of mud, and has to be towed out, often resulting in two more vehicles becoming stranded during this operation.'

To alleviate living in cold, wet, muddy tents 239 Wing took over three hotels in Naples: the pilots and ground crews were given rest and down time for a period of ten days, leave starting from 10 December.

Leave over, in a break between rain, cloud and mud, on 20 December, Sparky Black led a flight of nine up at 1125. Two German convoys were bombed, but heavy ack-ack prevented a strafing run. Major Venter attacked an 88mm battery the following day but recorded no claims. During the attack, Sergeant Russell was crippled by ack-ack. Realising he had no option but go over the side or burn alive, he parachuted into the sea. Seeing his Kittyhawk plummet into the sea in flames, Italian fishermen, in an act of mercy, motored to him in their little fishing boat and dragged a soaking wet Russell from the freezing Adriatic. Housed by the fishermen for several days, he was passed through German lines by partisans. The end result was that Russell returned to base in time for Christmas. These 'Boys Own adventures' seem unbelievable each time I write them, yet they are perfectly true. Many pilots owed their life to brave Italians who gave them food and sanctuary from the Germans and Italian Fascists: the bravery of these men and women who put their lives on the line to rescue downed pilots deserves greater recognition.

Under canvas for Christmas Dinner, the squadron was back on operations on 29 December. By the end of December 1943, the allied advance had ground to a halt with thousands of allied soldiers killed or wounded. To try and break this stalemate, Operation Shingle was originally conceived by British Prime Minister Winston Churchill in December 1943, as he lay recovering from pneumonia in Marrakesh. His concept was to land two divisions at Anzio, bypassing German forces in central Italy, and take Rome, the strategic objective of the current Battle of Rome. In an attempt to assist the offensive and cut German communications from Rome, an Allied amphibious landing was carried out on the west coast of Italy at Anzio. The landing took place on 22 January 1944, some twenty-five miles south of Rome and seventy miles behind enemy lines and was carried out by the 1st British and 3rd US Divisions.

At first, the Allies met little resistance. But they were too few in number for a major drive inland, and were quickly trapped in their beachhead by German reinforcements. Bitter fighting was to continue for months before the Allies were able to break out of Anzio.

With the attack at Anzio stalled, a major assault to try and take Cassino took place between 17 January and 11 February 1944, with heavy losses and no success for the Allies. Facing stalemate at Anzio a second assault of Monte Cassino was launched between 16 and 18 February. As a prelude, on 15 February, the famous historic abbey of Monte Cassino was destroyed by American bombers. Allied command was convinced that the ancient abbey was a German observation post. Ironically, German troops occupied the ruins only after the air raid.

A third battle commenced on 11 March, but despite the bombing and total destruction of the town of Cassino by the Strategic Air Forces, on the evening of 19 March the Allies were forced to call off their attempt to break through the Gustav Line. In five days, the New Zealand and Indian Divisions had lost nearly 5,000 men. All immediate offensive plans were shelved. What was achieved in return for a heavy loss of life and casualties? Three incursions made in the Gustav Line seemed a paltry reward. A small bridgehead across the Garigliano had been established downstream, about half of Cassino town and Castle Hill had been captured. In the east the Americans and French – at great cost – had taken more mountains. It was stalemate for the time being.

CHAPTER
9

CUTELLA

THE 'POWERS THAT BE' realising that Mellini was more mud than dry land, ordered 239 Wing was to move to the Adriatic coast and establish itself at Cutella on 3 January 1944. Again, the pilots and ground crew found themselves under canvas in the midst of the Italian winter. 112 Squadron joined the rest of the wing at the end of the month. About Cutella, Bert Horden of 112 Squadron relates:

'It was a very cramped area and all our tents, huts and equipment were compacted around the PSP strip. For months and months we had been promised that prefabricated wooden huts were on the way, to improve our living conditions. Rumour had it that they were on the way from England but the walls had been loaded on one ship and all the roofs on another. Not many ships survived the journey through the Med and it was said there was a plentiful supply of roofs but no walls to hold them up! However, at Cutella we were supplied with one corrugated iron Nissen hut. This became the pilots' and officers' lounge/bar. A separate tent for pilots to eat was arranged. The problem was that we were cold. We set about solving this with a marvellous heating system. We stood an empty 40-gallon drum on bricks in the middle of the hut and cut an air inlet and a hole for a chimney, which pilot Ken Stokes made out of about thirty 2-gallon cans beaten into shape. Outside we stood a 90-gallon belly tank of petrol on trestles with a small-bore pipe running through the wall of the hut and into the 40-gallon drum. Very simple. We just turned on a tap carefully so that petrol dripped into the floor of the drum. Lighting the petrol was a bit hairy, but after a few minor explosions we got the petrol dripping just right to heat up the drum to a suitable temperature […] for our tents we had a more economical method of heating. There was a plentiful supply of charcoal locally, so we punched holes in an empty potatoes tin and fitted wire for swinging it around. We filled with charcoal and a modicum of petrol to set it alight and we had a useful little brazier […] At the end of our

Nissen hut was a bar manned at nightfall by Corporal Brown for when Ops were over for the day. We had a radio, of course, as well as a gramophone with the usual selection of Glenn Miller and other pop records of the time.'

The bar of 112 Squadron would be the scene of a prank led by Shep Sheppard later in the year. Each squadron from 239 Wing had a Nissen hut, no doubt that of 260 Squadron was decked out in a similar manner.

As before, 260 Squadron's roll was interdiction of German troop movements both by road and rail, as well as German armour. Bad weather prevented many of the pre-designated attacks from succeeding, but one that did was on 23 January when Flight Lieutenant Leo Malins led off ten Kittyhawk's at 0740, objective German armour. A column of German motor transport accompanied by Mk III and Mk IV tanks along the road leading to Capistrano. Warrant Officer Nick Nichol, 260 Squadron's 'scrounger in chief', who we met earlier flew as Malins No. 2. Malins gave words that 'every man for himself', allowing his pilots to select their own targets. No tanks or lorries were hit, but the road was heavily cratered. The flight carried out six strafing runs: one MK III tank was set on fire, one lorry blew up and another was badly damaged, so too an armoured car. All pilots landed safely at 0925. Malins, with four other pilots, was back in the air at 1125 returning to the scene of the earlier attack, attacking the same group of tanks. A bomb fell between a tank and flanking lorry, destroying both. The formation carried out four strafing runs, and were joined by a flight of Spitfires. Malins also attacked a staff car, and damaged a German 15-tonne lorry.

Tragedy came at the end of the month. Flying Officer David Finley from Rosebank, Cape Province, South Africa, was killed on 31 January, aged twenty-two. He lies in Moro River Canadian War Cemetery. 260 Squadron had been detailed to sink a two masted schooner at Porto Civitanova: the boat was strafed five times. Heavy flak had brought down Finley.

For the first six weeks of 1944 Blomfield attended a gunnery course at El Ballah – where he was rated as 'Exceptional' as a 'Marksman (air-to-air)' – following which he resumed operational flying with 260 in mid-February. Returning for a second tour of duty with 260 Squadron was Shep Sheppard, who arrived soon after Blomfield had done so on the twentieth:

'On the twenty-first I set off to rejoin 260 Squadron. It was cold, raining and muddy; it was miserable weather but I felt elated, especially as whilst being driven through the dispersal area many of the ground crew looked, waved and gave me the "thumbs up". I was returning to the family and there to greet me at the mess was none other than my old flight commander who I had clued up when he had re-joined, Sparky Black. The squadron was based on the east coast of Italy, virtually on the beach just south of the village of Termoli and called Cutella. There were two airstrips; you could not call them anything else, one each side of the river Biferno, not that it was much of a river, and 239 Wing was sited on the lower strip. It was a metallic link strip with dispersal running to the left and living quarters in the field up the railway line. There was a large ditch between the dispersal area and the fields and although we lived in tents, the mess was actually a Nissen hut.

'I was disappointed to find that the standard of messing was not up to the standard we had enjoyed in the dessert, but it did not take me long to get it knocked into shape again. We went out with some of the tins of meat and fish paste, etc. that were hoarded in the Mess Cook Wagon and traded them for fresh eggs and cheese with the farms.'

In between the arrival of these two veteran flyers, a Mustang MK I was delivered on 15 February to allow 260 Squadron to begin familiarisation flights in the type before the squadron was weaned off its Kittyhawks. The Mustang Mk I by this date was already obsolescent. It had been proposed on 24 November 1943 to swop out the Kittyhawks for Spitfires and Warhawks: with all effort being placed on Operation Overlord, the Spitfires went to squadrons based in England who were to participate in D-Day, 260 Squadron therefore received Mustangs. The process of re-equipping the wing would be slow, the last 'kitty' going out of service by autumn 1944.

Mustangs

I had seen Mustangs first hand in flight at Duxford when accompanied by my uncle, possibly for D-Day anniversary in 1994, or VE Day 1995. Memory 30 years later does play tricks alas on when, but not the who or where. Seeing a Mustang flying alongside both a Tomahawk and a Kittyhawk, too a none-pilot, the Mustang in flight looked the better machine: faster and much more agile. It certainly sounded better with its Packard Merlin! I can remember my uncle's emotion as a Mustang rocketed passed the crowd at 100ft or less, and then climbed almost vertically to hang on its prop, before zooming down, twisting, turning and 'dancing' in the air before it exited stage left to land, its display over.

Moving on two decades almost, on a visit to Duxford, I asked one of the gallery guides about the type. After talking about Mustangs and explaining my project about 260 Squadron, the guide later found me and handed me a printed set of notes which proved invaluable in writing this comment. The P-51 Mustang was designed to a British requirement in 1940 by a relatively new company, North American Aviation. Desperate for fighter aircraft of any sort, members of the British Purchasing Mission had been touring US manufacturers placing orders, but it was obvious that most of the products on offer would be of limited use and would soon become obsolescent.

The President of North American, which was about to commence production of the Tomahawk under licence, persuaded the British that this would be a waste of time and that his designers could come up with something much better; indeed, what the company designed was indeed much better. Although initially committed to using the Allison engine like many of its competitors, the company's creation of a low-drag airframe, employing a radical laminar flow wing, raised performance expectations. The clean lines of the aircraft were directly copied from the ME 109 – both aircraft had the same designer – and were further enhanced by the particularly neat design of the radiator, which was set well back under the fuselage centre section. The performance of the first pre-production model, which first flew 26 October 1940, was way ahead of any other contemporary American fighter, and large contracts for production aircraft, to be named Mustang I, were soon placed. The first machine for the RAF (AG345) was flown on 1 May 1941. The Mustang I, when tested alongside Spitfire VB, was found to be 30-35 mph faster up to 15,000ft, reducing to 1-2 mph faster at 25,000ft. Its rate of climb at all heights was not as good as the Spitfire. At low altitudes the difference was only slight, but was more marked with height. With an inferior rate of climb to that of the Spitfire, the Mustang could not make use of climbing turns to obtain a tactical advantage, unless it had already dived from a higher level. The best tactic for the Mustang was to engage from above and to use the speed gained in the dive to zoom up out of range for another attack. The issue was the Allison engine. Realising the airframe was excellent, as an experiment an airframe was fitted with a Merlin 61. Mustang (AL975/G) was flown by Rolls-Royce Chief Test Pilot Captain R.T. Shepherd on 13 October 1942. With its uprated engine, the Mustangs performance was totally transformed into one of THE best aircraft of the conflict. Merlin-powered Mustangs as flown by the RAF were designated the Mustang III (equivalent to the USAAF P-51B and P-51C) and entered service with the RAF in February 1944.

On 17 March, fifteen of 260 Squadron's Kittyhawks were passed to 112 Squadron, as Shep Sheppard remembers:

'Our dear old Kittyhawks, Is, IIs and IIIs, had done valiant service through the Desert campaign, right the way of El Alamein to Tunis and up through Southern Italy, although in the early months of '44 they were mostly bogged down because of the appalling weather, and now we were going to hand our best aircraft over to other squadrons on the wing and get Mustangs as replacements – great.

'The CO of 260 Squadron at that time was a South African, Major Hunter [sic Venter], who very rarely flew, but decided that he would take seventeen pilots with him down to Casablanca to collect the new Mustangs and bring them up to Italy. Whilst they were away, nearly two weeks, we arranged the aircraft changes with the other wing squadrons, receiving some of our clapped-out kitties for training purposes. These aircraft really were the dregs of each squadron.'

It was one of these clapped-out Kitties my uncle had to fly at 239 Wing Training School. A real 'feather in the cap' for 260 Squadron was when Group Captain Brian Eaton, known as 'Skeeter', the Commanding Officer of 239 Wing, lodged his brand-new Mustang with A flight. That gave the squadron three single pilot aircraft, the other being for the Squadron Commander and the other for the A Flight Commander. All the other Mustangs on the squadron had two pilots allocated to them.

Keen to know more about the Mustang, I spoke at length to my uncle who remembers:

'The first thing you notice when you get in the Mustang is the great long nose. It sticks out there a good way. I'm 5 feet 11 inches tall. Even sitting on my chute, I could just about see over the nose. Some of the short fellas like Shep had to use booster cushions till the adjustable seats were fitted. The Merlin had an electric primer which was VERY sensitive, instead of the old push-in-and-lock type we found on the Kitty or Warhawk. The Merlin will usually take only a few seconds of primer before it's good to go. The mixture is automatic.

'The Mustang was a bit of a devil to start... you needed six hands on three arms. You hold the starter with your right hand... start counting the prop until six blades pass... at "six" you throw the mags to "both" with your left hand... hit the fuel boost pump switch on the left of the starter with your right hand (this requires a finger shift while holding the starter engaged)... now hit the electric primer to the right of the starter with another finger switch of the right hand... remembering not to over-prime the damned Merlin... and as it fires, reach with the spare hand you don't have and push the mixture up into "NORMAL."

'She will idle over at 2,300revs. For take-off you need 40" of pressure in the manifold. As you begin to accelerate, the Merlin needs 60". At this point, you can stop talking to yourself because you can't hear anything else in the world but that great big Merlin up front. The exhausts line up almost directly with your ears. You anticipate a left swing of the nose by easing in just short of what you need to keep it straight. The last thing you need on a full-power take-off is to apply too much rudder correction for torque, or it would have you off to the side with no warning.

'Climbing was 170 mph, you're at 2,700revs. On the level you could get away with 250 mph. Flat out would be 300 to 325. Not as fast as the text book, because this was not ideal conditions. Not an easy plane to fly, but once you got used to it, they were very good indeed. Some of the best planes of the war.'

Shep Sheppard notes:

'The Mustang MK I differed from the MK III in having an Allison engine which lacked sufficient surge in power to make it the equal of the Spitfire or the latest ME 109. Someone had the brilliant idea, however, of putting a Packard Merlin engine in to replace the Allison, and what a difference it made. Official figures were something like 430/440 mph at around 25,000ft, with an operational ceiling of 42,000ft. All these figures are great under ideal conditions, but, because of various factors, you rarely achieve them on operational trips.

'Notwithstanding this, there is no doubt that the P51 as the Americans called it, the Mustang Mk III and IV, was the finest piston engined fighter of the war, and probably of the period. To me, there were two small faults with the Mustang and we discovered them when we had the MK I for familiarisation.

'The first fault was the gunsight, which was American. It was square, literally with jagged corners and no protection as on British gunsights or even as on the Kittyhawk's. If one bashed one's hand or face on it in a crash you would have little left of hand or face.

'The second fault I found out in my second trip in the Mark I. The brakes tended to overheat and bind and this happened after I had landed and was taxiing in – the starboard wheel simply went solid! The first fault was easily overcome. The CO at 53 Reserve and Servicing Unit some short distance from us had once been the flight sergeant fitter on 260 in the desert, and he took all the gunsights from the clapped out Kittyhawk's and modified them to fit the Mustangs, and in a matter of a week before we began ops in the Mustangs all the new aircraft were fitted with this gunsight which had a huge rubber protection pad around it. The second fault was later eliminated at source, but not before it had caused some heartache. In spite of all this, it was a lovely aircraft to fly and I was extremely comfortable in it.'

Lyall Fricker, who flew with 260 Squadron from October 1944 to VE-Day, also had great admiration for the Mustang and gave his reasons as follows:

'It was designed later in the war than any of the others so it had all of the previous experience. And it had a different type of wing, it had a Davis air foil with laminar flow which gave it much better lift and drag ratio. It also had the Merlin engine even though it was built in the United States, Packard Merlin instead of a Rolls-Royce Merlin. It was still the same engine; more power and so forth. And the various features of it meant that it had greatly increased speed, for one and also greatly increased endurance so we could do a four-hour trip with long-range tanks, whereas the Spitfires could do about an hour and a half, and we could carry a thousand-pound bomb under each wing, we didn't do it very often but we could do it. Whereas the Spitfires carry one two hundred and fifty pound bombs mid ship, we had ours out on the wings.

'Also, the Mustang had a better rate of roll and so forth than the Spitfire. But as I say they were designed for different purposes, the Spitfire was designed to be able to take off from an airfield in England, climb up high quickly, intercept the bombers, shoot them down, come back and land again. They only carried fuel for about an hour, hour and a half, they carried ammunition for about thirty seconds, *thirty seconds* of firing time. The Mustang was about the same. None of the fighter aircraft could carry much more than thirty seconds of firing, since you only fired in one second bursts, that gave you a lot of time [...] on the Kittyhawk, you had to close the radiator gills before you dived otherwise you would cool the engine right down. The Mustang had a thermostatic control so that if you went into a dive and the coolant started losing heat then the radiator gills would close automatically and you maintained a constant engine temperature. All around it was a better aircraft.'

It did have its defects as Shep remembered and Fricker notes:

'For example, one of the features of the Mustang was that the tailwheel locked into position so that when you were on take-off, if you kept your tail down on the tarmac or once you landed and your tail was down, it stopped you swinging, it was a plus, a safety device. On the very first trip I did in a Mustang, as most of my colleagues said, you spent half of the time trying to slow it down as it was going so fast. You weren't accustomed to the rate at which you were moving over the ground. Having got used to the feel of it and so forth, curved around and came down, landed on the runway and I wasn't quite straight. So, I automatically touched the rudder a bit to bring the nose around and it didn't come around. I pushed a bit harder on the rudder and still, by this time there is a line of parked Thunderbolts either side of the runway and I am heading straight for them at about a hundred miles an hour, and there are blokes running in all directions trying to get away. And then I realised of course, the tailwheel was locked.

'So, I pushed the stick forward in a hurry and of course pushed it too far and nearly drove the propeller into the ground in front of me, but at least it got the tailwheel of the ground and I already had rudder on so it came around very quickly. And by that time, I had got my sense back together again and having got it right up onto the runway I then eased it onto the ground and we were right. But for that second or two I was really looking down the barrel and wondering what the hell was going on. It was my own fault; I had been told. This was one of the big problems, if you like to call it a problem, going from a training aircraft which is a two-seater, into these things, you really are on your own. And if you haven't read the instructions and remembered them one hundred per cent then you are in trouble and I had forgotten the bit about the lockable tailwheel.

'However, we survived.'

As well as being a better aircraft to fly than the Kittyhawk, the Mustang was also a huge improvement for the ground crews. Sergeant Pountain, leading A Flights team of armourers remembers that the Mustang was the best designed aircraft of the war for reasons beyond its handling once airborne. Perhaps the most important, was that the Mustang was an incredibly well designed and ergonomic aircraft. The gun bays on the Mustang were closed by a single door, opened by two handles and 'shoot bolts'. The gun bay door also provided access to the ammunition bay doors on either side of the gun bay. The three series of doors could be opened in fifteen seconds. On a Spitfire, twelve panels had to be opened necessitating fifty-six turn buttons to be activated rather than the two on the Mustang. Another improvement over the Spitfire was that bombing and gunnery trades were separated again making the turnaround of the aircraft more efficient and faster than a Spitfire. One problem, however, was that the American bomb trolley was designed to work on a perfectly flat and level surface. The armourers on 260 therefore, had to devise their own method, welding up their own lifting cradle. Despite this problem, the turnaround for re-armament, servicing and re-fuelling dropped to one and a half hours, an hour less in Pountain's estimation than a Kittyhawk: a huge time saving.

Non-Operational

With most pilots collecting new aircraft, the squadron was not operational: the opportunity was taken to rest the remaining pilots, sending them to the rest centres at Bari and Sorrento. Not all pilots went to the rest centres as Sheppard relates:

'During this period, I was acting squadron commander and with a nucleus of experienced pilots who had not gone to Casablanca, spent the time putting the inexperienced pilots through their paces and endeavouring to bring them up to operational standard.'

The squadron diary relates that most days in late March were taken up with flying training: seven pilots flying an hour a day, on a single worn-out Mustang, FB944, for familiarisation trips. Two Kittyhawks remained on the squadron as 'run abouts' for communication runs.

As the squadron was non-operational, Intelligence Officer Lee was seconded to the Army as he recalled:

> 'There was this extraordinary exchange that started in the desert and went on into Sicily and Italy whereby officers from RAF squadrons went up to the Army, and they exchanged an army officer for an air force officer. The army officer had a splendid time doing nothing. The air force officers on the other hand were sent up to divisional HQ and then were posted to some very bizarre units which was very alarming. We were given strict orders not to go on patrol and the first thing they arranged for us, was to see if the RAF chaps were up to it.'

The squadron diary reports Lee left on 18 March and returned on 25 March, his report being as follows:

> 'I reported to 5 CORPS HEADQAURTERS and continued to MAIN OTH INDIAN DIVISION. Under the guidance of a Major in the GURKHA RIFLES, I toured various parts of the front line, including a visit to a 25lb. FIELD BATTERY and a demonstration of firing by CANADIAN SHERMAN, I was permitted to fire a tank gun and observe the resultant hits on the target in GRSOGNA, 2000 yards distant ADVANCED OBSERVATION POST. I stayed for two days at a forward BATTALION OF PARA TROOP BRIGADE and was taken to forward COMPANIES SECTIONS. A visit was also arranged to a FORWARD OBSERVATION POST IN NO MAN'S LAND at the foot of the GUARDIAGERLE ESCARPMENT where the effects of our shelling was clearly seen. Enemy activity was slight, being confined to MORTAR AND SHELL FIRE which was directed from an OBSERVAION POST on the ENEMY LINE, itself under heavy fire from OUR ARTILLERY. During the last night of my visit, the nearest company was under HEAVY FIRE FROM ENEMY ARTILLERY and ATHOL CLASHES were reported.
>
> 'Altogether this was a most interesting visit and very much appreciated.'

Quite what the purpose for this exchange was, I know not.

Major Venter flew into Cutella at 1430 on 1 April, having left Tunis at 1000, flying in fifteen Mustang MK III. The squadron dairy records:

The arrival of the new aircraft caused a great deal of excitement amongst all ranks of the squadron and the following fortnight was the scene of great activity. The armourers were kept busy because the guns required harmonising and there was a great deal of practice bombing.

With the new Mustangs, training was the primary occupation as the diary relates, about which Sheppard recalls, 'we spent about ten days on dive-bombing practice, formations, turnabouts etc. and on generally getting to know the aircraft.' Outside of training, the pilots at Cutella found time to relax and unwind as Shep vividly remembers:

'Apart from training we were taking time to relax. This invariably took the form of minor parties with friends from the four other squadrons on the wing, or going over to their mess and generally visiting around.

'One squadron on the Wing with whom 260 were particularly friendly and also great rivals when it came to numbers of enemy aircraft shot down, was 112 squadron, known as the "Shark Squadron" because of the insignia on their aircraft of a shark's mouth painting on the nose of the Kittyhawk. Added to this, they were a peacetime RAF squadron so, naturally, they were wanting to build a score of kills and they were a "hungry" squadron, mostly chasing 260 in the "kill" table – some even said they got their shark motif because it was their nature!

'However, we were invited over for drinks one evening and, before going decided we do a bit of sharking ourselves. They were probably the only squadron that had really nice glasses in their mess, obviously appropriated from somewhere, and we decided that we were going to pinch them [...] we had a pleasant evening and at a prearranged signal from me, all the 260 boys walked out of the 112 mess with their glasses, full, half full or empty. I had gone out fractionally before, started up our vehicle which was the standard 15cwt Ford light van, and out came everyone who piled into the garry, some standing on the running board. Who should be last, none other than Christopher Lee – he jumped onto my side of the garry and away we went, driving at a rate of knots around the dispersal area and eventually up the narrow track, over the ditch – the "bridge" being two heavy railway sleepers – and up to our mess.

'The sleepers over the ditch ran into a field that had a typical farm gate, always open, in fact hanging on its hinges, but the hook to close the gate was simply a nail driven into a post to which the gate hooked on.

'When we went into our own mess with our prizes, everyone collapsed with laughter to see a tear right across the rear of Christopher Lee's pants. Driving through the gate with him hanging on the side, the nail had ripped right across his rear. He took it all in good part […] The next day we received a visit from 112 and there displayed on our bar were their very nice glasses which, of course, we then gracefully returned, having put one over them.'

On 11 April, a test flight was conducted with a Mustang carrying two 1,000lb bombs. The test was considered a success. Veteran 260 pilot 'Sparky' Black, on completing his second tour with the squadron, was posted as commanding officer of 250 Squadron on the 13 April, the same day as five pilots set off for Casablanca to bring in more Mustangs. Sparky hung around for a few more days. Major Venter also became tour expired as April began. An old hand from the squadron returned as Commanding Officer, Leo Malins DFC.

Back on Ops

The first operation on Mustangs took off on the 14 April, with Malins in the lead, as the squadron diary relates:

> At last, the pilots were to be carrying out OPERATIONS AGAINST THE ENEMY WITH THE MUSTANG IIII AIRCRAFT.
>
> On this date six pilots were briefed to attack 30+ MOTOR TRANSPORT which were reported to be moving south to TERANO FROM SAN BENEDENTO. The formation was led by […] L.A. Malins DFC. Unfortunately, the pilots did not meet with any great success for there was nothing to be observed in the target area. After a considerable amount of reconnaissance, the formation returned to base.
>
> Early in the afternoon SQUADRON LEADER L.A. MALINS, together with seven other pilots went out to attack railway bridges […] this operation was successful, one direct hit being registered on the railway line immediately north of the railway bridge, the road was also hit.
>
> The third operation of the day was another attack on the railway bridges. Eight pilots took part in this operation. This attack was made on the same target as the previous operation of the day. Bombing was carried out with excellent results. FLYING OFFICER (ACTING FLIGHT LIEUTENANT) L.J. SHEPPARD DFC returned at 300' to within 30 yards of the target and carried

out an assessment of the damage. He was able to plot a direct hit, half-width of the bridge in the centre of the railway, which appeared to have torn up the track and taken a large bite out of the east side of the bridge. There was a direct hit on the road bridge and midway between both bridges.

During the course of the 15 April, the squadron was sent on three operations. Shep Sheppard was in the air at 1620, flying 'top cover' to a flight from 112 Squadron, to attack a railway viaduct, which survived two attacks that day. On the way back, Shep spotted a B17 Flying Fortress ditched in the Adriatic. The stricken bomber was floating with the crew in rubber dinghies at the tail. Sheppard's flight circled the B17 until an RAF Air-Sea Rescue Walrus arrived to pick up the USAAF crew. Attacks on railway lines and other infrastructure occupied most of April as Shep relates:

'Between 14th and 18th April 1944, I did seven ops. We were carrying two 500lb bombs, bombing bridges and railway lines, strafing MT, all to prevent material from reaching the German troops. With two 500 pounders, you needed to get up to 100 mph to get airborne and the airstrip was not terribly long. The procedure was for the six aircraft to be in echelon right tucked in fairly close; stand on the breaks and then give the signal to go. We generally climbed at 200 mph and around 500ft per minute.

'After take-off we turned left fairly quickly because to have continued for a couple of minutes would have brought us into the circuit of the other airstrip. We circle around our own airstrip gaining height over the water and then set course.

'On April 20th I did an airtest with one 1,000lb bomb under each wing to check the practicality of it. You needed a small amount of flap to assist on take-off and climbing at 500ft per minute only achieved 190 mph with the same throttle setting that achieved 200 mph with two 500lb bombs, but the aircraft handled well in flight having climbed to 10,000ft, I dived on full throttle before releasing the bombs at around 1500ft into the sea. I think my speed went up to well over 500 mph, possibly climbing to the 600 mark [...] the next day we did our first op with all aircraft having two 1,000lb bombs on board, one under each wing. Cruising on weak mixture, I would estimate we probably used about forty-five gallons of fuel an hour which, in theory, would give us a range of some 800miles and four, perhaps four and a half hours flying. In practice, however, with the bombs on I would put the flying time available nearer three and a half hours. The op we did on the 21st was to bomb a railway bridge and we did some strafing on the way home with good results, four flamers and two left smoking. The show lasted two hours ten minutes and in the small cockpit of a fighter that length of time is long enough.

'I was leading and so was first into land, and as I touched down probably at 80 – 85 mph, my brakes seized and up came the body of the aircraft and over it went, down on its back. Being upside down on the deck is not quite the same thing as being upside down in the air and the first thing you want to do is to get out because of the almost certain fire hazard. What you must not do is panic and release your safety strap, because if you do, you will probably drop on your head and break your neck.

'Very slowly I put my hand on the deck. The hood was open and I carefully released the strap, letting myself inch down and by then there were a dozen airmen at the aircraft including one of the fight sergeants who put his hands in, and as I released the parachute harness, pulled me out.

'The problem with the brakes was a serious one and we stopped pilots using them in the dispersal area, but it meant the fitters seeing you out had to pull like hell to turn you when taxiing.'

The squadron diary reports Shep was flying Mustang GB276 and that on landing 'it ran about 400 yards, then swung right, turning over as it ran off the runway strip. The pilot was not injured.' Bad weather meant no flying took place over the next few days, and it was not until 28 April that Leo Malins led a flight of eight Mustangs to attack the German aerodrome at Forli. In the air at 0910, weighed down with 2,000lb of bombs, top cover was provided by a flight of Spitfires. Shep Sheppard tells us what happened:

'The rest of the month was spent bombing bridges except for a show on the 28th when we used a full squadron to attack Forli aerodrome in northern Italy. Leo Malins led the show, whilst I led top cover. It was early morning and we literally caught Jerry with his pants down. We made two runs across the aerodrome and I personally got four flamers, a JU 88 and three ME 109s. Both Leo and Russell got hit on the second run but both made it back to base.'

The Operations Record Book confirms that a group of nine plus ME 109s, a large aircraft not identified and a JU 88 were severely damaged or destroyed. And as Shep remembers, intense 20mm flak damaged Malins Mustang: flak had destroyed his hydraulic system and a fire broke out in the starboard wheel housing, which he managed to extinguish by side slipping before returning to base. Again, confirming

Sheps memory, Pilot Officer Russel's Mustang suffered flak damage to its flaps and was considered a CAT III repair, i.e. almost but not quite a total 'write off'.

Friendly fire

Saturday, 29 April 1943 began as any operational flying day did: after breakfast and briefing, Flight Lieutenant Blomfield was airborne at 0920 leading a flight of eight Mustangs to target a railway bridge. Shep Sheppard led Blue Section. The flight left Cutella heading north-west to the Gran Sasso mountains at 10,000ft. The German aerodrome at Perguia had been designated as the primary target, but was observed to be deserted, possible abandoned by the Luftwaffe. The flight continued to Umbertide to attack the secondary target, to destroy a railway bridge. Two bombs fell directly under the most western of the three spans, and blew away an estimated three-quarters of the bridge. Another bomb made a direct hit on the railway line leading to the bridge, tearing the track, ballast and embankment to pieces. Other bombs fell on the nearby road making it impassable by German transport. Blomfield then turned the flight to rendezvous with 250 Squadron at Spoleto to escort them to Bastia, providing top cover at 12,000ft whilst 250 dived down to drop their bombs. All 260 Squadron pilots landed at 1055hrs.

After the operation Sparky Black, and now Commanding Officer of 250 Squadron, came over to thank the pilots of 260 for their support as Shep Sheppard remembers:

> 'I was sitting outside the mess having a cup of tea with Sparky Black [...] the weather was getting much better and quite warm, and one enjoyed sitting outside our mess because it gave you a complete view of the whole site. You were able to watch the various squadrons taking off on a show and then criticise their landings on return.
>
> 'Our squadron was particularly proud of its formation flying, on returning from an especially good show we would do a very tight six formation; no one was allowed victory rolls or other foolishness. Although it was a warm day there was quite a lot of cloud about and it was fairly low cloud, not unusual for the Adriatic at that time of year. Suddenly there was a roar of aircraft coming down through a break in the clouds, and we both thought it was a strafing mission by the Germans.
>
> 'It was a strafing mission alright, but not by the Germans. Down came the two American aircraft, guns blazing, right down the runway and along the sides. Everyone was shattered, ground crews diving for cover, scrabbling to get out of the way. Reaction was and is very quick where self-preservation is concerned.

'Sparky and I were stunned by the suddenness and the speed of it all, and we just hoped they were not coming back for a second run, but no, they were up into the cloud and off. Fortunately, there were no serious casualties but some of the Wing squadrons did sustain a fair amount of damage.'

An eye-witness to all of this was Mervyn Talbot who had just arrived with the squadron:

'Some events during those years are etched in my memory with a vividness that takes me right back, others are more vague. One of those indelible memories was very soon after I had joined 260.

'After leaving Naples training continued, but now flying Kittyhawk's which was the aircraft I would be expected to fly on the squadron. It was now time to join 260 Squadron, which was part of the Desert Air Force, and face up to the real business of war!

'I'd arrived at Cutella on Friday, 28 April. I was a spare wank. No flying training or anything. So, Saturday afternoon came. I was laying on my bed in the tent, smoking. Back home I'd have probably been doing the same thing, before going out to the pub in the evening with my mates. There was this mighty roar, pilots and ground crew were screaming at us to take cover, the bloody Jerries were after us. I ducked out of the tent to find somewhere safer. The poor lads in 3 RAAF were shot up. Several of their Kitties were demolished: we could see the flames and hear the panic. Several of their fellas were badly burned, the ops trailer was a write off. The Walrus air-sea rescue pilot was killed and I think some of the ground crew.'

Shep Sheppard again:

'I heard afterwards that the pilot concerned, leading the pair, received a sentence of twenty years imprisonment, but was also told that he would undoubtedly be released at the end of the war.

'It is difficult to feel sorry for the captain involved. He was an experienced pilot, so it was somewhat of a mystery how he could have made such a mistake as there was no other aerodrome up the coast of the Adriatic that even resembled the two airstrips at Cutella. In fact, I do not believe there were any other than ours.'

The squadron diary for 260 tells us that 'slight injuries were sustained by two airmen of the squadron and damage was caused to two aircraft.' About Warrant Officer Glew, the Walrus pilot killed in the attack, the squadron diary reports:

A letter of appreciation has been received from Colonel L.A. Wilmot DFC, Officer Commanding No. 239 Wing in present of the amount raised by the various for the widow of Warrant Officer Glew of Air-Sea Rescue Flight. The total figure realised was £422-13-6 of which the sum of £57-8-6 was raised by this squadron.

On the last day of the month, Shep Sheppard led a flight of eight Mustangs to attack a bridge at Fossombrone. Due to cloud and rain, visibility was described 'as nil'. Flying alongside 250, the two flights attacked the second target at Pedaso, another railway bridge. The bridge was left standing, but by happenstance a small ammunition dump was detonated.

As April ended, 239 Wing had amassed a significant tally. In the air, one ME 110 was damaged, three FW 190's were shot down and six more damaged. Moreover, twenty-four aircraft had been destroyed on the ground and nine damaged. In addition, two steam engines had been destroyed, eleven damaged, twenty-nine ammunition or petrol dumps had been destroyed, a gun position silenced, two motor cycles, two barges had been sunk and four damaged, and over sixty items of railway rolling stock damaged or destroyed in 2,128 operational sorties. This equated to 198 missions, 2,970 bombs dropped and 399,842 rounds of ammunition fired.

CHAPTER
10

NEW PILOTS

ANY WARTIME RAF squadron was in a constant change of flux: pilots were made POW, killed, wounded, or became tour expired. It meant a constant coming and going of personnel. Joining 260 Squadron at the start of May was Dennis Varey. Having not flown since December 43, it was standard practice for pilots being sent operational to undergo a few weeks intensive training and a much-needed refresher. Dennis recalls he arrived at:

> Viano, was more of the same as at Portici: I was stupefied by the lack of organisation and urgency in what went on. After a week, it was off to 239 Training Wing. I think this was at Termoli. We were here for a week to ten days. Again, under canvas.
>
> 'This was a refresher course for us. We were put through our paces for ground attack, but this time on Kittyhawks and Warhawks that were totally clapped out.
>
> 'We trained to dive at an angle of 60 degrees from about 6,000ft or 8,000ft, down to 2,000ft or 1,500ft. With the target under the leader's port wing, he would radio us to arm our bombs. Having acknowledged this, the leader would radio "going down left (or right) now!" and would then wing-over into a diving turn. 60 degrees down felt near vertical I can assure you. The section bombed individually from line astern. Using our reflector sight, we would steady or kite on the target and commence pull out at about 1,500ft, counting to 10 and then releasing the bomb. When diving, the aircraft would pick up speed very quickly, but it had a great tendency to roll to the right. When you pulled up, it wanted to roll to the left quite violently. Ghastly thing.
>
> 'Lessons were in two parts, both air ops and classroom work. As well as dive-bombing, we had to learn formation flying in sixes and learn your colour in the flight. Each six had its own colour, red and blue and then broken down into others. We flew in boxed twelves, Red Section of four, would be 400ft above Blue (left) and Yellow on the right, each kite 75yards distance line astern.

'In battle we had to learn fluid 4s or 6s. In fours you had Red leader and his No. 2, and Green leader with his No. 2. The second four would be Yellow leader and his No. 2 and White leader with his. No. 2 served to protect the number 1 who was navigator, Yellow Section would be 500-1000ft above Red. In Six's, it went white, red, yellow, and then blue, green black. If flying with Red and Blue Section up, we would have four Spitfires 2,000ft above us.

'For close escort we would form a box around the bombers, the object of this was to drive away any planes that attacked the bombers, and we flew level with them. If only four escorts were detailed, they flew alongside and weaved.

'The two trips in the Warhawk showed what a better plane it was to the Kittyhawk: it had a Merlin not the god-awful Allison. Quite why we trained on Kittyhawk's when we were going onto Mustang's, heavens know. They were totally different to fly. I suppose as they had just gone onto the frontline squadrons, they had none spare to use as training aircraft. It meant when we arrived, we had very little time to get used to the new type.

'The past two years of training seemed to have lasted forever. There were five of us waiting to join the squadron, all of us felt the same excitement at the thought of getting into action. Mervyn was posted with two other lads to 260 on 26 April, I went with another a few days later. There seemed no sense of organisation to any of it.'

Dennis's logbook records, that part of his training on 12 April included a sector recce, classroom training occupied the next three days before taking back to the air on the sixteenth for a refresher training on aerobatics. More classroom work on the seventeenth followed before putting theory into practice on formation flying the following day. Dive-bombing theory occupied the nineteenth, with practice taking place the following day. The 24/25 April was occupied by battle formation and dog fighting practice aboard a Warhawk. The last day, 29 April, was spent on battle formation, back aboard a Kittyhawk. Total air time, six hours forty-five minutes. The next time Dennis would fly was in a different type, the Mustang.

Dennis and Mervyn were much needed reinforcements for 260 Squadron in the coming battle for this most famous Italian mountain, Cassino.

Towards the end of March 1944, the Desert Air Force (DAF) commanding officer Air Vice-Marshal Broadhurst departed. Broadhurst had led them from the deserts of North Africa to Italy's Apennine mountains and was replaced by Air Vice-Marshal Dickson. Exactly one year before, at El Hamma in Tunisia, Broadhurst had pioneered DAF's innovative use of fighter-bombers in close support of a decisive breakthrough on the ground. He also had ensured that, despite the massive growth of Allied air forces in diverse roles, DAF retained its powerful and unique identity. At the time of DAF's operation at El Hamma in Tunisia, Dickson had been making an inspection visit of DAF with Air Marshal Leigh-Mallory, command in chief of Fighter Command. On completing the inspection, they returned to the UK with lessons to be quickly implemented by fighter commanders before Operation Overlord was to begin. Lessons learned from DAFs organization and tactics, which were put to good use by the RAF over the Normandy beaches, perhaps the most important being DAF's operations using fighter-bombers.

During his Tunisian visit Dickson must have been impressed with what he saw and learned of DAF's close support tactics for the Eighth Army: on taking up his new command of DAF in late March 1944, he ordered the conversion of more fighters to fighter-bombers. He also ordered the replacement of the Kittyhawk with the Mustang. The process of change was slow, as resources were directed to support the impending Operation Overlord, the Allied invasion of Normandy: 260 Squadron was the first to get the new aircraft in 239 Wing. DAF was left to persist with many outdated models such as Baltimores, Bostons and Kittyhawks. The use of obsolescent equipment was only viable because of the Allied air forces' superiority over the Luftwaffe's meagre strength in Italy. The dependable Kittyhawk, during April and May, in support of ground forces at Anzio and Cassino, carried a 1,000lb bomb under the aircraft's belly, and two 500lb bombs under the wings.

To increase operational flexibility, the Rover David Cab-rank system was expanded. As well as the Mobile Operations Room Unit (MORU) named David, in recognition of its introduction by Group Captain David Haysom, five more MORU Rovers were established, code named Paddy, Jack, Joe, Tom and Frank. Each MORU would normally have an RAF officer in command, and preferably one who had some army experience. Each MORU was manned by eighteen Eighth Army men which include two officers, a sergeant, a radio operator, a cipher clerk, technicians, drivers, mechanics, a cook and guard troops. Their vehicles and equipment, typically comprising an armoured car and trailer, a light truck, and three jeeps with trailers, these units had a high degree of self-sufficiency.

During April the command of the Tactical Air Force (TAF) raised the tempo of the air war, with the instigation of Operation Strangle. The objectives were the interdiction of Rome, the battlefields at Anzio, Cassino, and the enemy's communication routes leading to the Gustav and Adolf Hitler Lines. It could not entirely prevent the flow of some supplies, and the movement of some reinforcements. What it did do was to severely weaken German defences, and undermine their capability for sustaining indefinite resistance. Of course, Operation Strangle was not without its consequences. To counter the growing air-to-ground onslaught, which clearly preceded another major offensive by Allied armies, the Germans increased their ground-to-air defences. More intensive anti-aircraft fire of various types imposed greater losses on Allied air forces, particularly the fighter-bombers in their low-level dive-bombing runs.

Right: Flight Sergeant Dennis Varey (1922–2007), Italy, December 1944. He joined 260 in May 1944 and left the squadron in November that year for a training squadron in England after being severely wounded.

Below left: Edward James 'Stocky' Edwards (1921–2022). The highest scoring Canadian Ace of the Second World War and veteran pilot of 260 Squadron in North Africa.

Below right: William 'Ron' Cundy (1922–2019). Australian Ace, who flew with 260 from 1941 to 1943: his last flying with 260 was at the controls of HE IIII MkV 'Delta Lilly'.

Above left: Christopher Lee (1922–2015), Intelligence Officer of 260 Squadron.

Above right: Mervyn Phillip Talbot (1922–2007), Abu Seuir, December 1943. He completed a tour with 260 from May to October 1944, before taking up a position as an instructor at RAF Rednall.

Dennis Varey like thousands of other pilots was trained to fly in Africa, in what is today Zimbabwe. Landing at Durban, Dennis travelled north by rail, to Bulawayo. This is the view countless hundreds would have seen

New pilots arriving at Initial Training Wing, Bulawayo, January 1943, complete with 'Bombay Bowlers'.

Training in Bulawayo comprised square bashing and theory lessons about flight, the laws and ordinances of the RAF.

Left: 27 Elementary Flying School at Induna, February 1943, is where Dennis learned to fly. His first flight, like for countless thousands of RAF pilots before and after him, was on the de Havilland Tiger Moth.

Below: After learning to fly on the Tiger Moth, the next stage of flying was aboard the American Harvard MKII, this example at 22 Service Flying Training School, Gwelo, summer 1943.

As well as the Harvard, pilots learned to fly on the Miles Master, seen here flying over Abu Sueir in October 1943.

Joining the RAF gave many new pilots experiences they would not normally have ever encountered. Dennis Varey was posted to Gaza at the end of 1943. Here we see Dizengoff Square.

Posted to 22 Personnel Transit Centre at Almaza at Heliopolis, Dennis, like countless thousands of others who passed through the base, explored the wonders of ancient Egypt.

Jerusalem was home of 2 Aircrew Rest Centre, which allowed RAF personnel a chance to relax and unwind in the Holy City. Here we see the Jaffa Gate.

The Kittyhawk was the workhorse of the Desert Air Force from 1941 to 1944. This example, piloted by Mervyn Talbot at 73 Operational Training Unit, Abu Sueir, November 1943, was photographed by Dennis Varey. The two pilots met here and formed a strong friendship.

The Mustang began to replace the Kittyhawk and its Merlin engined sister, the Warhawk, in front line service from new year 1944. This example, HS-D, photographed at Saint Angelo Landing Ground, Italy, was the personal mount of Dennis Varey.

Above: 260 Squadron was based at Guidonia, near Rome in summer 1944. They operated alongside the Regia Aeronatuica. Here we see a fitter working on a Fiat BR2C.

Right: The relaxed atmosphere of the Desert Air Force is captured here at Falerium in summer 1944. Left to right we see Flight Sergeants Duke Kent and Dennis Varey along with South African Pilot, 2nd Lieutenant 'Larry' Johnson, following ablutions in a bath tub improvised from a 40-gallon oil drum.

Pilots were able to enjoy the sites of Italy on leave. On three occasions, Dennis Varey was posted on leave to Sorrento.

After completing a tour of 200 hours, pilots were sent on 'rest tours' of 200 hours as instructors. Here we see 61 Operational Training Unity personnel at Montford Bridge in March 1945. Dennis Varey, promoted to Warrant Officer, is seated, third left on the right hand group.

Just as it had at El Alamein and for the invasion of Sicily, the massive air superiority of the Allies also created a No-Fly Zone. This allowed the Eighth Army to move west with impunity over the Apennines to join the Fifth Army for the major offensives at Cassino. It aimed to do what its name suggests, to cut off all rail, road and river routes across Italy, and prevent supplies reaching the German armies. An unforeseen and beneficial outcome was the near paralysis of any tactical mobility of the enemy forces. Tracks at rail-tracks, overpasses, tunnels and bridges, in central and eastern areas along the Teni-Perugia and Terni-Sulmona-Pescara lines. Trains were being hit or halted as far as 120 miles from Rome.

Joining 260

After completing ten days at the wing training school, Mervyn Talbot arrived with 260 Squadron on 28 April, in the company of Flying Officer J.H. 'Jack' Green, who had been with Mervyn and Dennis since arriving at Portici in January. Dennis remembers:

'I watched Mervyn drive off for a second time in the back of the 8-tonner with two other lads, Jack and Streety. They were all off to Cutella to join 260. We called it two sixty.

'I had been posted to 260, but for some reason, the paperwork was delayed and I followed three days later, with "Duke" Kent. We were all on the same course at Abu Sueir and had hung around as a group since then. One of the officer pilots from 260 was also at Abu Sueir, Duplesis, a rough speaking Boer. Later, Captain Mahee joined us, again he had been at Abu Sueir. Duke and I arrived on 1 May. The RAF was like that: if the paperwork was not right nothing could happen. What was the sense in sending a driver from Cutella to the wing training area, leaving two 260 pilots behind, only to come back a few days later! It made someone happy I suppose.

'I was two months into my twenty-second year. What a difference to the climate to where I had done my flying training, in Southern Rhodesia! Italy was altogether different. I've never known rain like it, or heat in the summer. Cutella was at the coast, amidst sand dunes, with the Adriatic on the far side of the two strips.

'On clambering out of the back of the 8-tonner, I reported to the adjutant. The office was filled with other pilots. I was asked my name. Told the squadron already had a Dennis, I was christened Gus. I never understood why, but Gus I was to be. The squadron was a mix of fellas. Us English lads mainly, but we had a New Zealander, an Australian and a good number of South Africans, some of whom were Boers with strong accents. I was up before the CO, Malins. A tough type, who drove the squadron and himself hard. Once leaving the office, and being told to dump my kit in one of the six-man tents I was met by Shep Sheppard, my flight skipper. After saluting he replied, "Cut that crap out, we don't do that in the Desert Airforce. I'm Shep, Come on I'll show you where the kites are, do you know the Mustang?" or something close to it. You must remember it was all a long time ago, and memory is not always what it should be.

'I had to admit that I didn't know the Mustang and as we walked toward the aircraft lines, I felt a bit concerned. I'd heard of this aircraft. It was reckoned to be one of the best fighter-bombers in the world. It had the Packard Merlin and not the lorry engine which the Allison was. I think the Mustangs specification was still on the secret list. The Mustang was a pure thoroughbred and not some lumpen carthorse like the Kittyhawk. I also felt a bit uncomfortable about my dress. I was wearing my blues, cap and boots, but all the fellas I'd seen so far wore any sort of rough gear, some in blue, others khaki, or a mix of both. Nearly all the pilots had scarves, few had hats, none had gaiters or puttees and certainly no webbing. I had seen no sign of a gun of any sort. This was The Desert Air Force. I had a lot to learn...After this it was the usual questions, where's the mess, karzi, cookhouse, etc the cookhouse was in a lorry with a tent rigged up at the back.

'The CO had a trailer, so too had the intelligence officer. I lost no time hooking up with Mervyn. We are all allocated to a single tent, five new pilots in a six-man tent. It would be our home for the coming months. We improvised a shower from a petrol tank with holes banged in it with nails. We cut up a large oil drum to make a bath. At night for heat, we filled a petrol can with sand and petrol. Cutella landing ground was among sand dunes between the beach and the river Tangro, so it was simplicity itself to get sand. It burned for a few hours. To give us head height, being almost 6ft I needed it, we dug down a pit, about 2ft. It made our beds about level with the ground. We had a fly sheet over the tent to keep it cooler inside, and draped our Mossie nets on the inside. The entire wing was at Cutella. We had the lads from one one two next door. Two fifty was on the other side, with the South African lads and Aussies in three squadron. We all intermingled between each other's mess. We had a degree of rivalry between squadrons as I soon learned.'

As Dennis explained, 260 Squadron had a pilot called Dennis on the books when he joined. Flight Sergeant Dennis Copping, had been missing since 28 June 1942.

Officially not killed in action, 260 clearly entertained the hope Copping would be found alive, and thus forbade anyone else using the name in the squadron, either out of bad luck or name association. Copping was part of a two-plane formation flying defective aircraft from the landing ground at Biur el Baheira to 53RSU, a Recovery & Service Unit at Wadi Natruna. The wreck of his Kittyhawk was founded in 2012. Dennis Copping clearly survived the initial crash because his body was not in the airframe, nor had he bailed out, as the remains of his parachute lay near the aircraft's nose. The use of the parachute in this manner has suggested it was perhaps erected as a sun-shelter by Copping himself after the accident. Since no skeletal human remains were evident near the Kittyhawk, it seems likely that Copping wandered off into the desert, with no food and no water, in an ultimately futile attempt to reach salvation. He must have died alone, in truly awful circumstances. He was just 24-years-old. It had been hoped to bring Copping's Kittyhawk back to England under the auspices of the RAF Museum. International tensions meant that the airplane remains in Egypt on display at El Alamein. My uncle Dennis's arrival with 260 clearly triggered all the memories both of personnel who knew Copping, like Sheppard, and the inherited folk memory of the squadron.

The day job

No. 260 Squadron's Operations Record Book tells us that both Dennis and Mervyn flew on their first operation on 5 May. Mervyn Talbot remembers:

> 'After three familiarisation trips in the Mustang, I flew my first operation, which was an armed attack on a bridge, using two 500lb bombs, then looking for other suitable ground targets. The anti-aircraft fire was described as intense. We had a Spitfire escort for that and the following three operations which were all attacks on bridges at different locations. This set the pattern for the future operations where we carried a bomb under each wing, usually 500lbs, although occasionally 1000lbs for special targets and we approached the target in "boxed six" formation at 8000ft before peeling off and diving to 1200ft to release the bombs. After this we were free to search and destroy ground targets at low-level.'

Dennis Varey again:

> 'On my second trip, one of my bombs hung up. I had to joggle my wings to get the thing to drop off. On other times you had to get back to base and fly around until you were out of petrol, then land as gently as possible, then bail out and run like hell in case she blew

up. Twitchy job that. These sorties as ground-attack took me back to my training days in Southern Rhodesia, where I completed my flying training on Harvard's and Kitties at Abu Sueir. There, we had a bombing area where we tried to hit ground targets with little success. This sortie made me realise that our training hadn't been as useless as we thought at the time.'

About operations Dennis remembers:

'We could be on standby for 60 or 30 minute take-off waiting for targets from Rover. In other cases, once we were in the air, on a Recce, an army forward observation post called a "Rover" gave us clear directions as to our target, sometimes laying down a smoke marker for us. These directions were given to us on the radio. Quite often there would be several squadrons in the same area at the same time and the "Rover" control would call us in consecutively. Mostly if we were not Cab Ranking that day, we were briefed about the op before we went up and given a series of pre-defined targets in scale of importance if the primary target was obscured.

'In the morning, our intelligence officer, in this case Chris, or to give his proper name Pilot Officer C.P. Lee, gave us a briefing as to the role which we were to play in support of the PBI. It was up to us to provide close support to the troops on the ground, clearing a way for them to advance past mortars, heavy guns etc. We either attacked pre-assigned targets, or went on armed recces to prearranged target zones that had been requested by the infantry by Rover David control. Facing flak was, in the scheme of things, no worse than the PBI being mortared or shelled every day, and slogging up muddy mountains in torrential rain to be mown down by German MG fire. We gave them the support they needed to clear the Jerries out. We were trying to fight a war in Italy without adequate support, and tried to overcome this with air superiority and artillery.'

As we noted earlier 'cab-rank' operations were a new form of close air support introduced by the Allies in Italy during the winter of 1943-1944: formations of patrolling fighter-bombers were maintained over the front lines to be called down upon targets by RAF liaison officers embedded with the forward elements of the Army. From June 1944 air spotters replaced the rover teams on the ground. The air spotters operated at an altitude of 3,000 to 4,000ft, ranging above small arms fire, roving up to twenty miles inside German lines, and marking targets with smoke bombs. To aid the strike pilots in seeing the tiny liaison craft, the upper wing surfaces were painted red, green, yellow or blue. In both cases, infantry encountering resistance that required air support radioed the Rover unit, which passed the request to the fighter control centre. If a request was approved, the Rover unit contacted designated aircraft on station and the forward air controller identified and pinpointed the target to the circling aircraft, which then dropped their bombs on the targets, sometimes just a few hundred yards ahead of the advancing Allied ground troops. After the bombing run, the pilots would pull-up, turn around and roar back down onto the target to make low-level strafing runs at any vehicles or anti-aircraft gun emplacements that were left intact. As Dennis hinted at, about operational flying, Shep Sheppard recalls:

'Much depended in Italy on what the Army required from us on the following day. If it was to be taxi rank, then two or three squadrons would be given rough times for take-off. We had a system of coloured flags on the operations trailer telling us which flight was to go next. You would know if the squadron was required for one six flight or two, and whichever flight commander was due to fly first would make up his own team and tell them what time he wanted them down the ops trailer. We could choose who we wanted. At full strength in Italy we had about thirty-three pilots, split into A and B flight. Each flight commander had about sixteen pilots to choose from, although the flight commander would fly on every trip, he had available to him four, possibly five, pair leaders. Pair leaders would fly every other show, leaving a pool of ten pilots to slot in as number twos. The number two's at first would fly every third or fourth trip. It gave a reasonable amount of rest and familiarisation of new pilots, who probably did one show in every five or six outings. As the number two's gained experience, and were considered up to the job, they would move up to section leader, and fly every day, sometimes twice if we were short on pilots. Once the first flight commander had picked his team, the second did so, and give them a time to assemble at ops. By now, we would know if Malins, the CO wanted to join, which he frequently did, in which case one of the flight commanders might not go, depending on what was suspected could come up during the day.

'If you were not on the taxi rank, you might get a request for a special one-off show, or perhaps HQ wanted a special armed recce or sweep; most usually these would be a flight of six rather than twelve. Much the same rigmarole went on choosing teams, except that details of the show might not come through until very late in the day. I remember on one occasion; it was well past midnight when the job finally came through. When this happen, our procedure was simplicity itself. The flight commander who was not on the show, would stay up to get the detail and the flight commander on the show would get off to be with his team. This was necessary because it often meant a five o'clock kick off. The batman, the duty flight sergeant for the ground crew and the cooks of course, all needed to know so they could get a brew up on for everyone.

'Regardless of the care and attention, we put into this, we were often caught off guard. Your time to join the taxi might be say, nine o'clock in the morning, and suddenly you went into a blind panic because an earlier show had observed a large convoy of MT which needed knocking out, so you would get a call to come to five minutes readiness.

'It is then all panic stations. Old Jock rushes to the flight commanders tent to call him. You both rush around the team's tents, waking them and hurrying them, and then get down to ops. I always found timer to clean my teeth, having that slight edge of being called first, but if it was the other flight on their call, I then got my team together for a quick breakfast because it was certain we would be in as replacement, at short notice […] on these occasion's I spent a lot of time in the ops trailer going over troop dispositions, both Allied and German, the latest intelligence on enemy aircraft placement, and any other gen that was available. Equally, you could be chasing the engineering officer on serviceability or the Equipment Officer who had not given a new pilot a whistle or camp bed – the whistle was more important because we did fly up and down the Adriatic a great deal, and one hoped it would attract some attention if anyone was near you, and you were in the drink.'

I asked Dennis what his memories of the taxi or Cab Rank were:

'Cab Rank. Well, that was the big thing at the time. Who did what and why was all sorted by Chris in his van. He knew what was going on as he was in contact with Wing intelligence. He would disappear, and then come back and suddenly it was all hands on deck.

'The target was chosen by folk on the front line. An Army liaison officer and a RAF liaison officer worked in a modified tank known as a Mobile Ops Room. Chris Lee went off to command one. They were right up on the front line, which could be very dodgy. An army unit finding a Jerry tank, mortar battery, or whatever, would call up the army liaison officer, describe the target, then the attack would take place and the target would have marker smoke. That would all be discussed with the RAF officer, who would issue instructions to one of the squadrons already Cab Ranking. On some jobs we had an air spotter. One flight would bomb the target, he would fly over and say more north, south etc and then the next flight would drop onto the bomb run. It made sure we got the target. It was only possible as the Luftwaffe did not exist in any real sense.

'Each pilot carried a large-scale map divided into squares, numbered from south to north, lettered east to west. A block of squares formed a larger unit which was given a letter as designation. When the Cab Rank leader reported the position, the Rover would brief him, telling him the which map sheet was needed "target in square B4" the leader would reply "understood target B4". Rover would reply "see the main road running south-east to north-west? Over" The leader would reply "yes", Rover would respond with details such as "a third of the way down the road from north-west is a bridge over a river that runs roughly east to west". "Yes, got it," leader would reply. Rover, "Follow the river east to a wood, your target is three Mk IV tanks in the wood. "Roger, target three tanks in the wood." And so, there we would go. Of course, in a Mustang it was the devil's own job for the leader to juggle the maps, often shoving them in a boot. Can you imagine anything as stupid as being asked to fly a kite and juggle a map, look for a target square. Someone very clever had come up with it, but failed to get to grips with reality. We had a lot of that during the war. Good ideas that were less than obvious to put into practice. We tended to keep our maps tucked into the top of our boots The cockpit had nowhere else for it.'

Dennis showed me a map he had kept from this time on 260 Squadron. Neatly folded around the edge, it was still a large and cumbersome item. I could not begin to imagine how time consuming it must have been to extract it from a boot, check position and keep on going to target. 'How did you navigate?' I ask:

'The elements of aircraft navigation are the air speed and heading of the aircraft, the wind velocity and direction at the current altitude, and the speed and track of the aircraft against the ground. Of these the accurate determination of wind drift is the most difficult problem, especially on long flights where there was no visible ground reference. We'd be given bearings and headings at Ops. It's all down to maths. At Thornes House, cousin by marriage Wilfred Emery taught me mathematics and music: he gave me a good grounding in what I needed to know to navigate about the place.

'To help us we had the Dalton Computer do a lot of the hard work for us. It was not an electronic computer, but a very advanced type of slide rule.

'We had a compass in the cockpit and we had a good idea of the route from the briefing, and for which way markers to turn at: it was important we kept amental note of speed and time. On a Lancaster the navigator had the luxury of his own little cabin, for us, we had to juggle the map, remember course, time, speed, keep a look out for Jerry, flak and manage the engine. It all became second nature as our instructors and the RAF intended. Once you were based anywhere for a length of time you go to know landmarks, rivers, bridges, that sort of thing, so you had a good idea, dead reckoning we called it, of where we were all the time, and how to get home if we had engine trouble.'

What happened next? Did the Germans ever try and interfere?

'Once Rover had talked to flight leader about the target, we called him skipper, or Skip, some of the South Africans called them Kanga, skipper would radio through what we were to do, giving us details visible from the air, and our direction of attack. Often, he would drop down to 3,000 or less, swoop around looking at the deck and then climb back up to us at 10,000. He would then line us up all behind him like a mother duck and her ducklings and we would start the bomb run. We would dive at around sixty degrees, at up to 400mph from 2000ft. If the Luftwaffe had turned out, they would have had us as easy targets. What the Germans were deadly at though was ack-ack.'

To make up for the lack of air cover, the German's increasingly relied on ground fire. As a result ground attack became increasingly more dangerous due to flak: diving through 88mm flak was riskier than a dog fight with a 109. As well as the feared 88mm, the 37mm and 20mm and the quadruple barrelled Flakvierling 38 firing 900 rounds per minute, provided a ground fire far thicker than the 88mm. Pilots also had to face the threat of machine-gun fire and small arms. A particular danger in Italy was from the Breda. This was an Italian light machine gun, but it had the range and hitting power for anti-aircraft use, especially as dive-bombing necessitated a low escape point, sometimes under 1,000ft, well in range of machine guns and rifle fire. Mervyn Talbot again:

'Ground fire was encountered, of course, as well as high level stuff so it was not unusual to suffer some occasional damage to the aircraft. Most sorties were greeted with the black puffs from bursting 88mm shells at high level and during the dive onto the selected target there was usually plenty of 40mm and 20mm fire followed by ground fire. On one occasion my fitter pointed out a bullet hole in my cockpit cover just a few inches from where my head was and this must have been fired from a rifle on the ground. Some places were more heavily defended than others so we were met with quite intense fire throughout the operation although on occasion there was almost nothing sent up at us. It was all pot luck really.'

Although by spring 1944 the Luftwaffe in Italy were depleted by demands of the Russian front and the defence of Germany, some fighters were still in the theatre of operations. For this reason, most operations by 239 Wing were escorted by four Spitfires as 'top cover.'

The Dam Busters

The second operation carried out on 5 May 1944 was a major bombing action carried out by 239 Wing in order to breach the hydro-electric dam on the Pescara River. The task-group comprised three dozen aircraft from three separate squadrons: 260 Squadron, 3 Squadron (RAAF) flying Kittyhawks, as did 5 Squadron (SAAF), which also participation on the operation.

It was thought that the German Army intended to open the sluice gates of the Pescara Dam and flood the countryside to impede the advancing Allied troops after the new assault had commenced. Allied Command decided to strike first, prior to starting their advance. Shep Sheppard, who flew on the raid recalls:

'To take Rome would be not only a great victory in itself, but also a great victory psychologically. Our attack on the Pescara dam was to help the situation along.

'It was the best show of the month when on 5 May three of the squadrons from the wing bombed the Pescara dam. This particular effort did not receive the applause in the UK that it warranted, but it probably contributed more to the war effort than the much-vaunted Ruhr "Dam Busters" raid in May 1943.

'This is not sour grapes in anyway, because the flying, especially at night, that the aircraft in those Ruhr raids achieved, was absolutely fantastic and they achieved their objective in destroying the dams, but unfortunately the losses were terrible. Every one of the aircrew in those raids is to be commended for the magnificent job they did, but I do not believe it achieved the end result envisaged by the boffins who thought up the raid, i.e. the dismantling of the Ruhr industries which apparently were back in production in a couple of days. The raid was meant to put them out for good. One effect of the

Ruhr Dam raids was that the Germans placed very heavy ack-ack defences on all important dams and this applied to the Pescara Dam, which was part of the system for hydroelectric development of the Adriatic coast of Italy.

'The objective of the bombing of the Pescara Dam was twofold: one, to disrupt the power from the hydro-electric system and secondly, and most importantly, to flood the valley down to the coast, thereby making it virtually impossible for any counter-attack by the Germans on the east coast whilst the push for Rome was getting underway on the west coast of Italy. Apparently, this effort by DAF enabled the allies to move a large number of Army divisions to the west coast of Italy for the push on Rome, in the knowledge that the Adriatic coast was comparatively safe from attack.

'We used three squadrons for the attack on the dam, led by 260. The whole show was led by Colonel Wilmot (SAAF) who was the Wing Co. I was to lead the top cover of 260 Squadron and, after bombing, was to climb to provide cover for the other two squadrons to make their runs without any interference from enemy aircraft.'

One sluice gate was destroyed by bombs from 260 Squadron, those of Duguin. In 260's wake came 3 Squadron (RAAF). Carrying two 500lb bombs, one under each wing, and a 1,000lb under the fuselage, this was the first time the squadrons Kittyhawks had carried such a payload. No. 3 Squadron diary reports Flight Lieutenant Richards made a direct hit on another sluice gate and the hydro-electric power station complex was also hit by their bombs. No. 5 Squadron (SAAF) followed, reporting that the water level in the dam was dropping as they came in on their bombing run. The result was that the immediate area, containing German supply and troop concentrations, was flooded and one of Italy's main sources of hydro-electric power was temporarily disabled, which helped the Allied advance. The town of Pescara was reported to be under four feet of water. No. 260 Squadron diary reports:

Colonel Wilmot DFC of headquarters, No. 239 Wing DAF led a formation of 11 aircraft of this squadron to attack the Pescara Dam [...] Bombing was extremely good and very accurate, the first five bombs that were dropped were all right on the dam construction knocking down the masonry and apparently caving in at least one gate of the three.

The Squadron Operations Record Book continues:

There was a flash from one hit and a large quantity of water was seen rushing through what remained of the gates. The masonry of the superstructure was also seen to be crumbling and the obvious result in that the dam was very thoroughly demolished, 6 streams of water cascading over each other were seen to be swelling down river towards PESCARA, losing in volume somewhat as they progressed in distance, the maximum rush of water was about 150yards long. A great deal of spray and smoke together with quantities of debris was thrown up from dam obscuring a large part of it, making it difficult to assess individual results, except that for the second bomb, that of F/S Duguid, was a direct hit straight on to the superstructure. After bombing formation climbed to 17000', orbiting target as remaining 2 squadrons went into bombing dive. No definite results are reported, though it appears that bombs were in general target area.

A primaeval surge of water had been unleashed. But unlike the more famous dams raid which failed to inflict upon the German war machine a devastating economic blow, but instead temporary disruption, together with a human catastrophe, the 'other dams' raid helped win the war. The 617 Squadron raid was a huge boost to moral, yet the more significant raid in Italy went unnoticed, compounded by Lady Astor describing all those in Italy as 'D-Day Dodgers'. Veterans of the Italian campaign are quite rightly bitter of this accusation, and 260 veterans, like Shep in particular, felt let down that their war and success was virtually ignored. The *Yorkshire Evening Post*:

R.A.F. dive-bombers have been dam-busting in Italy today. Mustangs and Kittyhawks attacked the great Pescara dam on the river of that name behind the German lines, on the Adriatic sector. Twenty minutes after the first Mustang had cracked the iron sluice gates a wall of water was seen sweeping downstream towards the town of Pescara at the river mouth. All our planes returned.

However, the Australian Press reported:

The blasted dam is about 10 miles ahead of the Eighth Army positions on the Adriatic coast, and 20 miles from the port of Pescara.

Kittyhawks, led by Flight Lieutenant Kenneth Richards of Warrigul, Victoria, took part in the daring attack made in daylight. Waters from the dam supplied power for the whole area around Pescara, and also supplemented the Rome power supply. The dam was a massive iron and concrete structure, and held millions of gallons of water.

The attack was carefully planned, and for weeks before the actual raid selected pilots studied a small-scale model of the whole area. Finally, a plan was decided on, and all was made ready.

It was realised that only a terrific underwater explosion would smash the huge steel sluice gates in the centre of the dam, and the pilots of the Mustangs and Kittyhawks briefed for the mission were ordered to make a power-dive on the sluice gates, no matter what flak met them, and drop their bomb loads in a very small area.

The first flight of Mustangs was led by Sergeant Pilot Alexander Duguid, of Aberdeenshire, Scotland, and he made a brilliant precision bombing attack. Power-diving low over the dam he dropped his high explosives with deadly accuracy, and watched the waters begin to surge through the breach he had made. Other Mustangs followed, and dropped their bombs right on the target area.

Kittyhawks led by Flight Lieutenant Richards then swept in over the dam, and as he zoomed up after releasing his load of bombs, Flight Lieutenant Richards saw that the water was surging through the breaches, and the area at the base of the huge structure was a mass of roaring, muddy water.

Another flight of Kittyhawk's made the final attack, and wreckage from the sluice gates flew high into the air as the heavy loads of bombs fell away from the planes.

Twenty minutes after the first plane made the breach, flood waters were roaring down the valley more than a mile away.

Heavy anti-aircraft fire was encountered over the target area, but this did not deter the RAF pilots. A number of the Kittyhawks came from an Australian squadron based in Italy.

Although this attack was made on a big enemy dam, it had little in common with the blasting of the Moehne and Eder Dams in Germany last year by Lancasters under the leadership of Wing Commander Gibson, VC. This attack was made by the Lancasters in moonlight with mines which blasted the concrete walls of the twin dams, and shattered the whole system.

The attack on the Pescara Dam was carried out in broad daylight, and all the planes engaged returned safely from the mission.

Unlike the raids of 1943 which killed up to 1,400 people – more civilian deaths than had been generated by any previous RAF attack on Germany – this attack in 1944 is reported to have killed no civilians and destroyed a key hydro-electric power station crippling power supplies in the region and to Rome. It also flooded farmland which prevented a German attack in the area. The Italian Dams raid achieved all its objectives. And was conducted with standard aircraft and armament. That it was a triumph speaks of the training and courage of the pilots in 239 Wing.

On 7 May a message reading: 'Please give my best congratulations to the Dam Busters in 3, 5 and 260 Squadrons. We are all proud of their splendid bombing.' Duguid was awarded the Distinguished Flying Medal on 20 May.

Basking in the success of a 'job well done' 260 Squadron did not 'rest on its laurels.' Mervyn Talbot was in combat on 6 May attacking a vital rail bridge. The flight was again led by Malins, and was airborne at 0835. Again, the flight rendezvoused with its escort of Spitfires off Penna Point before heading to Pesaro. Two bombs overshot the railway bridge damaging the station, but no direct hits were made on the bridge. The 7/8 May were marked with rest days. No operational flying took place. Operations resumed on 10 May. Denis flew as Blue 2, to Flight Sergeant Billy Johnson on an armed attack on a bridge at Pesaro. The squadron diary tells us, the flight of twelve mustangs took off at 0800, the target was a railway bridge at Pesaro, it had to be destroyed. Escorted once more by six Spitfires, second time lucky 22 x 500lb bombs were dropped, one making a direct hit, severing all four rail lines. The rubble of the bridge blocked the track. Dennis was back a Cutella at 1000. Mervyn was in Italian skies flying alongside Shep Shepperd the following day. He was Blue 2 to Pilot Officer McParland. On the same operation was Duke Kent as Green 2, and Lieutenant Larry Johnson as Black 2. Mervyn and Dennis shared their tent with Duke, Larry and Jack Green. The other in the six-man bivvy was Sergeant Street. Shep led a formation of twelve Mustangs into the air at 0940 to attack and cut the railway line between Fabiaro and Possaro, and if possible, to destroy the bridge at Cebaro. Picking up the Spitfire escort at Perna Point, the formation climbed to 15,000ft, making landfall at Porto Recanati. Cloud started at 9,000ft and descended to hill tops obscuring the primary target. Shepperd ordered the formation to the secondary target at Cebaro. The bombing run was north-west to south-east, the flight dropping from 8,000 to 2,000ft for the run. The bridge was damaged but not destroyed. The railway was blocked with fallen masonry but not cut.

CHAPTER
11

CASSINO

IN ANTICIPATION OF the Allies' build-up for spring offensives at Anzio and Cassino, the Luftwaffe garnered its remaining numbers to try and blunt Allied air attacks. However, air superiority had given DAF a lethal tactical advantage. Rather than being drawn into individual dogfights, DAF squadrons were able to shift to an emphasis on formation group work. This does not mean the Luftwaffe was yet totally eliminated.

The night of 11 May 1944 was set for the fourth battle to begin, they hoped for the final battle for Cassino and the Monte Cassino Monastery. With the bulk of the Eighth Army now added to the US Fifth Army, the Allies planned to throw overwhelming force at the mountain bastion. In a concentration of numbers, firepower and a massive artillery bombardment, they intended to smash their way through the Gustav Line and north onto Highway 6. It was not just a pincer movement of breakthroughs out of Anzio and Cassino. The German Army found in retreat that they were under constant attack from Allied air forces. The goal was for air power to cripple the German's lines of communication and supply. To achieve a decisive advantage on the ground, General Alexander planned a build-up with a number of deceptions. The vast bulk of the Eighth Army was gradually moved at night-time from the Adriatic coast to the Cassino front. False information on planning for another seaborne landing north-west of Rome at its port of Civitavecchia was leaked to the Germans. It must have had an effect, for Kesselring kept strong reserves north of Rome until a few days after the start of the Eighth Army's Operation Honker, scheduled to begin on the night of 11/12 May which was to be the next attack on Cassino and the Gustav Line. The Canadian Corps of two divisions was brought into the Eighth Army reserve without announcement. At the same time fictitious information was issued which indicated that the Canadians were relocating to Naples to embark for the fake amphibious operation to land at Civitavecchia. A member of 3 Squadron RAAF, a sister squadron to 260 wrote in his diary:

Friday, 12 May 1944

Fine. Artillery barrage opened at 10.40pm last night – biggest one the 8th Army has ever put over – 500 more guns than El Alamein.

They put over about 11,000 ton in 40 minutes. Planes did one op at dawn – bombing guns near Cassino. Poles made good progress but were heavily counter-attacked and had to give a bit of ground.

As well as the artillery barrage, the Allies' overwhelming air superiority meant that DAF could bomb targets at will. Air superiority had another important advantage for the allies, it reduced to a bare minimum reconnaissance undertaken by the Luftwaffe. This meant that the Allied build up went largely unobserved. The concealment of forces was not just to give the benefit of surprise, it would hide the reserve capability to exploit the capture of Cassino and Monte Cassino, so as to surge forward up the Liri Valley in Operation Diadem, to combine with an Anzio breakout – codenamed Operation Buffalo.

The timing of the attack was significant. Together with the simultaneous break-out from Anzio, Operation Buffalo, there would be less than a month before the planned D-Day landings in Normandy. The hope was that the offensives would draw German attention and their forces to Italy, and away from Normandy and north-west Europe. It was essential that Operations Diadem and Buffalo succeeded. Any further stalemate or defeats in Italy could be catastrophic, and allow the Germans to divert divisions to Normandy. A strategic loss in Italy would be a huge psychological blow to the Allies in all theatres.

Cassino had to be taken and with it the road to Rome.

During 12 May 1944 the operations of 239 Wing intensified, supporting the Fifth Army's big push on the Gustav Line and the breakout from the Anzio bridgehead. The fighter-bombers were only able to go about their destructive work because of air superiority which was asserted and sustained around the clock by Allied fighters. The first of many operations against targets at Atina by 260 Squadron was in the air at 1045, led by Squadron Leader Malins, the Squadron's Operations Record Book reports:

> The target showed up quite clearly, all 5 gun pits being seen, with wheel tracks leading up to them and to the farmhouse nearby. After bombing, leader recced area and reports that the majority of bombs landed well in target area, which was completely covered by smoke and dust, observation results were therefore impossible, although one was evidently firing before it was attacked as flashes were seen.

Blomfield was airborne at 1120hrs, again heading back to Atina, again targeting German artillery. Mervyn Talbot flew his first sortie at Cassino on the thirteenth. No. 239 Wing Operations Record Book reports:

> The principal role of this Wing on this day was that of keeping enemy guns quiet in the ATINA area to prevent them interfering with

the 8th and 5th Army push on the CASINO area. IN all, 13 missions were carried out on these targets and there is no doubt that the desired result was obtained. The army report stated that attacks were most effective, and guns quiet throughout the day.

It was on one of these thirteen operations that Dennis Varey received his baptism of fire flying as Black 2 to Flight Sergeant Duguid: the objective to take out German artillery at Attina. Squadron Leader Malins led the flight into the air at 0840, Blomfield led the second attack at 0920. No guns were observed, but an ammunition dump was obliterated. Dennis landed at 1030 and watched Squadron Leader Malins get airborne at 1245 heading back to Cassino on his second operation of the day. As in the morning, the primary target was to silence German artillery, but as before no guns were observed so the second target was attacked. This was a large ammunition dump which was bombed from 1500ft: the resulting explosions, flames and smoke, rose up to 3,000ft. More of the same followed on the fourteenth. Dennis was in the air at 1550, as No. 2 to Warrant Officer Bill Nelson, the flight was led by Blomfield. The target was a German artillery battery near Cassino identified by Rover David as lodged in a dried-up stream bed. No guns were observed, but possible blast walls were obliterated, with six bombs falling on the target. Throughout the bombing run intense 40mm and 20mm anti-aircraft fire was encountered, but no Mustangs were hit. For this operation, each Mustang carried two 1,000lb bombs.

Other operations flown by 260 that day was against a column of German lorries at Subiaco, by the day's end there were an estimated 120 destroyed or damaged. On 14 May Shep was in the air at 1135, the target mortar positions. He led a flight of six to target at 9,000ft. The area was 'pitted with bomb and shell craters making observation difficult.' Despite this the flights twelve 1,000lb bombs fell on target, with eight direct hits, one bomb fell on a house which was totally demolished. Flak was fired from nearby houses: already partly ruined, the Germans used the shell of the houses to conceal 40mm and 20mm flak. Shep led his flight in a strafing run against these targets, silencing the guns. A total of 1360 rounds of 0.50cal was fired. Sergeant Street, flying FB 268, 'was shot up in the tail-plane. a/c Cat: 2' meaning it was repairable, but not serviceable again that day.

Shep landed at 1250, just after Blomfield had taken to the Italian skies at 1155 to head back to the same position Shep had attacked. Mervyn Talbot, flying FB 274, was No. 2 to Pilot Officer McParland on this run. No mortars were observed, but the target was again bombed and strafed.

The bridge at San Giovannie was identified as a key objective to demolish on the fifteenth. Blomfield led the flight of six Mustangs off at 1650, and recorded in his logbook: '15 May: Cab-rank – Cassino – bridge: Bombed 1 Mk. IV tank

and set on fire. Broke bridge across Liri. Army sent "Bloody Good Show!"'
Dennis flew on this trip as Yellow 2 to Warrant Officer Bill Nelson as Yellow
1, recording in his logbook 'bombed tank. Flamer. Cloud bad. Four direct hits
on bridge. Intense, accurate heavy and light ack-ack, small arms fire.' Also
flying that day, Shep was airborne at 1655, Mervyn was No. 2 to Flight Sergeant
Duguid. The target chosen by rover was a 40ft bridge over the Mela River. The
bridge was already damaged, so a nearby railway bridge was targeted. Again,
the Germans concealed anti-aircraft guns in houses. 20mm was put up from the
window of a house which was silenced by a strafing run. The Operations Record
Book reports: 'It was impossible to recce the bridge area as extremely accurate
bred and slight accurate 88mm was being fired continuously at formation.' Shep
landed at 1820. The 15 May had been a busy day for 260 Squadron. Cassino was
again the target on the sixteenth. All twelve mustangs of A Flight were dispatched
to attack mortar positions. Red Section, led by Flight Lieutenant Sheppard was
airborne at 0850, Blue Section led by Blomfield was in the air by 0900. The
flight gained height to 9,000ft as it headed to Cassino, close to the mountain,
Red Section dived to 2,000ft to come in and bomb in a line east to west which
was obscured by a smoke screen. Of the twelve bombs dropped by Red Section,
six were 'hung ups', two eventually fell on what was assumed to be German
positions. Coming round after the bombing run, Sheppard dropped to 1,500ft
and led a strafing run under the protection of Blue Section. Blue Section then
turned their attention on a battery of three German artillery pieces, bombs were
dropped from 2,000ft into a bombing zone of 50ft from target pinpoint. At the
end of the run, the flight turned and strafed the area. Both flights landed by 1030,
twenty-four bombs dropped and 2970 rounds of 0.50 ammunition. Dennis again
flew as Yellow 2, noting 'Bombed Observation Post, near misses.' Mervyn Talbot
and Duke Kent both had a brush with death that day. Mervyn got lost in dense
clouds and struggled to find his way back. Duke Kent found that HS-Q had not
been thoroughly serviced. The Mustang had a glycol leak, billowing white smoke
almost as soon as he took off, he attempted to get his kite back on the deck before
it exploded. He crashed but was uninjured; however, HS-Q was a write off.

More of the same came on the seventeenth. Blue Section was airborne at 1525 in
bad weather, heading to Cassino at 3,000ft. The squadron diary notes: 'Sgt. Varey
left formation with engine trouble before bombing target and landed at Santa Maria,
returning to base.' Two days later Dennis was back in the air on a reconnaissance
patrol. In the air at 1030 flying at 9,000ft below the cloud, the flight headed to
Cassino. The target was a gun position at Grid Reference 734278. All bombs
missed the target and on the return trip came under intense 88mm flak as well as
from 40mm and 20mm ground fire. All landed at 1155. Dennis's logbook records
'Yellow 2. Armed attack on gun positions in Cassino Area. Engine trouble over
target. Broke formation and landed at S.Maria (USAAF). Repaired and returned to
base. 10/10 cloud cover, visibility bad on hills.'

The following day, observation posts on Monte Trocchio, staffed with a mix of RAF and Eighth Army Air Control officers, directed the Kittyhawks and Mustangs on 239 Wing. Shep Sheppard again:

'In May I did 23 ops covering thirty-five and a half hours, mostly on Army Support at the Cab Rank as we called it. We flew over to a point just below Cassino and then bombed on the grid reference given to us by Rover control. We received a lot of congratulatory messages, both from the Army and the Poles and, on the 15 May we received three congratulatory messages directly to the squadron – I had led two shows that day so felt pretty good about.'

The breakthrough at Cassino came on the eighteenth when the last of the German defenders left the ruined monastery. In total 100 sorties were flown by the wing on Cab Rank attacking gun positions, roads and bridges.

The monastery may have fallen but it did not mean the way to Rome was open. Kesselring organised a German counter-attack on the early morning of the nineteenth. Four divisions of the Eighth Army were moved north along the Liri Valley on Highway 6 in pursuit of the Germans. The Allies had to act quickly to prevent the Germans retreating back to the Adolf Hitler Line. 260 Squadron and all of 239 Wing were to the fore. 3 Squadron (RAAF) attacked the ruined village of Pontecorvo, and were fired upon by 'rocket-like projectiles in groups of fire thrown up from south of Atina' reported the Wing Operations Record Book. Dennis flew as Black 2 aboard HS-T FB 277, an armed recce over Cassino. The secondary target at Roccasecca was bombed as the primary target of Cassino was not evident. The flight came under intense, accurate machine gun and ack-ack fire. HS-T was hit, with holes punched into the fuselage and wings, which damaged both bomb racks, meaning he had to land with two 'hang ups'. This was the first time he had come under fire and his airplane been damaged, but not his first hang up, that had been on his second operation on 5 May. Seventy-eight sorties were flown that day

The following day it reported:

Further attacks on enemy strongholds in PONTECORVO were carried out which apparently had every effect as the Army signalled as follows: 'GROUND REPORTS STATE THAT ATTACKS ON PONTECORVO BROKE UP ENEMY COUNTER ATTACK – MANY THANKS.'

As the Operation Record Book relates, 239 Wing had stopped dead the German offensive. A contemporary report from 3 Squadron (RAAF) gives a flavour of intensity of operations over Cassino:

During the three weeks' battle which began at Cassino and ended at the gates of Rome, our fighter-bomber squadrons experienced possibly their busiest operational period since El Alamein. Daily our pilots ranged over enemy territory, blasting his gun positions, smashing his bridges, cratering his roads, dislocating his rail communications, destroying his mechanized transport. The first faint streaks of dawn found pilots strapped in their cockpits, ready for a first light take-off. Night had almost closed in before the last of the Kitties had taxied back to its dispersal point. And from well before dawn until long after dark, armourers, fitters, riggers, stores assistants, cooks, stewards, clerks, ground officers and those scores of others whose efforts are seldom headlined, worked at pressure to keep the aircraft flying.

The losses in men and machines suffered by our fighter-bomber squadrons in the Italian campaign have been remarkably small, compared with the results achieved, and many of the pilots forced to crash-land, or bale out over enemy territory, managed to walk back, some to relate stories as enthralling as any to be found in books of adventure fiction.

Despite the success in Italy, all thoughts of Allied Supreme Command were now focused on Overlord. Delays in strategic planning and operation in Italy allowed the Germans to escape the trap set by Operation Buffalo. The attack against the Adolf Hitler Line began on 23 May in bad weather. That day, Blue Section was in the air at 0615 in poor visibility and had to climb to 10,000ft to get above the cloud cover. The target was to cut a road at grid Ref 435526. A gap in the cloud cover allowed the flight to drop to 2,000ft and commence a bombing run from north to south. One 500lb bomb made a direct hit on a German 3-tonne motorised transport. After the bombing run the flight carried out five strafing runs expending over 4,500 rounds of 0.50cal ammunition fired. The flight destroyed four motorised transports and a 20ft petrol bowser. The other vehicles in the convoy were 'well shot up.' Landing at 0735, after re-fuelling and re-arming the mustangs of Blue Section were airborne again at 1025 to attack German gun positions. The weather was still fairly bad, the cloud base was at 2,000ft and the top around 8,000ft. The flight headed to Cassino at 10,000ft, on reaching Cassino, cloud top was estimated 15,000 and base was ground level. The target was totally obscured and the flight retuned to base, jettisoning bombs over the target zone. Blomfield recorded: '23 May: Bombed road – Alatri: Road cut. Five M/T "flamers" and a petrol bowser!' Dennis flew alongside Blomfield's HS-E as Blue 2. In the strafing run Dennis claimed six lorries as flamers and a petrol bowser. Anything that moved was attacked by 260.

Aboard HS-E later that day, flying as Yellow 2, the flight of six was led by Shep Sheppard who remembers:

'We had taken off to join the Cab Rank and been told that there was broken cloud from about four or five thousand feet up to ten thousand, but it was reasonably clear over the other side. Off we went climbing up through some patchy cloud, but it was obvious to me that the "met" people had it wrong and we were going to hit some really thick stuff before long. I played safe and put everyone on cloud flying – the leader sets his gyro compass on nought degrees, those on the right set at 001 degrees and those on the left at 359 degrees and so on. Instructions are rigid: climb at 190 mph, 500ft per minute, do not deviate.

'Sure enough at 5000ft we hit the cloud 10/10 and for ten minutes my heart was in my mouth. Should I have turned back, single engine pilots are not thick cloud flyers, but it was too late now when suddenly out I came into strong sunlight. As I looked around for the flight, it was like watching corks fly out of a bottle; up through the lovely white layer came first one, then another, four, five and number six well off to the left. We reformed, setting course for "Rover David" but as the cloud got higher so did we and when we arrived at the rendezvous point, at least where I pinpointed it to be, we were at 20,000ft! A complete blanket of beautiful white cloud covered the whole area and so it was decision time. Take the bombs back or to try and find a break in the clouds. If we took the bombs back, would we be able to find a decent break in the clouds to get down?

'Although you have 10/10 cloud there are often small breaks that enable you to fix your position, but it is not possible to fly six aircraft down through them, and so having pinpointed my position, I flew the flight on a north-westerly course for five minutes. This meant we were well over the line and finding a small break in the cloud through which we could see a gaggle of transport, instructed everyone to release their bombs. My concern was to save the pilots and aircraft, and it proved the right decision, because when we got back to the Adriatic side of Italy, the cloud was almost as thick. We were fortunate in picking up a bit of a break and I led them in line astern down through a valley where at one point we literally lifted wings to clear a church steeple in a village, but we came out almost on our own airstrip. The desert homing built-in instinct seemed to have worked even in Italy.'

Up again the following day flying HS-C, and flying as Green 2 as wingman to Bill Nelson, Dennis flew as part of an armed attack on the Avezzinao-Altari road led by

Blomfield. Larry Johnson brought up the rear as Black 2. The road was cratered, so too a nearby railway line. The squadron diary relates; 'after leaving target area formation sighted 2 small cars and a truck loaded with fruit [...] stationary and were thoroughly strafed, resulting in 8 motor transports destroyed, flamers, and one smoker. Slight machine-gun fire from target area.' Dennis claimed one direct hit with a 500lb bomb and claimed three German lorries on fire.

To keep the pressure up on the Germans, 239 Wing began its move to San Angelo, twenty-five miles north of Naples on the twenty-first to support the drive north. 260 Squadron was not fully operational here till the twenty-fourth. Mervyn Talbot adds:

'During May we moved to San Angelo, again we were on ground attack. Some places were more heavily defended than others so we were met with quite intense fire throughout the operation, although on occasion there was little opposition. Ground targets included roads, railways, bridges, trains, airfields, transport of any sort and anything else requested by our ground forces through the very effective cab rank system.'

The new location for the landing grounds was chosen by the intelligence officer as Christopher Lee remembers:

'The destruction of buildings and mechanised transport, with people in them still, often burned and charred corpses. One certainly did see a lot of that. It was inevitable. I had to drive through these places. The pilots flew from one strip to another but I had to drive through these places, so I could see the damage on the ground. We had awful experiences.

'I think the worst I've ever seen in my life was Casino.

'The small town had only one road, it was heavily mined on either side and masses of huge shell holes filled with water along both sides. It was highly dangerous but it was the only way through. The entire village had been literally blasted off the face of the earth like the Monastery above it. You couldn't believe there had ever been any buildings there. It was appalling.

'The pilots flew from one strip to another but I had to drive through these places, so I could see the damage on the ground. Sometimes, I went in an aircraft to spy out the land you might say, find a suitable spot to lay down the track for the so-called air strip and having done that I returned. Then I would go out in my truck and jeep, and on arriving liaise with the engineers who would lay down this metal strip called PSP.'

Dennis Varey again:

'The airfields were built for us by the Royal Engineers and consisted mainly of a runway made from PSP. PSP stood for Perforated Steel Planking, this consisted of a series of sheet steel plates designed to be interlocking, which were laid on a foundation. These runways were a great success and enabled temporary airfields to be established quickly and to be usable in all but the most severe weather. On landing, we were left to sort ourselves out, find suitable places to site our tents and mess marquees. The settling in started again, with foraging parties going out to find food and drink to make our stay more acceptable. In a remarkably short space of time the mess tents were up and food was being prepared. Washing facilities were minimal as you can imagine, our tin hats made a useful bowl for washing and shaving and about once a month a mobile shower and bath unit run by the Army would appear and we could luxuriate for a few minutes and get rid of the BO with which we were usually surrounded!

'As it was the first day at the new land ground, to supplement the tinned rations, Mervyn and I went out on foraging parties to see what could be bought from the local farms as our supplied rations were not of the best! We managed to purchase some poultry, vegetables and a couple of demijohns of the local wine, so by sunset the whole squadron felt well refreshed. We didn't stay up too late as we were due to fly the next morning.'

With the Germans now falling back, Canadian and Polish forces advanced on the Hitler Line during 23/24 May. However, initial attempts to penetrate the defences before they had been effectively manned failed and a set piece prepared assault became necessary. The action was hard fought and the Germans launched repeated counter-attacks over two days, attempting to retake their former positions.

Dennis Varey once more:

'During my first month with the squadron, we had concentrated on ground attack. Bombing and strafing gun pits, mortars, railway lines, bridges, as well as attacking anything that moved. You'd start off at 8,000ft & pull out at 1,500. The goal was that we got in as close we possibly could without hitting the ground. Targets were trucks, halftracks, staff cars. We had a job to do. We knocked out vehicles: if we stopped to think about killing men, that did not really come to mind. It was them or us, and we made certain it was them. Not long after moving to San Angelo, my skipper, Flight Lieutenant Sheppard

DFC was shot down and belly landed in our lines. He was the first casualty I experienced: we all carried on as normal. We had no time to stop and think. Friendships were superficial, you never knew when your number may be up.'

About the mission Shep Sheppard remembers:

'On 25 May I did my 189th op but I did not know when I got airborne that it was to be my last. We had moved a couple of days previously from Cutella to a landing strip nearer the battle on the west coast. I believe it was called San Angelo, somewhere near Carazzo and Telese. The show was ostensibly an armed recce, but we had been briefed to pick up a convoy that was travelling along the Frosinone-Cassino Road and to take it out completely. Apparently, there was a fairly high-ranking German officer in the convoy who was going to Cassino to conduct is defence – Cassino was the doorway to Rome.

'We came around the back of Cassino and picked up the road, and also the convoy, fairly easily. I put the flight into close line abreast and we bombed the road in fairly tight formation coming down from 8,000 to 1,000ft before releasing the bombs. We gave them a burst on the guns just to make them happy. We pulled out of the attack, low on the deck, and then turned south-west up into the sun and as we did so Bill Nelson, who was flying on my right called over the R/T, "We missed him guv." We had obviously done a fair amount of damage but we had missed the one car that was important to get.

'I then did what I had always stressed when lecturing at the CFS on ground strafing that you must not do – go back over the target, because they are waiting for you.

'We came out of the sun, guns blazing and really hammered them, but they were sheltering under a line of trees and it was very difficult to be absolutely sure we had collared every vehicle in the convoy. It was pointless to bring out another flight to be sure the convoy was wiped out, so I made a decision, probably right in its application, and within the brief, that it was vital to write off this convoy, but the end product wrong for me personally.

'I said we would go back for a third run and this time to go slowly and make sure we wrote off completely what was left of the convoy. This we did; we were only doing about 250 mph on the attack, but on the pull out some light ack-ack not connected to the convoy clobbered me. The consolation was that Bill Nelson, again doing the observation, called me to say we had done it. My reply to Bill was that I had been hit and for him to take over.

'We came out of the attack on a south-westerly course and around a kind of a saddle back hill, and turning eastwards I decided to stick with the aircraft and get as near to the line as possible. I knew if could get between the two bumps of the hill or hills that it was almost a certainty that I would come down on our side of the line [...] I managed to coax the aircraft through that gap with about fifty feet to spare and my instruments were now telling me that in a very short space of time the engine was going to seize up and/ or catch fire, and I thought I was a bit low to jump, so desperately I looked for a nice flat field to put it down.

'What looks nice and flat a couple of hundred feet up is not quite the same when you go to put down and I could see the ground below was deeply furrowed. Not surprising really, as I was later told it was the edge of a minefield, but I did not know that when I put it down. Straps to lock, all switches off, a little flap, which as I was touching down [...] with the force of the landing it appears the armour plate behind the seat must have bashed me forward and I was jerked onto the gunsight and somehow, I know not how, I next found myself lying out on the wing [...] I have a vague recollection of the Mustangs flying around and then of being up off the wing as if I were a baby. I had come down in the French sector of the Line and a French major and a giant Senegalese soldier had come to pick me up, and seeing me condition, had immediately driven to the forward casualty clearing station.'

The Squadron Operations Record Book observes the flight came under intense ack-ack from over sixty guns, both 88mm, 20mm and 40mm. In the barrage, Pilot Officer Russell's Mustang was damaged CAT 1.

Dennis flew his first sortie from San Angelo during the twenty-fifth. Heavy cloud had started to disperse by 0600 that day. In a reconnaissance patrol to Cassino, with six mustangs heading to the observation area at 1000, Dennis flew as Yellow 2, being wingman to now Pilot Officer Bill Nelson, Blomfield led the flight. The Squadron Operations Record Book tells us that on reaching Fiuggi, they observed a column of German motorised transport heading east on the main road, and a further two vehicles on a road heading north. Attacking from the north from 1,500ft, two bombs scored a direct hit on the road, and one fell on a motorised transport. As the mustangs dived down from 9,000ft, the 0.50cal machine guns opened up. The vehicles were strafed but did not explode. Heading to Avezzano, ten plus heavily camouflaged motorised transports were spotted. The column was strafed three times, in total 3260 rounds of 0.50cal were fired, but many pilots reported gun problems. The flight landed at 1150. Dennis's logbook tells us one of his bombs made a direct hit on a German lorry, and he conducted two strafing runs, claiming one flamer.

Whilst 260 Squadron was in the air, the Germans began their retreat from the Gustav Line: after five months of stalemate the road to Rome lay open. The costs were high. It is estimated that the Allies (Australia, Canada, Free France employing also Moroccans, Kingdom of Italy, India, New Zealand, Poland, South Africa, United Kingdom, and the U.S.) suffered about 55,000 casualties, Germany and the Italian Republic about 20,000.

Dennis picks up the story:

'The day after Shep had bitten the dust, a dropped fag end caused a fire to break out in the Officers' Mess and our mess. In less than the time it took to make a brew up, the whole lot had gone up in smoke: chairs, matting, tent, all gone. Nothing but a charred mass.'

On the 26 May, Red and Blue Sections, all of A Flight, a total of twelve Mustangs, headed back to Fiuggi. On reaching target, a German 3-tonne lorry with infantry in the back was spotted. Flight Lieutenant Blomfield led Red Section, which included Dennis and Mervyn Talbot, to attack. Dennis was flying as Yellow 2, Captain 'Jack' Davis was Yellow 1, and Mervyn flew as wingman to Lieutenant 'Larry' Johnson, a South African pilot like Davis, at White 2. Zooming down from 8,000ft to 1,500ft, four 500lb bombs hit the road leaving large craters, but leaving the lorry unscathed: I cannot imagine the occupants were particularly 'happy bunnies' though with bombs raining down around them. Climbing up from the bombing run, Red Section turned and strafed the lorry. The lorry was destroyed and the German soldiers shot down as they tried to run. Coming out of the strafing run, Blomfield ordered that a 15cwt German truck which he had spotted emerging from cover was the next target. The Mustangs dived down, the 0.50cal kicking up dirt as they hit the ground. The lorry was immobilised and left smoking but not destroyed. Next in the Mustangs gun sights were four more motorised transports which were strafed, but none destroyed. Red Section, which had been airborne at 0800 landed at 0945. Blue Section remained in the combat zone, attacking six motorised transports in seven strafing runs, expending all 0.50cal ammunition. All the vehicles were damaged but none destroyed. Dennis claimed one German lorry as a flamer. In total 239 Wing flew 173 sorties that day, destroying thirty-six motor transports, damaging forty-seven more and knocking out two motorcycles.

Preventing a German retreat to prepared positions became the primary objective for 260 Squadron, and meant a stepping up of operations. Squadron Leader Jandrell took off at 0530 on Saturday, 27 May with six Mustangs, Sergeant Varey, acting as his No. 2, flying Red 2. The objective was to attack a column of twenty plus motorised transports at Frosinone. Dropping down from 8,000ft to 2,000ft, Jandrell allowed each pilot to choose their own bombing target. No bombs hit any of the vehicles. Completing the bombing run, Jandrell radioed to the flight that they were free to choose their targets and inflict as much damage till ammunition was expended. The flight attacked the column for forty minutes, destroying three vehicles, setting seven on fire and seriously damaging the remaining vehicles. No ack-ack or ground fire was encountered either, on target, or on enroute. Dennis's logbook reports; 'found 20+ motor transports north of Frosinone. Bombed motor transport and road, but no direct hits. Results of straffe 3 flamers, 3 smokers & several hits. Visibility poor. 3 gun stoppages.' Blomfield recorded in his logbook:

> 27 May: Bomb and strafe M./T. Alatri. 2 hit bombing. 1 ammo. wagon. 1 petrol truck. 6 M./T. 'all flamers'. Hit tele. wires - a./c. cat II.

It was FB269 that was almost wrecked on the telegraph wires. The Squadron Operations Record Book reports two German lorries were destroyed in the bombing run, and then during the strafing raid, eight caught fire and blew up, one caught fire and ten more were severely damaged. Blomfield was airborne again at 0935 aboard FB287 at the head of a flight of five, an armed reconnaissance, attacking eight motor transports between Guargino and Arsoli, the survivors of the earlier attack. Dennis was airborne again at 1755, again flying Blue 2, but this time to Pilot Officer Bill Nelson. The flight of six Mustangs climbed to 7,000ft to intercept a German column heading between Charcino and Chariaco. Despite poor visibility, the column was spotted and Nelson ordered a bombing run. Diving down to 2,000ft, all ten 500lb bombs were dropped, none hitting any vehicle. On diving, Pilot Officer Nelson observed twenty plus more vehicles, heavily camouflaged in a wood. Calling on the flight to attack, eight strafing runs were made: two German transports were destroyed outright, one was left burning, another caught fire and others were damaged. An ammunition lorry was targeted which blew up. For a second time, no ack-ack or enemy fire was encountered. All planes landed at 1925. 239 Wing Operations Record Book picks up the story:

> May 27 1944. Operations. A great day of armed recces and Army targets on the 'Battle for Rome' fronts during which 153 sorties were flown, spread further havoc among enemy's transport. In a total of twenty-seven shows, which included attacks on gun positions in the LIRI Valley and an enemy strongpoint at POFI, the following scores were added to the already long list of M/T etc destroyed or damaged during the previous days:

66 M/T destroyed
38 M/T damaged
1 40 feet M/T destroyed (disintegrated)
1 railway tanker destroyed
1 tank destroyed
1 bus damaged
1 motor tri-cycle damaged
1 motor cycle damaged
1 motor cycle destroyed
1 HDV (halftrack – ed) destroyed

239 Wing and strategic bombing was proving itsself a battle winning weapon.

Not every trip was as easy. Sister squadron in 239 Wing, 250, lost six of twelve planes on one operation that day.

No flying on the twenty-eighth for Dennis – 239 Wing carried out 114 sorties that day – but he was back flying on the twenty-ninth, taking off at 0530. Dennis was Green 2. The target again was German motorised transport: four bombs landed on a 5cwt truck, four bombs missed the road the convoy was using and two cratered the road. After the bombing run, a convoy of twenty plus transport were spotted, but terrain meant strafing runs were not possible. Intense ground fire forced Mervyn Talbot to jettison his bombs and return to base due to damage. Dennis claimed one large German lorry destroyed and a bus. The flak damaged his Mustang HS-Q, classified as CAT I, a quick repair by ground crew. This was the second time his Mustang had intercepted German fire with it causing damage. Was it becoming 'second nature' I wonder? How do you get used to flying through flak and ground fire, feeling your airplane get hit and wondering if 'this is it' and the plane erupts into a sheet of flame. It is hard to comprehend for those who have not experienced it, to be 'dancing with death' every time you flew. The psychological strain must have been intense.

Corporal Colin Faehse, a fitter with sister squadron in 239 Wing, 3 Squadron (RAAF) jotted in his diary:

30th May 1944

Intensive ops. Dawn till dark ops, harrying the fleeing Hun, hope he breaks this time, he sure should!!! Terrific air pounding, sky is black with our kites, we alone toting about 30 tons per day!!! Work!!!
260 cop it heavy 8 kites.

On this operation Dennis's logbook reports:

May 30. Mustang III FB 272 Q. Armed Rec on Sora-Guercino Ferrentino roads. 2x 500lbs. Broke Road near Ferrentino with

3 direct hits. Also 1 large house and motor cycle. 1 Flamer, 2 Smokers from Straffe. Intense very accurate high and low Anti-Aircraft fire. Sandy Hit. CAT II

For pilots, aircrew, infantry, artillery and tank crews, the Italian campaign was not D-Day dodging: 260 Squadron had lost eight mustangs in a single day: this was over fifty per cent of the squadrons compliment damaged. In reply, the Wing that day destroyed eighty-six lorries and damaged thirty-seven more as well as an armoured car: the previous day fifty-two lorries had been destroyed, eighteen damaged, a MK IV tank destroyed and two damaged. Thanks to the ground crew, the eight damaged Mustangs were repaired and Dennis was back in Italian skies at 1330 on the last day of the month, again flying wingman to Jack Davis, the flight commander, Red 1. Yellow 1 and 2 were Duguid and Jack Green, Cunliffe and Mervyn Talbot flew as Green 1 and 2. The target was a column moving north of over forty German lorries and other vehicles. A group of five were attacked, ten direct hits from twelve bombs were made on the road in front of the convoy, guns hammering as the Mustangs followed their bombs down, they levelled off at almost deck level and shot up anything that came into their gunsight before pulling up into cloud to head home. 239 Wing flew twenty missions that day claiming sixty-three German lorries destroyed, twenty-three damaged and one MK IV tank damaged, an armour car destroyed and a machine gun nest eliminated.

During the last six days of May, Allied fighters and fighter-bombers claimed 1,148 German vehicles of all types destroyed and 766 damaged. Not glamourous, but Blomfield, Dennis and Mervyn were taking part in the strategic evisceration of the German army.

After our first interview, I spoke to Dennis on several more occasions about his wartime experiences. Armed with tea, pencil, pad of paper and tape recorder, I asked Dennis what it was like attacking ground targets:

'Unlike fighter pilots, we were faced with multi-tasking which had to become second nature; bombing, strafing, tactical, reconnaissance, escorts. Once your bombs had gone you didn't waltz around thinking about what to do next; that was just asking for it from the flak batteries. You had to make up one's mind in a matter of seconds as to your next target. Often, we would open the throttle, climb, turn and then dive down with the guns hammering at what came in front of us. We'd been taught the rudiments of how to aim a Kittyhawk with a bomb on board: the Mustang was a different beast entirely.

'If we were given our head by the skipper and told to choose our own targets, the squadrons speciality, a trick learned in North Africa, was to follow the bombs down, banging away. Down we would go from 6,000, dropping the cookies off at about 1,500, and then carrying on down to 500, some went to treetop, and as we dropped down, we would open up. Officially this was an opportunity to "test our guns", but rather than sodding about climbing back to height just to come back, we just followed the bombs and gave em as good as they gave us squirting at whatever moved. The 0.50cal we had made the 0.303 on most of our kites look like pea shooters. Even with our six 0.50cal if we came across a 109, they had better guns than us with that 20mm cannon firing through the engine block. Deadly, totally deadly if flown well. The lads in 112 thought they were the bee's knees and painted silly gaping sharks' mouths on the front of their kites. They believed they were better than us. We knew we were better: you never heard them talk about copying our tactics. It took real balls. If you cooked it up, you flew into the explosion of your own bombs and that was that. Once the cookies had gone, the kite bucked like a mule and you'd gain a few hundred feet unless you really held onto the stick.

'Of course, being at 100ft or much less made you vulnerable to rifle and other ground fire. Merve came back with bullet holes in his hood. But it was our thing of course. We couldn't go around with the shark lads saying they were the best and not do anything about it. Some of the fellas in 260 were mad as hatters in the air. Blomfield was the nicest guy you could hope to meet, in the air he was ruthless and a bit of a daredevil. He took risks few would do. Bagshawe was another. More than once when I flew with Blom, and we followed down the bombs to strafe the place up, in doing so he got so low he caught his tail unit in telegraph wires. How the hell his kite was flying I'm not sure. He must have been down to 10ft off the deck. From my point of view, he could have opened his hood and shook hands with the jerries as he went past.

'Once your down, you have to have eyes all over. If a flight of twelve splits, kites were zooming all over the place. I am amazed no one ever ran into another kite in these melees. With the Kittyhawk and Mustang rear visibility was bad, like the Spitfire. But the later Mustangs with the greenhouse canopies were something else. You could see all round, no problem. The Mustang always needed a bit of leg on the rudder, a lot less than the Kitty, which was not as manoeuvrable as the Hurricane. In a dive the Kitty flew like a brick, and you had to wedge your right arm against the cockpit to hold the thing straight: you aimed the bomb by pointing the kitty at the target. It took most of your strength to get it out of the dive and for it not to rotate off to the left. We did target bombing on floating targets in the Adriatic. Holding the thing straight was a challenge in itself, it wanted to fishtail or skid as you came down. It was complicated to fly. It had electric landing gear, not the reliable hydraulics on the Hurricane. It had no boost either, which, when with 1500lb of bombs, you needed it to get it into the air.

'Those days at 239 Training Wing taught me a lot of respect for what the lads in 260 had achieved on that type. The Mustang was not as light on the controls as the Spitfire, but the latest Mustangs were as good as a Spitfire, if not better as they were more stable as a gun platform due to the shape of the wing.'

Dennis, in his first month on squadron, flew nineteen operations, totalling twenty-eight hours fifty minutes. His aircraft had been damaged twice, and twice he had suffered the intense anxiety of contending with Hung Up bombs. The 'Bag' for May with 239 Wing from 424 missions – of which sixty-five were Cab Ranks – represented 8,029 bombs dropped and 476,685 rounds of 0.50cal machine gun ammunition fired. In total 866,784 miles were flown. In terms of damage inflicted, 468 German motor transports were destroyed and another 268 probable. In addition, were four tanks destroyed and three damaged, twelve motor cycles destroyed and two damaged, two half-tracks destroyed and two armoured cars destroyed in addition to two steam locomotives and twenty pieces of railway rolling stock, one Siebel Ferry and five barges sunk. This intensity of operation was maintained throughout the summer, as little by little the German war machine was eviscerated.

NEW OBJECTIVES, NEW PILOTS

12

AS WE NOTED earlier, personnel on a squadron were in a state of constant change with an almost continuous fluctuation in pilots. One such joined 260 Squadron on 29 May, Pilot Officer Gordon Brown. One of his first memories of life in 260 is associated not with going to war, but altogether different concerns:

> 'We lived under canvas and I remember watching some horses which were grazing in the same field and saw one drop a foal. As a very young city boy I was amazed.'

The San Angelo landing ground was backed by the Italian mountains and flanked by lush meadows and pasture. Brown flew his first operation on 1 June, two days after half an hour familiarisation. Eleven Mustangs in two sections were airborne at 1600 led by Captain Maree. Maree had replaced Blomfield, who was stood down from operations, but was still on squadron until the middle weeks of June. Brown was 'tail end Charlie' as Yellow 2, in Red Section. Pilot Officer Russell led Blue Section, in which was Mervyn Talbot as Black 2. The operation was an armed recce in the San Vito area. Flying in poor visibility at 10,500ft, Maree dropped to 3,000ft to reconnoitre the area. Spotting a group of five or more German lorries, he gave the order to Red Section to commence the bombing run from 2,000ft. Ten 500lb bombs plummeted onto the German lorries, three of which were direct hits and exploded. Blue Section was ordered to attack the remaining lorries, one was destroyed. No flak was encountered and Russell returned with both bombs, as they had 'hung up'.

The squadron suffered its next casualty the following day. Shep Sheppard remembered Bill Nelson as a raucous Londoner, who had been his understudy, and it was on Shep's advice that Nelson was promoted from sergeant to officer in April. He adds, 'the tactics he used would be exactly those I would have used.' Nelson was flying as Red 1; Flight Sergeant Ferguson was his no. 2. The Squadron Operations Record Book reports:

> Very intense and accurate light and heavy AA fire came from target area. Formation orbited lake Canterno and P/O Nelson said he was going down to strafe an MT […] His No. 2 went down with him and

as he pulled out of the strafing run noticed a puff of black smoke very near P/O Nelson's a/c. Another pilot reports seeing the a/c go to pieces and crash into the ground [...] P/O nelson was not seen to bale out.

Sixty years later Dennis remembers:

'Following briefing where our primary target had been explained, and our secondary objective if we could not get onto the first, Pilot Officer Bill Nelson led us into the air at 0930. We climbed to 10,000 on what was described as an armed recce to Ferrentino. The target was a tractor unit with trailer. Heavy and accurate ack-ack came up from target area. Skipper told us that after the bombing run, we were to break and strafe any target we could get onto. After unloading our bombs onto the target drop zone; down we went with our guns going. At treetop level, we all broke left and right, zoomed up to gain height into the sun, rolled and came back down and strafed anything that moved. As I banked left on full throttle, Bill zoomed down guns hammering, as he did so, the Jerries opened up. We were all low, about 1,000ft and under.

'Their shooting was deadly accurate. Ground fire hit his kite.'

Dennis goes quiet. After a pause he continues:

'It went to pieces. It just exploded. He was hit at nought feet, both his wings blown off. A ball of flame and smoke. What remained of it crashed into the deck. He had no chance at all to get out. I guess a lucky round had hit the reserve tank, detonating instantly.

'It was the first casualty I'd seen first-hand: yet I was not cut up about it, not at first anyhow. Self-preservation came first. Emotion came later.

'I guess we all were a conflict of emotions. If you'd told me he had been hit by a tram on Dewsbury Road, I'm sure I'd have been upset, as it was, we had a job to do. It was one of those things, but you never got used to it.'

After a pregnant pause in the conversation, where Dennis fiddled with his pipe. 'Do you find you think about the war a lot?' I ask. 'I do, if I am triggered,' he replied.

Dennis's logbook records: '1 MT probably damaged by bombs but not claimed. Bill Nelson shot down in strafe. VERY intense, accurate heavy & light AA & MG fire.' He flew as White 2, as wingman to Pilot Officer Russell. Maurice Gordon 'Bill' Nelson, was the son of John and Hilda Nelson of Finchley. By the time of his death aged just twenty-two he had already been awarded the DFC. He lies buried in the

Cassino War Cemetery. Perhaps the best description of what the war was really like for fighter-bomber pilots in the campaign comes from the pen of Bobby Gibbes, Commanding Officer of 3 Squadron (RAAF) who starkly and honestly writes:

'ENEMY ATTACKING FIERCELY – ONE HUNDRED TANKS – OUR LOSSES HEAVY – FRENCH LEFT FLANK CUT OFF – SEND AIR SUPPORT.'

'Armourers are sweating, cursing, toiling – bombing up while pilots are briefed. Last bomb snaps on – last plane starts up. The leader's arm is raised; it drops and powerful engines roar into thunderous life. Dust swirls back. Sweat-lined dusty muddy ground crews gasp for breath, engulfed in a man-made blizzard of dust and sand. Their charges move forward into the air – on course.

'Vicious snap of attacking Messerschmitt's. You turn about. Their attack is foiled and one of them goes down a flaming torch. They attack again. Once more you turn about. They break and give it best. On you fly, still with your bombs.

'Yes, there's the landmark below us. Turn left. You fly towards the distant churning spot. That spot shown on your map as a peaceful nothingness; a waste of barren sand. Your approach is unnoticed. The enemy is too busy to look above.

'Yes, there are the Frogs. My God, they're taking hell. And there are the tanks – tanks passing through the gap of smoking fire and running blood, intent on attacking those battling troops from the rear.

'Your decision made, the squadron dives down – speed builds up – good God the target's small. We must not miss and get our troops, already sorely crippled.

'Number one bomb goes, the others too within a second. Far best to trust the leader – his skill is greater than yours. You break and climb and turn to port to keep the sun ahead. The air is clouded with one or two black puffs that hang. He's missed by miles. He didn't know our speed would be so great.

'A cloud of dust. Too thick to see properly, but it looks like smoke as well. Away and home for still more bombs. The next lot out report fires still burning, three tanks at least, and transport. They could not see the damage for the dust which their bombs raised.'

Once an operation had ended, and the flight returned, the first pilots looked skyward counting:

'Those circling planes, but where are the other three? Theirs not the luck of yours. They never will come back or be taken prisoner either.

The last man in saw them go. One hit a tank and disappeared – a mass of burning breaking metal. The other two? Why, number one, the leader of a pair was hit and burnt while near the ground and tried to climb for height. Just height enough to jump and trust his safety to that small tightly-folded pack of purest silk. He didn't make that height. His plane exploded. Debris, flames and little pieces.

'Number two? Well, it's funny about that man. He climbed away, quite straight, then slowly rolled inverted and dived into the ground. Dead of course; dead before he hit. Dead before he started his climb away.'

Gibbes' honesty about the never-ending cycle of operations, 'brings it home to me' about the experiences of my uncle, and all those caught up in the hecatomb of Italy. It was a case of kill or be killed.

The Wing was putting pressure on the battle front around Rome. In total, twenty-three missions were flown the day Bill Nelson was killed, claiming thirty-one German motor transports destroyed and thirteen damaged, along with a MK II tank. So successful and important was the Wings contribution to the battle that day, General Gordon P. Saville, Officer Commanding 12th Tactical Air Command sent the following:

'Please accept and express to your personnel my very great admiration and appreciation for the perfectly splendid job you have done and are doing on enemy Motor Transport. The "Jackpot and Handle" can't be very far away and if we can all put on shows such as you have been putting on. Well done and good hunting.'

Dennis again:

'Soon after Nelson had gone west, we had a party to mark the squadron being operational overseas for three years. We had a soccer match of England v Scotland, which we won two to one. After the birthday cake was cut, I can't remember much except the hangover.'

The following day, 3 June, was intense again for 260. Squadron Leader Jandrell led Blue Section of B Flight, up at 0555 with six Mustangs. Sergeant Talbot was aboard FB246 on an armed recce to Subiaco. Approaching target, Jandrell observed a dispersed group of German lorries accompanied by a Mk IV tank. Diving down to 2,000ft, none of the twelve 500lb bombs hit any of the vehicles, but did destroy large sections of the road. Captain Davies led an armed recce into the air at 0625 of five Mustangs. Again, targets were German troop convoys.

Shortly after lunch Captain Maree led all twelve Mustangs of A Flight to attack a reported German HQ. Dennis flew as White 2 in Red Section. The flight was led to target by a Tactical Reconnaissance Spitfire. Due to bad weather, Maree dropped down to 1,000ft to recon the area, observed twenty or more German lorries and headquarters tents, but due to low cloud, it was impossible to attack the target. The Subiaco area was explored for targets, eighteen German lorries were spotted and bombed. Red Section destroyed one lorry, and green section's bombs destroyed two lorries outright, set two on fire and an ammunition lorry exploded. Blue Section bombs recorded no observable hits on targets. One strafing run was carried out despite ack-ack fire from 88mm and 20mm anti-aircraft guns. On the operation Dennis claimed one German lorry (flamer) and another (smoker). He observed in his logbook 'Intense Accurate high and low AA. Rocket Guns?'. These may have been German Nebelwerfer or 'moaning minnies.' Limited height and range meant that this weapon was not ideally suited for the anti-aircraft role.

Pilot Officer Brown was airborne at 1840 on a Cab Rank patrol flying FB287, the target being a German troop convoy of ten or more lorries. Just one lorry was destroyed. The flight was led by Captain Davis. At 1855 Captain Maree was airborne again, with Mervyn Talbot flying FB265, on a Cab Rank patrol, the target a bridge a mile west of Subiaco. The bridge was damaged, but not destroyed. Flak from 40mm and ground fire was put up by the German defenders which failed to damage any of the Mustangs. The next two days were occupied with attacking German troop convoys and destroying road and rail infrastructure to hinder the German retreat.

Captain Davis led Blue Section into the air at 0535 on 4 June. All of A Flight took to the sky that morning, led by Captain Maree. Larry Johnson flew as Red 2, Gordon Brown as Blue 2 to Davis, and Dennis flew as Black 2 to Lieutenant R.B. Bishop. Bishop, a South African, had joined 260 in February. Led to the target, a German Headquarters, by a TAC/R Spitfire, on arriving over the target area Captain Maree flew with the Spitfire on a low-level recce, observing a group of six tents. Red Section then bombed the target, one bomb detonating an ammunition dump with flames leaping 2,000ft into the sky. Blue Section also bombed. Dennis recorded 'several hits on gaggle of tents. No anti-aircraft fire.'

Rome was captured on 4 June by General Mark Clark and the American 5th Army. This was the first European capital to be liberated. 239 Wing's contribution to the capture of Rome was recognised by General Cannon, commanding the Mediterranean Allied Tactical Air Force, who sent a message of congratulations to the squadron on 16 June:

'I wish to express my deep gratitude and appreciation to all members of your command for their splendid work on the current Italian Operation culminating in the capture of ROME. They have given super best and the results were magnificent. Congratulations to all of you and good hunting.'

The Air Officer Commanding DAF added, 'I am sure all ranks in DAF realise my pride in the great effort they have put out in recent weeks and the success it has achieved.' Dennis was moved back to Red Section as wingman to Captain Davis, section leader. Davis led a patrol on 5 June, which was airborne at 0840. The objective was to attack a German column at Rieti, blowing up a German lorry during the bombing run and a troop carrier was strafed. The German soldiers bailed out before it exploded. Squadron Leader Johns flew on the operation as A Flight was down to eleven Mustangs and fewer pilots. Dennis found himself now allocated to a single Mustang, HS-D. The wing flew seventeen operations that day, sixteen were armed recces interdicting German tanks and other vehicles, claiming a halftrack damaged.

On 6 June came news about Operation Overlord as Dennis remembers:

> 'We heard after breakfast the long awaited second front had opened in the north of France. Everyone excited and the wireless sets were very popular all day as we listened to the news. 30,000 paratroops, 4,000 landing craft and 13,000 front-line aircraft had landed – so it is a very big do. We had a bit of a do that night in the Mess to celebrate the occasion and finished up about 4am.'

The brutal slogging match continued in Italy, almost unnoticed: overshadowed then as now as the eightieth anniversary of D-Day and Arnhem have shown. Up at 09:30 Red Section was down to five pilots due to pilot unavailability: hungover? Dennis was again Red 2 to Davis. A group of German lorries and other vehicles dispersed under trees was the target identified by Rover Control. They were bombed by Davis and Dennis, but no claims made. The remaining three pilots bombed the road, one direct hit on the road being made, blowing half of the carriage way to smithereens. Slight 88mm fire was put up as the flight dropped back down and strafed the area, again no claims made. During the course of D-Day, 239 Wing flew 150 sorties, claiming amongst its 'bag' one German spotter aircraft and three Mk IV tanks destroyed.

Despite the fighting in the sector, 260 was given twenty-four hours down time from operations: just twelve sorties were flown due to bad weather across the entire Wing. Operational flying resumed the followed day, when Squadron Leader Johns led Red Section of B Flight into the air at 0715. The flight headed to a target designated by Rover Control on intelligence from the front-line infantry: five Mk IV tanks. Despite low cloud and German 20mm ground fire, four direct hits were observed to two tanks. The tanks were damaged, but none were destroyed.

Captain Maree led Red Section of A Flight into the early summer sky at 0720. Dennis flew as Green 1 and Gordon Brown as his No. 2: despite the difference in rank, it was experience that mattered. As pair leader, it was Dennis's role to shepherd the new boy. Being pair leader was an increase in responsibility and participation in flying combat operations.

The flights primary target for the day was obscured by cloud, so were instructed to attack their second target, the objective to crater a road between Rieti and Terni. Light and heavy ack-ack was put up, and in the barrage Mustang HS-C, piloted by Dennis, was damaged CAT II: damage that was serious and required taking the Mustang out of service. This was Dennis's third and closest brush with death – all in the space of a month. Landing at 0845, Dennis was back in the air again at 1705, with Captain Davis leading the flight of six Mustangs. Dennis was Green 1 again, with Gordon Brown his wingman. Despite bad weather, two German half-tracks and a lorry were bombed. Dennis claimed 'one flamer' and noted the road was holed by three direct hits. All landed at 1905.

The ninth was the busiest day yet, seven missions were flown by 260, the Wing flying thirty missions in total. Due to his Mustang FB279 HS-C being out of service, Dennis found himself with a day off. Mervyn Talbot was in the air at 0525, in an operation lead by Squadron Leader Jandrell. The target was a German troop convoy on the Rieti-Terni Road. Pilot Officer Brown was likewise airborne soon after, heading again to Rieti and to attack anything that moved. Mervyn was flying again at 1020, attacking a convoy of 20 plus German lorries south-east of Tenni. Landing at 1155, Mervyn was once more in the air at 1430 again, the objective to bomb and strafe anything that moved. The days 'bag' included a 170mm German artillery battery silenced, forty-two lorries destroyed, fourteen damaged, one Mk IV tank obliterated, a motor cycle destroyed and a halftrack likewise converted to scrap.

Just two operations were made on the tenth by 260 due to bad weather. Squadron Leader Jandrell led Red Section up at 1250, the target Rover David had reported was tanks. Dennis flew as Yellow 2 aboard what would become his regular Mustang, FB269 HS-D. His No. 1 was Flight Sergeant Davoine, Pilot Officer Gorden Brown flew as Green 2. They were sent 'on a wild good chase', as following a low-level recce, the expected column of twenty or more tanks could not be found in the target area. Informing Rover David of this discovery, clearly someone had bungled, the alternative target from Rover David was a German HQ at Cantalupo. Jandrell led the section to the new target, ten bombs falling on target, but none made a direct hit on the houses sheltering the Germans. Ground fire and Breda fire was encountered. They landed at 1450. The episode showed the incredible tactical flexibility of Cab Rank and Rover David systems: rather than landing to get a new target, radio communication facilitated a rapid re-direction of airborne forces as the situation dictated.

During 10 June, 239 Wing moved out to a new landing ground, about which Dennis Varey recollects:

'It had been an Italian base. The Germans had done their best to break up the concrete runway, and had mined the grass verges. Some hangers remained, as did the gates to the place. It was with some trepidation that we got down. When we arrived, we found that we had been allocated an area on which had once been buildings which had been either bombed or demolished. When we came to put up our tents we found that the bases of the old buildings prevented us from using tent pegs to put up our tents and mess marquees. We therefore used old lumps of concrete and bricks for securing the guy ropes of our tents, and as it was getting dusk, left the mess tents until the following morning. The weather was looking very threatening when we turned in, and it didn't come as much of a surprise, when at about two in the morning, the wind got up and things started to fall down about our ears.

'Having struggled out from our collapsed tents, we all looked for somewhere to spend the rest of the night, so I ended up trying to sleep in the cockpit. The mood was lifted in the morning when the sun came out, and we could get things sorted. It seemed to me that no one really knew what was going on. The mood was lightened further with the news that we would be given leave in Rome. The cinema in Guidonia, more by bad bombing than luck, had survived with little damage. The Army Kinematic Corps took the place in hand. Off duty we were allowed into town and could watch a film in relative comfort. I think it was here that one of those terrible gang shows turned up, Every Night Something Awful. We gave them a good barracking. Alongside us was the Italian Airforce with Fiat and Caproni tri-motors. We got matey with the fitters and pilots. I managed to get an unofficial flight. They were good lads.'

No operational flying took place on 11 June as ground parties were moving to the new landing ground, but on the twelfth Dennis was Blue 2, with Captain Davis leading the flight of six. Up at 0655 the operation was an armed recce in the Avezzano-Rieti-Fligno-Pergia area. Dennis's logbook reports:

Blue 2 [...] Found five MT south-west of Todi. Broke the road with several direct hits. Four MT (two flamers & two smokers) were claimed. Slight 88mm. CAT I.

All of A flight was airborne at 1055, led by Squadron Leader Jandrell. Dennis was flying Green 2 to Flight Sergeant Mansfield as Green 1 in Red Section. The objective was to bomb a factory being used to conceal a petrol dump. Dennis's logbook records:

Armed attack on petrol dump north of Spoleto. 2 x 500lbs. Heavy concentration of bombs in target area which we completely destroyed. Slight Low ack-ack. Moderate 88mm.

As June dragged on into the warm Italian summer, on 13 June, 260 Squadron's new Commanding Officer, Squadron Leader George Binmore Johns, led his first operation in lieu of Jandrell, who was tour expired. Donald Percival Jandrell had replaced Malins as May had come to a close, and had had command for six weeks Jandrell was awarded the DFC on 7 July, the citation read:

> This officer has participated in many sorties, including attacks on a variety of targets such as locomotives, trucks and shipping. Much of the success achieved during these operations can be attributed to the determined efforts of Squadron Leader Jandrell, who is a skilful and daring leader.
>
> He has recently led formations of aircraft in operations which have resulted in the destruction of many mechanical vehicles and in the effective bombing of numerous gun positions. Squadron Leader Jandrell has set an example worthy of emulation.

Johns had joined the squadron some weeks earlier as an almost supernumerary, before taking command. The day Jandrell formally handed over to Johns, Dennis flew as Yellow 2, Flight Sergeant Duguid as his No. 1. Gordon Brown flew as Red 2. A group of ten plus German lorries were bombed: the road was destroyed and, in the strafing run, a number of lorries were damaged, but none destroyed. Throughout the operation, intense and accurate 88mm and 40mm ack-ack was put up. The following day was a Cab Rank on a convoy of fifteen plus German motor transports north of Orvieto was the objective for Red Section led by Squadron Leader Johns. Dennis flew as Yellow 2 to Pilot Officer Russell. Due to cloud and intense accurate 20mm and 40mm anti-aircraft fire, the outcome of the bombing run was not observed.

Dennis claimed a German lorry on the following day as a flamer and one a smoker, flying as Yellow 2, back in the Spoleto area. One of his 500lb bombs failed to drop, and he had to dislodge it with some aerobatics before returning to base. He had had an early breakfast: he was in the Italian sky at 0530 and landed at 0715. Almost twelve hours later, Dennis was on a Cab Rank patrol. Flying Black 2 to Flight Sergeant Corcorran, Blue Section was to bomb German gun emplacements north of Fabro. On operations during 15 June 1944, Larry Johnson's Mustang was holed by flak, CAT II damage being recorded: the mainplane being shot through by 40mm fire.

More of the same followed on the sixteenth, again attacking German convoys: after spending most of the day drinking tea, smoking and playing cards, Dennis, as Green 2, with Larry Johnson as his No. 1, was in the air at 1810 with Red Section of A Flight. Flight Sergeant Mansfield led the flight, with Sergeant Ferguson as Red 2, Flight Lieutenant Bagshawe flew as Yellow 1. The target was a convoy of fifteen plus German lorries. Dennis's logbook claims one lorry disintegrated and one flamer despite heavy ground fire and cloud cover. On coming in to land at 1955 Flight Lieutenant Bagshawe was almost killed: the tail wheel burst, which catapulted the Mustang on its port wing, and came close to being totally inverted. The aircraft was written off. Even when not damaged by flak, accidents could spell death.

The same day as Bagshawe was rescued from his pranged Mustang, Peter Blomfield was posted to 3 BPD in Naples. He was rested until August. Up with the lark on 17 June, Dennis was Yellow 2, again to Larry Johnson, Captain Maree led Red Section into the hazy morning sky at 0530. Duke Kent flew as Green 2. Due to haze and cloud cover, the target was bombed on the pinpoint, cratering a road and demolishing a house. Strafing in the dive, the flight encountered intense and accurate 20mm anti-aircraft fire as well as machine-gun fire from the ground, Dennis's Mustang, HS-D, was holed, CAT I, for a second time in six days, and was the fourth incident since Dennis had gone to war with 260 Squadron. It would not be Dennis's only close brush with death that month.

No. 260 Squadron, along with the entire Wing, was off operational flying from midnight of 17 June, to midnight on 20 June due to bad weather. It gave the pilots and ground crew much needed rest. Maintenance could also be 'caught up with', laundry and other 'odd jobs' attended to. Dennis remembers:

'Operations were now habit, and it all seemed to blend together. After the excitement of joining the squadron and going operational, it all became routine, as was expected. We had a job to do after all. As ground attack, for us it was all Jerry troops in trucks or halftracks, gun positions, mortar pits. Or it was trains, bridges and railways. Anything that allowed the Jerries to move were our targets. We had all settled in our routine and habit. The gaggle board in the mess told us which section, or at least colour we were, and when we would be up. Our day was our own, but you could not relax until you'd been on ops. If we were called up on short notice, the Army needed a specific target taking out, we would all dash around at panic stations, hurried out of our beds with the most abusive comments, we'd grab a mug of tea made from foul tasting chlorinated water and then off we went. If it was very early, breakfast and the necessary ablutions were hasty. Occasionally it was all a total waste of time. You'd be on call all day: you'd do nothing nor could you, just in case the red flag went up. I was even afraid on days like that of doing my laundry. Sometimes it was all madness running around like headless chickens and then nothing.'

During 21 and 22 June, the Wing moved to Falarium, recorded in Dennis's logbook as Civita Castellano. After three days rest, B Flight, led by Squadron Leader Johns was airborne at 0515. Mervyn Talbot flew the operation as Red 2. Captain Davis led A Flight up at 1250. Mervyn flew as Red 2 to Davis. Dennis flew as Yellow 2, with Pilot Officer Russel as his No. 1. Captain Maree led Blue Section, Duke Kent flew Black 2. Blue Section was up at 1310, both sections heading to the same objective, a railway junction north-east of Arezzo. Cloud was almost total above 5,000ft, which exposed the flight to 88mm ack-ack.

On 22 June, Captain Davis led Red Section of A Flight up at 1555. Dennis flew Green 2 to Sergeant 'Billy' Johnson. Cloud forced the flight to come in low at 5000ft, below the base of the thick cloud. After a recce of the assigned primary target, Rover Control directed Davis to a group of German lorries and other vehicles on a road north of Perugia. Bombed and strafed, Dennis claimed two lorries destroyed and five bombs destroyed the road: bombs fell on the hillslope above the road causing tonnes of rocks and soil to cascade down the slope and block the road for a length of over forty meters. One bomb was a direct hit on the road itself. Moderate 88mm ack-ack was encountered as well as 40mm and 20mm fire.

A Flight took off at 1830 to make the half hour flight to Falarium, recorded in Dennis's logbook as Civita Castellano. A Flight was reduced to ten Mustangs through aircraft attrition. The road party and B Flight arrived during the course of the following day.

Squadron Leader Jandrell, being granted an extension to his operation tour, was still on squadron and led Red Section up from Falarium at 0635 on 24 June. Just four pilots, Jandrell, with Lieutenant Stone (SAAF) as his No. 2, and Pilot Officer Russell flying as Yellow 1, with Dennis as his No. 2. The target was gun pits and an ammunition dump. Cloud meant that the pinpoint was bombed through cloud and results were not observed.

For the third time that month HS-D was damaged, this time CAT II on an operation on 25 June, an armed attack on a bridge at Farno. Again, flak was the culprit.

Mervyn Talbot again:

> 'The area of operations ranged from just north of Naples up the length and breadth of Italy as far as Venice, including an attack on shipping in the Gulf of Trieste. Communications between important towns such as Pescara, Terni, Ancona, Florence, Rimini, Bologna, and Venice were particularly important as targets. We went after a ferry and oil tanker, but missed both.
>
> 'We were also tasked with bombing trains. If we got in too close, the steam explosion from the boiler going up, could knock you kite out of the air. Again, depending what was on the train, determined the outcome. We bombed and strafed an ammunition train: it was like Guy Fawkes night. The explosions continued long after we had left. Gus got a little close on times, and had bullets pinging through his kite as the ammunition on the train blew up.'

Dennis was allocated HS-Y on 26 June. Captain Davis led A Flight up at 1635. Due to lack of aircraft and pilots, just eleven Mustangs took off, with Mervyn Talbot from B Flight as Black 1. He had flown an operation already that morning. Dennis flew Green 2, to Gordon Brown, again from B Flight. Dennis records in his logbook that the Royal Yacht was bombed at Arcona Harbour. Three bombs overshot, two made direct hits and blew the bows off. Intense, accurate 20mm and 40mm ack-ack was put up. The following day, flying as Green 2, on an armed attack in the Siena area, three motor transports were found north of the town. The convoy was bombed and strafed, two lorries were damage. Thick could covered from 15,000ft to 2,500ft, forcing the flight into the path of 88mm ack-ack as well as 20mm and 40mm fire.

Dennis was back aboard newly repaired HS-D on the morning of 27 June, Captain Maree led Red Section up at 1015. Dennis flew as Green 2 to Flight Sergeant Mansfield. Cloud was 10/10 i.e. total cover above 5,000ft. The operation was an armed recce. Three German lorries were found north of Siena. Forced to fly at 2,500ft the flight were obvious targets for anti-aircraft fire. Intense and accurate 88mm fire was encountered. The flight followed their bombs down and claimed two lorries as damaged. For the fourth time, Dennis had to coax a damaged Mustang back to base. The Operations Record Book notes two Mustangs damaged CAT I, one was Dennis, alas, we do not know the other Mustang which was damaged.

Dennis flew with Blue Section the following day, 28 June, his 'trusty steed', HS-D, having been repaired by ground crew and was airborne at 0530. The flight was led by A Flight skipper, Jack Davis. Cloud cover was total above 2,000ft. A group of five or more German lorries were spotted through breaks in the cloud, and the flight attacked from 1,500ft. All bombs fell on target with one lorry damaged. Intense and accurate 40mm and 20mm anti-aircraft fire was put up by the Germans, one aircraft being holed, classed as CAT I. The weather closed in on the run back, with heavy rain and wind, despite this 239 Wing Operations Record Book reports:

> Whilst on an armed recce in the URBINO area, No. 260 Squadron RAF, led by S/Ldr D.P. Jandrell, sight a locomotive and ten trucks moving NW. These were bombed and strafed with great accuracy, one bomb cutting both lines in front of the train, and the loco was left belching steam although not claimed – four of the trucks were ablaze and two pouring yellow smoke. Nearby were many more trucks and a locomotive, and these were also straffed, leaving the engine riddled and two trucks smokers.

Jandrell had led Blue Section to the skies at 0655. Tragedy struck as the flight took off. Canadian pilot, G.H. Bernier was lucky to survive as Christopher Lee remembers:

'His port wing dipped and hit the strip. His aircraft was catapulted off the strip into a kind of big dell where there was an army post office. One of his bombs went off and we had to rush over there, myself and the doctor, we tried to keep the pilots away. We had to get this chap out, there were dead bodies everywhere with red hot bombs still sizzling in the grass.'

The Squadron Diary notes that the landing strip was wet and greasy and with a side wind, the aircraft was buffeted on take-off. Bernier found it impossible to correct for the side wind and about 400 meters from the end of the runway, the Mustang:

Swung left in a gully, striking a vehicle and tent. The aircraft then came to rest and burst into flames; one bomb having detonated on impact with the vehicle causing casualties amongst personnel in the vicinity. The pilot suffered burns but was able to get clear of the aircraft.

Bernier did not return to 260 Squadron. Neither the Squadron Operations Record Book or squadron diary gives us the full details of the casualties suffered that morning.

On 29 June, Jandrell led 260 on another armed recce: the squadron attacked the Forli-Faenze railway line. A Flight was up, led by Squadron Leader Johns at 0700 with Dennis as his No. 2. A large steam engine moving a goods train was the primary target. Three bombs were near misses, one hit the track 100 meters in front of the engine, the loco ploughing into the crater. Two strafing runs were made: the locomotive exploded in a sheet of steam and flames. Intense and accurate 80mm and 20mm fire was put up by the Germans. All landed at 0830. Johns led B Flight into the air again at 1810, Dennis flew as Black 2 to Flight Lieutenant Bagshawe. The Squadron Operations Record Book notes: 'Sgt Very's a/c hood came open and he had to return to base after jettisoning bombs in Lake Bolnaro.'

With its hood repaired, HS-D, with Dennis back at the helm, was up at 0605 the following day, the thirtieth, Jack Davies led Blue Section on an operation to cut railway lines between Forli and Faenza. Dennis, flying as Black 1, claimed two direct hits on the line. Throughout the operation, 20mm anti-aircraft fire was put up along with intense and accurate 88mm ack-ack. All of A Flight were led up by Davis at 1550 on an armed recce later the same day. Dennis was Yellow 2 this time. A train consisting of a locomotive and over sixty wagons was spotted by Davis and attacked. The line was severed with three direct hits from 500lb bombs and in the strafing run four wagons were destroyed – Dennis claimed two of these plus 'two smokers and one flamer.'

As June came to an end, Dennis had flown twenty-six operations, some forty-two hours twenty-five minutes flying time, and been hit by flak four times.

Mervyn Talbot was in the air at 1000 on 1 July, with Squadron Leader Johns heading the flight of six: the operation was to cut railway lines around Bologna. Top cover was provided by four Spitfires. After the bombing run, three strafing runs were carried out, detonating a steam engine in a cloud of boiling steam intermixed with flying debris. Two railway wagons were also demolished. All laned at 1150. Captain Davis led all of A Flight's twelve Mustangs up in the afternoon haze at 1515. Dennis was Black 2 flying HS-D as No. 2 to Lieutenant Bishop. Mervyn was White 2; Larry Johnson and Duke Kent were Yellow 1 and 2. This was part of a rolling airstrike on the railway network around Bologna. Due to dense cloud the flight came in at 2,000ft and attacked forty railway wagons. Bomb run over, twelve Mustangs from 250 Squadron dropped down and bombed the same target. All landed at 1755.

The operation for the following day was an almost repeat performance. Flight Sergeant Mansfield led Red Section up at 0700. A railway bridge between Imola and Bologna was bombed; damaged, it remained standing. The six Mustangs then turned and strafed 100 plus railway wagons and coaches in the station area at Castle Saint Pietro. The Germans put up 88mm flak during which Dennis, flying as Green 2 to Billy Johnson in Blue Section, reported for the fifth time that his aircraft HS-H was CAT II damaged.

Landing at 0950 after a drink and ablutions, Captain Maree led A Flight to Imola. Jack Davis led Blue Section. Dennis was promoted to Black 1 and was flying HS-E FB 267, Mervyn Talbot was his No. 2, Duke Kent flew as Green 2. The same target was bombed and strafed. During one of the strafing runs, Flight Lieutenant Bishop, Blue 2, clipped his tail unit on a telegraph wire: the damage was considered to be CAT I. To hit a telegraph cable, on 30ft poles, means Bishop was low; but this was 260 Squadrons 'party trick.' Follow the bombs down, guns hammering away and get in as low as possible on what was officially classed as a gun's test. Mervyn flew a Cab Rank action in the late afternoon, when Squadron Lead Johns led a flight of twelve to bomb a road junction. Heavy anti-aircraft fire was put up: two Mustangs were logged CAT I damage and one CAT II. All landed at 1800.

Flying as White 1, Dennis was aboard HS-X in an operation of eleven Mustangs flying in fluid 6 formation that took off at 0950 on 3 July. Mervyn Talbot was flying as Yellow 1, the third leading plane in Red Section. Again, the target was destruction of railway infrastructure around Imola and Bologna. Eight bombs were direct hits on the wagons in the marshalling yard. Despite machine-gun fire from the ground, a strafing run was carried out starting several fires amongst the railway vehicles. Squadron Leader Johns aircraft was hit by machine-gun fire, all returned safe and sound at 1150.

An armed attack on a petrol dump was the objective for 4 July. Squadron Leader Johns led A Flight into the air at 0830. Dennis was flying as White 2, being wingman to Larry Johnson. Mervyn Talbot brought up the rear as Black 2 flying as wingman to Captain Duplesis (SAAF), his and Dennis's former instructor at

Abu Sueir. Gordon Brown was up front as Red 2, and Duke Kent as Yellow 1. Encountering flak which damaged Mustang HS-K electrical systems, Dennis had to turn back. His landing gear systems were partially inoperable. The fairing doors had opened, and the fear was the gear was damaged. Dennis dropped his bombs over the German occupied area and returned early fearing an electrical fire. Landing HS-K at 1000, Dennis was marshalled into HS-P, taking off at 1215, flying as Black 1. Larry Johnson flew as Green 1. Lieutenant Storen (SAAF) led Blue Section. Captain Jack Davis took all of A Flight up, and encountered thick cloud from 3,000 to 15,000ft. It meant that the primary attack in the Florence area had to be abandoned in favour of the secondary target, the Poggi Bonsi – Florence Road. The road was broken with six direct hits. Intense and accurate 40mm and 88mm flak was fired, but no Mustangs were damaged.

After twenty-four hours off duty, Dennis found himself rostered to fly as Yellow 2 flying the repaired HS-D. Mervyn Talbot flew at Green 2 to Lieutenant Cunliffe (SAAF). Squadron Leader Johns was airborne with A Flight at 0850, on an anti-shipping raid north of Rimini. Accompanied by twelve Kittyhawks from 112 Squadron and fifteen Spitfires, this large wing was expecting to interdict a German oil tanker. Clearly the intelligence report was wrong, as the only visible shipping was a hospital ship. The secondary target was attacked, which consisted of large transport barges in the harbour at Gatteo. All bombs dropped on the target area, but no results were observed. Dennis remarked that when 260 had Kittyhawks with them, 260 had to slow down their cruising speed. He adds that when 260 escorted Baltimore bombers, along with 112 flying Kittyhawks, the Mustangs AND bombers had to slow down to keep pace with the slow, lumbering Kittyhawks: a far from ideal combination. The Mustangs could keep pace with the Spitfires easily enough, but anything else was left far behind.

Mervyn was airborne at 1250. Captain Jack Davis led A Flight to attack the German landing ground at Ferrara. After the bombing run of the hangers, the flight attacked five German aircraft standing on the apron in front of the hangers, seemingly 'sitting ducks' abandoned by the Luftwaffe to their fate, all of which were damaged and rendered unairworthy. As the Mustangs left, a plume of black smoke could be seen rising 1,000ft from the crippled landing ground from several large fires.

The Arezzo Line

In the aftermath of the Allied breakthrough at Cassino and the fall of Rome, Kesselring's forces managed to evade Alexander and retreated to the line of the Arno River, Florence, 160 miles north of Rome. Kesselring attempted to set up a series of defensive positions, in the hope that these would delay the Allies long enough for the defences of the Gothic Line to be completed. The first of these, the Dora Line, was brushed aside in mid-June, but the Germans had more time to work on the Tresimeno or Frieda Line. The Germans made a determined attempt to hold the Frieda line for as long as possible, but it only held out for two weeks. As a result, Kesselring decided to use the next series of lines for delaying actions only, holding each line for long enough for the bulk of his men to reach the next line back. The Germans would then make a stand on the Gothic Line in the northern Apennines, running from the Tyrrhenian coast midway between Pisa and La Spezia, over the Apennines in a reversed S curve, to the Adriatic coast between Pesaro and Rimini. The next line Kesselring held was the Arezzo Line, the objective was to protect the ports of Livorno and Ancona, and win precious time to improve the fortifications of the Gothic Line.

In order to support the battle of the Arezzo Line (3-18 July 1944), 269 Wing moved out to Crete in Tuscany during 7 July. The landing ground was south of Siena.

As the new landing ground was close to German lines, blackout precautions were put in place, and all tents and aircraft had to be camouflaged. Slit trenches were dug around the landing field by pilots and other ground crew, as improvised air-raid protection in case the Luftwaffe bombed the landing ground or the German heavy artillery sent over 170mm artillery rounds. Conspicuous use of trees and hedges on the landing ground, the squadron diary reports, were made of use to hide personal tented accommodation.

As part of the battle, gun positions close to the new landing ground were the objectives of the morning of 8 July. Squadron Lead Johns lead a flight of five Mustangs into the air at 0900, to attack guns west of Arezzo. Over the target in under half an hour, bombing was on the pinpoint position and the area strafed in the dive. Moderate 20mm anti-aircraft fire was put up. Thanks to the pilots accurate bombing, three 88mm guns were converted into piles of scrap. More guns were the objective of the ninth, again in the Arezzo area. Dennis, flying as Green 2, took off at 0900 into bad weather, which became so bad, the flight of twelve was forced to land at Orvieto, home of 7 Squadron South African Airforce. Landing conditions were described as 'twitchy.' After resting up with 7 Squadron, the pilots from 260 flew off Orvieto to the squadrons new landing ground at Crete in the early afternoon. After refuelling, Squadron Leader Johns led the flight into the air at 1905. The target was a German heavy artillery battery concealed in woodland. The pinpoint was bombed. Intense and accurate 20mm and 40mm anti-aircraft fire was put up to defend the battery: Dennis's aircraft HS-D was considered CAT II, and Duke Kent's Mustang was also hit, but considered CAT I. All landed at 2020. This was Dennis's sixth close brush with death from flak. Any one of those 40mm shells, as they exploded, could obliterate an aircraft and its crew without warning. As Mervyn Talbot observed:

> 'We seldom knew we were under fire until the anti-aircraft shells
> began exploding in proximity to us, usually in simultaneous bursts
> of four black puffs from a single battery if it was light, or in thick

concentrations of random explosions if several batteries were zeroed in on us. The 88mm stuff was deadly. One shell could destroy an aircraft in an instant. On a bomb run, we could take no evasive action regardless of how intense the flak was.'

Attacks on gun positions occupied the second week of July. On the tenth of the month, Dennis flew as White 1, Jack Davis leading Red Section. Cloud forced the flight to operate below 5,000ft, which made them easy targets for 40mm and 20mm anti-aircraft fire. Three bombs failed to drop, and two pilots had to land with bombs on. The following day Dennis was Black 2, again Johns was Blue 1 attacking German heavy artillery. Direct hits were scored: the pilots followed their bombs down strafing anything that moved on the ground. 239 Wing reports 'stepping up of operations' on 12 July with 'twenty-six missions divided between gun positions, strong points, MT an Cab Rank.'

Dennis was given a rest day on 13 July, but was sent up to carry out an air test on repaired Mustang HS-A. He reported repairs to radio and electrical systems were good.

Back flying HS-D on 14 July, Dennis as White 1 with Sergeant Street as his wingman, was airborne at 1045. Squadron Leader Jandrell led Red Section to attack German mortar positions west of Ancona on the Polish sector, supporting General Ander's 2nd Polish Corps, supported by the Italian Corps of Liberation, as airborne artillery. For a seventh time Dennis recorded in his logbook he had been hit by flak, once again HS-D had been holed, recorded as CAT I. Flying HS-C, Dennis as White 1 with Lieutenant C.F. Howes (SAAF) as his wingman, followed Jandrell into the sky at 1735. The target was not apparent, German guns north-west of Arezzo. Bombs were dropped on pinpoint, all dropped except Dennis's: both bombs hung up. Armourers removed them after a 'twitchy' landing.

The Germans defended their position stubbornly on 15 July, during which day Dennis flew two operations. Flying as White 1, Mervyn Talbot was his wingman, flying his second operation of the day. Mervyn had been on an operation from 0905 to 0950. Like Mervyn, Davis was on his second operation that day, and led up Red Section at 1050, the objective to attack the same gun positions as the day before as the guns had not been silenced. Cloud and rain, meant that the pinpoint was bombed with no results observed. Intense and accurate 40mm and 20mm anti-aircraft fire was put up. Up again at 1805, Johns led Blue Section to the attack. Dennis was flying HS-L as Black 2 to Lieutenant Cunliffe (SAAF), the objective was to attack German artillery south-east of Citta De Castello. The primary objective was concealed by cloud, so the pinpoint was bombed. Johns then led a strafing run along the German lines shooting up German infantry. Some flak was put up, and Dennis returned to base at 1835, his aircraft for the day HS-L suffering CAT II damage. His eighth 'dance with death.'

After facing Allied infantry, tanks, artillery and bombardment from the air, Kesselring ordered his troops to withdraw overnight on the 15 July. Early on 16 July the 26th Armoured Brigade, 6th Armoured Division, was able to move into the upper Chiana valley to the west of Arezzo and advanced towards the city and the upper Arno. By the end of the day the British and New Zealanders had crossed a stretch of the Arno twenty miles from Florence (at the south tip of a loop in the river), and were ready to advance north towards the next German defensive position, the Arno Line. Arezzo was quickly turned into the Eighth Army's main railhead in the northern Apennines, and was used to support the advance towards the Arno and the early attacks on the Gothic Line.

CHAPTER
13

A HOLIDAY

MERVYN AND DENNIS were absent from the squadron for the rest of the month: they had ten days leave from Monday, 17 July, starting at 0900 to 2359 on 28 July. Destination: Hotel Minerva Sorrento. Having mentioned I had read Mervyn's recollections of his time on 260 Squadron, I asked Dennis what he remembered about this period with 260:

'For our good behaviour in keeping up moral through our nefarious dealings in obtaining decent grub, Mervyn and I found we were given leave in Sorrento. Lad's from Lupset don't holiday on the divine coast, but it was true and for a second time. It was ten days away from tents, dust, bombs and death.

'The journey to the Rest Camp was something of an adventure in itself. Before leaving the airfield, we stowed most of our belongings and placed them in locked storage so that the local thieves (a continual problem at the airfields) would be deprived of an easy target. Our tents were stowed in a similar manner: we took our personal clobber with us in our small pack. By now, what had once been pristine RAF issue uniforms, were battle weary like the rest of the fellas in the squadron. To be fair, if the Ities wanted to knock off our KDs that stank of BO they were welcome to 'em. Washing and laundry were mostly a thing of the past. Often the only chance we got to launder our shirts was in petrol. Water was for drinking, even then it was chlorinated and tasted little better than petrol.

'This jaunt of ours was all possible because the powers that be turned blind, but appreciative eyes to our out of hours commercial activities. In the end we had a driver and Italian cook with us as interpreter, but we all had some basic Italian. We kept the mess supplied with vino, beer, eggs, fresh meat: the good things in life rather than rubber egg and bully beef. It was all tame in comparison to what Blomfield and Shep told us had happened in the past on the squadron.'

Dennis pauses to laugh:

'It all began soon after we had joined. Mervyn had obtained our wheels; I think he swopped a bottle of scotch with the yanks… they would sell their aged grandmother or sister for scotch. A bottle of scotch and the right Yank could get you anything. Anyhow, Mervyn obtained a Ford 15-cwt truck. In the desert the squadron had borrowed from Hitler an HE111. That I'm sure you know is a twin-engine bomber. The lads called it Delta Lilly and used it to go shopping with: bringing back booze, chickens and the like.

'Once we had our Ford, Mervyn had the erks paint it in our camouflage and we used it to go shopping in, swopping our tinned rations for something edible. Lieutenant Shepperd was behind a lot of the underhand goings on before he went for a burton. Merv was mates with an erk, one of the ground crew who looked after our kites: for us 16 or so pilots, we had dozens of erberts as armourers, mechanics, engineers, making sure that after each trip our kite was in A1 condition. Somehow, Mervyn had convinced his mate to drive the truck from place to place when we were airborne. It was all very dodgy. We kept our mess well supplied with proper eggs, milk, meat that was not bully beef. It was all appreciated. It got so hot in the Italian summer that the bully in the tins could be poured out like soup with this thick orange scum of fat on top. Of course, some lads liked all of this, God knows why. I suppose you get used to anything. Not for us though.'

Dennis laughs again. 'You mentioned Sorrento?'

'Yes, it was a real boys own adventure. There was Duke of Kent, Sandy Street, Merve and I.

'We used our truck to motor down to Number 2 Rest Camp. This place was officially for the bomber crews, but us fighter-bombers had been found space. I can't imagine what it must have been like flying in a bomber night after night, or like the yanks in broad daylight suffering flak. It was bad enough for us. Some of the jobs we heard on the grape vine had crippling losses: a squadron of four engine Halifax's set off to bomb targets in the Balkans and most never came home. Those lads deserved a rest more than we did, but the powers that be sent us off on our jolly's.

'From our base it meant driving across mountain roads that twisted and turned on its journey across the hills and valleys on its way to Naples. A lot of the bridges had been blown, and the replacements were a bit dodgy to say the least. The landscape was rugged and barren, dotted with ramshackle farms and derelict cottages. There was virtually nothing from which the locals could scrape a living from. What little livestock that could be seen were thin, undernourished and uncared for. Chickens, goats and pigs rummaged around the vineyards or olive groves searching for food. Dirty children in ragged clothes, underfed and bloated, wandered aimlessly around or huddled together in the dirt. Everywhere there were small well-kept shrines built into the rock face or at the sides of the roads. We arrived at Salerno late in the afternoon before motoring into Naples. We headed to the Royal Palace which the Allies had commandeered and converted into a giant canteen/leisure complex. We enjoyed our first really decent meal in months, and checked the notices announcing various entertainments available for the evening. We could hardly walk a few paces without being accosted by prostitutes and women offering their young daughters for bars of chocolate. The poverty was shocking. It was a great relief to leave the squalor of the city for Sorrento the next morning.

'Driving at a steady 25mph we headed towards the divine coast. The views were spectacular. Was there really a war on? Was I really heading to the divine coast for a second time? It all seems to wrong. I was mixed up inside with emotion, mostly bloody relieved to be out of the range of the German flak. By midday we were on the coast and drove into Amalfi. The sunlight made the white, pink and blue houses with red tiled roofs glow, the sky was bluer than you could imagine. The sea was calm, with a few white dancing horses. It was all very different to my last trip to the seaside with mum, uncle Charlie and aunt Lily, and my cousins Jim and Eric, plus your grandmother Jeane and Shirley of course, all at Primrose Valley.

'We stopped at Amalfi for a brew up. The cathedral was right on the beach, or so it seemed. A huge baroque affair in marble with stripes. We had egg and chips in a little café by the steps that led up to the main doors. Above the town was another village, again with another huge church. All bright marble, cool and clean. A steady procession of the faithful came and went, their heads bowed, and veiled. Hard to think come the evening, they would let you sleep with them for chocolates and fags.

'The road twisted and turned and, at each turning, a new vista opened up before us. The views were breathtaking as the cliffs plunged ever downwards towards the sea, their tree-lined chasms blending with the splendid outcrops of rock and foliage.

'We were last here in the winter, it was nothing compared to what we experienced now in the summer. The sea nestling below the cliffs was a picture: deep Mediterranean blue as the sun sparkled over the crests of the otherwise almost unnoticed ripples. Each time we went round a corner a new and magnificent scene greeted us.

'We arrived in Sorrento, in the early evening, with its familiar narrow streets, shops and vino bars that we had come to know so well earlier in the year. Merve and I shared a room. A quick wash and brush up and soon we were joined by the others and were sitting on the terrace looking across the Bay of Naples sipping cherry brandy and drinking vino.

'Dinner was served in the hotel restaurant by young Italian waiters and waitresses. The battle front seemed very far away. Yet we all knew we had to return. We lived a carefree existence. As long as you never thought beyond the next meal, life was great. Even on squadron, so long as you lived in the now, tomorrow would never come and your number may not be up.

'It didn't take long for a pattern of relaxation to appear. Between swimming, walking and messing about in a small sailing boat someone had managed to acquire, more than likely Mervyn, he was good at things like that, we were able to forget the cares and squalor of war and enjoy our holiday. We were determined to enjoy it.

'One evening we had a concert on the terrace given by Neapolitan musicians and singers and I remember sitting outside listening to the strains of 'Turn'a Sorrento', 'Santa Lucia', 'O Sole Mio', 'Cuore ingrato' etc, which all meant nothing to me at the time.

'A dance organized in the hotel proved to be a very humorous affair. All the women present, reputedly of good reputation and brought in by the entertainments officer, seemed to be either an ex-countess or the wife of a count who had been captured by the Allies.

'The hotel staff told us we had to visit Capri and visit its famous Blue Grotto. We took the 15-tonner onto the ferry to explore the mountains of the island. It was another a day of complete relaxation and fun. Favoured by the Roman Emperors, Capri was another demi-paradise of narrow streets with white buildings garlanded with flowers and looking breathtaking in the glorious sunshine. It was hard to imagine there was a war on.

'The grotto was something else entirely. We were rowed out by an Itie guide in this little boat. He told us that we had to wait for the right wave, so we could scoot inside the cave. Once in, the water was so clear that the row boat looked to be floating. I dived over the side. It was like flying, the water did not seem to exist. It was really all too much. Back on Capri, we were warned about Gracie Fields, and her tendency to suddenly appear singing Sally.'

Laughing, the conversation paused:

> 'We always use to bugger up songs adding our own words. It was harmless fun. I don't think we were ever caught by her. Merve always had his accordion with him, and we had a whole repertoire of songs to well-known tunes, or from the earlier war.
>
> 'The days passed too quickly. We had tasted the good life and were now due back to reality. The final evening arrived; we were due to leave for Crete landing ground the following morning. We had good food, booze, women to dance with, comfortable accommodations in an excellent hotel and it had not cost us a penny. This was the kind of holiday that only the jet set of the 30s could afford; I had much to thank Hitler for.'

Dennis pauses to laugh:

> 'There was no discipline and virtually complete freedom of movement and activity. What was more we all had a lot of fun. But it was back to earth with a bump. Back to tents, no baths, crappy food until we got going on the egg run again. I had slept well and, except for the last night, we had hardly talked about operations at all. I guess it was all Dutch courage really: we were scared to go back and face the never-ending threat of being blown of out the sky by flak. As a matter of fact, it had been taboo in the mess to talk about operations and how we felt. If anyone had dared to start talking about them, shouts of "shut the hanger door" were hurled at them from all directions, more often than not coloured with more expressive expletives. We were all kidding ourselves.'

During our conversation my notes tell me Dennis had handed me a brochure of the hotel he had stopped in, and the open pages of his photo albums with images captured forever of this holiday. On the tape recording, the conversation fades away. Dennis gets listless again as he fiddles with his pipe.

The day job once more

Back at Crete on 28 July, the holiday party had to sign their big packs out of stores along with tents and go through the ritual of getting set up again. From sprung beds with sheets, to sleeping on make shift beds in tents was a substantial culture shock. Mervyn was back in the air at 1010 on 30 July. Squadron Leader Johns lead A flight of six to bomb a marshalling yard. No longer carrying two 500lb bombs, standard payload was now two 1,000lb bombs. Dennis was airborne at 1130, the flight of six led by Captain Maree to bomb five houses suspected of being a German strong point.

Whilst Dennis had been away, Jesi Road bridge was destroyed on 17 July, an ENSA concert party visited the following day, followed by a squadron party and 'in the evening squadron talent came to the fore. This was a most successful evening.' Was Mervyns accordion playing missed we wonder? The 19 July was an anti-shipping strike, when 260 was sent out to attack a group of fifty or more barges in Comacchio Lagoon: three were sunk and three damaged. On the twentieth the squadron was attacking gun positions, there followed twenty-four hours down time:

This brief respite from operations allowed the aircrew personnel to rest and afforded ground crews to have a little leisure and to attend to any of their domestic requirements, such as washing kit and doing necessary mending.

Operations resumed on 22 July. An armed attack directed on railway wagons in the Ravena area. This was the first operation for Pilot Officer Glen, and sadly his last. The flight of eleven Mustangs was airborne at 1655. Glen was flying No. 2 to Captain Maree. As the flight came over the target, German anti-aircraft fire opened up, both 20mm and 88mm. Glen was observed to dive down on this bombing run, release his bombs and as he started to pull out of the dive, he was hit by ack-ack. The stricken Mustang, FB 270, plummeted into the ground, exploding on impact. Glen had made no attempt to bail out, he was presumed killed or severely wounded by flak and thus incapacitated by his injury before the Mustang ploughed into the earth. Flying Officer Roland Glen was from Hull, gazetted in early January 1944. He was the son of Malcom and Emily Glen. Aged just 20-years-old when he died and is buried in Forli War Cemetery.

A German observation point was attacked by Jack Davies during the 23 July. The OP was located in a group of farm buildings. The bombing run scored direct hits, blowing the roof of both houses, but no enemy hits were claimed. A road bridge was the target for the following day, with 20ft of the bridge damaged beyond repair.

Bridges were again the target on the 25/26, and on the morning of the 27 July:

> No. 5 (SAAF) Squadron and No. 260 Squadron were briefed to attack big concentrations of troops and troublesome guns in IMPRUNETA – bombing was all well in the area and was much appreciated by the Army who signalled that 'all bombs in target area.'

Royalty

Whilst Dennis had been away, George VI reviewed the squadron during the course of 27 July, 'a historic day' reports 239 Operations Record Book:

For days in advance the general preparations and 'sprucing-up' had evoked considerable speculation; and despite full security measures, most people drew their own conclusions from the radio announcement that the King was already in Italy. The title 'General Collingwood', by which the distinguished visitor was announced, concealed little or nothing, and there were few who did not parade on the 27th in anticipation of cheering the king.

It was early afternoon when the King literally descended on the sun-bathed landing ground in a DC3 aircraft, appropriately named 'Freedom', there to be received by the Officer Commanding the Wing, Colonel L.A. WILMOT DFC (South Africa) who was accompanied by Wing Commander Flying, Lieutenant Colonel E.M. BAKER DSO DFC (South Africa). The party with the King included the Air Officer Commanding Desert Air Force, Air Vice-Marshal W.F. DICKSON CB DSO OBE AFC. (This was, in fact, the King's Day with the Desert Air Force exclusively).

His Majesty's first place of call was Wing Operations. Here, he was closely interested in the briefing of pilots by an Air Liaison Officer (Army) and caused not a little comic embarrassment among the company when he spotted, written over a map point for the benefit of pilots, the time-honoured RAF phrase 'Extract Digits Here', and, of course, inquired the meaning. For reasons of nicety, the King was respectfully dissuaded from his curiosity and was content to remain unenlightened.

From Wing Ops, the Royal Procession of many cars [...] drove round the landing ground perimeter, along which, at intervals, were paraded spick and span, the personnel of the squadrons and ancillary units [...] and smilingly acknowledged the roars of cheering with which the British, Australian and South African Units – coloured men and white – greeted him. He made only one halt [...] the detachment of the 87th Heavy Ack-Ack Regiment (London Scottish); whose skirling bagpiper gave the only musical touch to the occasion [...] Squadron Commanders and other officers were invited to a Wing Mess party; and in the Airmen's Mess too, drinks and snacks were 'on the house' – a hangover making wind-up to a memorable day.

The day after the review, 112 Squadron was detailed to bomb 'a house where General Heydrich was supposed to be holding a party at 2015 hours. At 2035 hours, three 500lb bombs finished up on the front of the house,' reported 239 Wing Operations Record Book. For 260, Impruneta village was attacked by a flight of twelve Mustangs led by Captain Maree. All bombs fell on target starting a large fire with smoke and flames rising 100ft into the air. Their followed a 'day off' when: 'The squadron was released all day and airmen not engaged in any special duty were permitted to visit the nearest village,' reported the squadron diary.

With Dennis, Mervyn and others returned, three officers were 'stood down' and allowed rest at a Hotel in Assisi. For those back on ops the principal target was the demolition of infrastructure to prevent German movements. Dennis was airborne at 1855 during the twenty-ninth, as White 1 flying HS-Q with Sergeant McGarry as his No. 2. Captain Davis led all of A Flight to attack a railway bridge. Despite intense and accurate 40mm ack-ack, all bombs hit the target, tearing up the railway lines.

Mervyn was in the air at 1010 on 30 July, Squadron Leader Johns heading the flight of six Mustangs. The target was a railway level crossing which was obliterated. Dennis was airborne at 1130, Captain Maree leading Red Flight. Dennis was White 1 with Sergeant Fergusson as his No. 2. The target was a German strongpoint: the Germans had dug into a group of houses. The bombing runs partly demolished one house and damaged a second. Dennis had flown twenty operations in July over seventeen days, with twenty-eight hours twenty-five mins operational flying. On four occasions the Mustang he was flying was damaged by flak or ground fire, the same tally as June.

The Arno Line

By the start of August, the Germans had pulled back into the Arno line. On 2 August, Kesselring decided to abandon Florence, and by 4 August the Germans had pulled back four miles to the Heinrich Mountain Line, in the Mugello Hills. The last German troops left the city on 7 August, and the Allies quickly occupied it. Once again, the Allies would pause before assaulting the new defensive position. The Eighth Army moved back to the Adriatic to attack towards Rimini, while the Fifth Army was given the task of attacking north from Florence.

A Flight, consisting of all twelve Mustangs, was in the air at 1755 on 1 August, led by Captain Jack Davis, both Dennis and Mervyn were on the operation, to attack a German strongpoint. Dennis was back in Red Section as Yellow 2 and wingman to Larry Johnson. Captain R.T. 'Roy' Rogers flew as Red 2, with Captains Duplesis and Maree and Green 1 and 2. Pilot Officer Maddison led Blue Section, Mervyn Talbot was Black 2, wingman to Sergeant Street. Flying low at 6,000ft, bombs were dropped onto the target of three houses acting as German strongpoints – which may have been a command centre – from 1,000ft: six bombs missed but fell close to the buildings, two hit one of the buildings and the remainder fell in the target area. The buildings were damaged but not totally destroyed. Some 790 rounds of 0.50cal were expired on a strafing run. The attack was watched by 2nd New Zealand Division, and sent the following dispatch to 260 Squadron 'Excellent bombing, Ammunition Hit. First Class Show' reports 239 Wing Operations Record Book.

Houses and farm complexes made ideal strongpoints for the Germans: the walls provided defence from small arms fire, 20mm or 40mm wheel artillery could be set up to fire through windows or doors, or in some cases flak was fired from roofless shells. Slowing down the allies, concealment of forces and giving ground inch by inch in a war of attrition was Kesselring's objective. The terrain of Italy did not favour artillery: hence ground attack and fighter-bombers provided aerial artillery. In the early stages of the campaign in Italy, strategic bombing failed to knock out bridges, railway lines and strongpoints. The US 15th Air Force, it was reckoned, hit one bridge every 190 operations, and even then, the bridge was not guaranteed to be destroyed. Dennis and his colleagues provided air cover, as well as ground attack, to allow the Allies to advance through Italy. Interdiction and destruction of infrastructure was vital to the success of the campaign even if it lacked the glamour of being a fighter pilot. By this stage in the war, air superiority meant the Luftwaffe was largely a 'spent force.' The operations by 239 Wing had both a physical and moral impact on the German's: 'reliable civilians report' states 239 Wing Operations Record Book that 'bombing of S Maria very successful. Enemy showing signs of panic when fighter-bombers come over.'

Daring escapes

Captain Jack Davis was airborne at 1130 on 2 August; the flight of six included Pilot Officer Brown. The target was a railway bridge. Flying through intense 20mm anti-aircraft fire north of Florence, as the group of Mustangs turned into the target, German 88mm flak opened up. All bombs were dropped from 1,000ft, but the effect was not seen. Davis reported to his No. 2 Sergeant Bell that he had been hit, adding Captain Duplessis was to take over. Davis informed the flight he was going to try and make for the Allied lines. White and black smoke was seen pluming from the stricken Mustang. The engine failed, and Davis had no option but to bail out. Gordon Brown picks up the story:

> 'The five remaining aircraft of his flight (including me) saw his aircraft blow up on hitting the ground and he was seen to land safely by parachute. The story has it that he was immediately captured by a German detachment and put in the back of a small German truck with an elderly German soldier.
> 'Jack was wearing Nuffield flying boots, which had a knife in a little pocket, with which to cut off the top of the boot and made them look like ordinary civilian boots which would not give away the identity of the wearer. Jack apparently stabbed the soldier with the knife, rolled out of the back of the truck and took to the hills, from where the partisans passed him through our lines.'

As RAF training had noted, the best time to escape as POW was between capture and being taken to internment and interrogation: Davis, well aware of this dictum managed to evade the Germans for several months. He was not allowed to return to Operational Flying in case he was shot down and captured again: the Germans would have shot him. With Davis being reported missing, Pilot Officer Bagshawe took command of A Flight. Davis returned to 260 Squadron at the end of the month, his operational flying days over.

Throughout early August, operations were the 'same old' attacking strongpoints, railway lines, road and any German vehicle or train that moved. Dennis was airborne at 1140 on 3 August, Flying as Yellow 2 to Billy Johnson. Squadron Leader Johns led Red Section on an armed attack on German gun positions. Flying in at 6,000ft, the target was reconnoitred at 3,000ft, no guns were observed, but the grid reference pin point was bombed. However, on the ground, the target had been eliminated, as an Army dispatch arrived with 239 Wing stating 'guns silenced after bombing', so clearly the objective had been achieved. Throughout the operation, intense and alarmingly accurate 88mm flak was fired at the six Mustangs, accompanied by 20mm ground fire. Two new pilots had joined that day, Sergeants Hughes and Lawrence, and had no operational experience. It is said a cat has nine lives: this may also be true of pilots. For the nineth time Dennis recorded in his logbook – a/c CAT II. Mustang HS-V was holed by shrapnel from 88mm fire. The tail unit and port wing had been holed by flak. The engine had a damaged radiator, glycol and oil leak. The following day was an early start. Mervyn was soaring in Italian skies at 0605 as No. 2 to Flight Lieutenant Cunliffe, as the third pair in Blue Section. Squadron Leader Johns led the formation of twelve with Captain Rogers heading Blue Section. Red Section flew direct to the target, taking off at 0535, conducting two identification circuits over the target whilst under ack-ack. Blue Section bombed the target as Red Section turned for home. The objective was to destroy a road, to prevent German troop and stores movements. Both sections came under intense and accurate 20mm anti-aircraft fire: the road was damaged but not destroyed. Four bombs with Red Section were hang ups, which were later jettisoned.

With no spare serviceable Mustangs on the squadron, Dennis found himself off operations for two days.

Dennis returned to the sky on 6 August, flying as White 2 aboard HS-V, with Captain Duplesis flying as White 1, Dennis participated in an attack on gun positions in the Polish sector west of Semigallia, about which 239 Wing records:

On the Polish Corps front, three artillery targets were attacked. Details of results were unobserved, but on the last mission of the day – a second visit within three hours to the same target by the same 6 pilots – the target is believed to have been well hit. These missions were also noticeable for the amount of accurate flak. One aircraft was holed in 26 places, one in 6, one through the cockpit, and three more aircraft were CAT 1.

The flak damaged five out of six Mustangs. Dennis, with HS-V was the only pilot unscathed. Given twenty-four hours rest, Dennis took part in no operations on 7 July, but was back flying on the eighth. Dennis used his day off to head to Rome.

Gun positions were the target for 9 August. Lieutenant Larry Johnson led off the six Mustangs of Red Section at 1920. Dennis flew as White 1, Pilot Officer Maddison as his No. 2 The target was obscured by thick cloud descending to 3,000ft. The pin point was bombed by Red 1 and Red 2 at 1,000ft, but no claims were made. Heavy, accurate 20mm flak was encountered. White 2 was hit, white smoke immediately billowing from his engine. Ten minutes later white smoke had turned to black and flames crept along the engine cowling to the cockpit. Dennis radioed him to jettison his bombs and head to the Allied lines. After dropping his bombs and seeing them explode, Maddison bailed out at 3,000ft, landing safely. His Mustang plummeted into the deck belching smoke and flames, exploding on impact. Maddison had landed within Allied lines, and made his way back to Crete the following day. Dennis's logbook comments about Maddison, 'Lucky son of a bitch. Returned down flak alley. Intense, accurate light anti-aircraft fire all the way.' Sixty years later I asked Dennis about what he remembered of 'Flak Alley':

> 'With the Luftwaffe almost non-existent, the Jerries increased their anti-aircraft provisions. We entered flak alley; it was an almost uninterrupted cloud of swirling black smoke filled with angry red explosions. Plainly, any one of those exploding 88mm shells could obliterate an aircraft and its pilot without warning. When the group ahead of us entered this inferno, they all but disappeared. My heart was hammering as fast as my guns did on a strafing run. It did not seem possible that anyone or anything could fly into that hell and come out alive on the other side. But somehow, despite being buffeted by thunderous explosions and the incessant clinking, clanging, and pinging of shell fragments striking our kites, we all made it through. We all had a big twitch on getting through that lot.'

Dive-bombing put a particular strain on the pilot as Dennis remembers:

> 'Starting at 6,000 or 8,000ft and dropping down hell for leather to 2,000 when we started to pull put a huge gravitational force on us, which we knew simply as "G". As we zoomed down, G would push us into our seats, and then as we pulled back once bombs had gone could cause us too momentarily black out. It was also painful on our ears because of the pressure changes. The other danger of course was

not pulling out in time, especially as we were often flying in hilly or mountainous areas.

'As we let go of the bombs we were often at 1,000ft: we had to be that low to attain some degree of accuracy for our bombs, the Mustang would kick unburned from considerable weight. Our bomb load was almost the same as the Boston's we escorted.

'As we dropped down in the dive, the altimeter would spin round so fast we could not read it to read how high we were: we had to judge visually from experience when to pull back on the stick to prevent us going thumping into the deck. All of this was in addition to the chances of being hit by ground fire at any stage. Flak really was our nemesis.'

260 Squadron moved to Roisgnoni on 10 August 'for special duties as fight patrol against high altitude enemy reconnaissance aircraft' reports the squadron diary. Dennis was part of the last group to leave Crete, he flew as White 1, in a flight of six led by Lieutenant Johnson. Duke Kent flew as Yellow 2, with a familiar face to Abu Sueir, Captain Duplessis, flying as Yellow 1. Airborne at 1210, the flight flew direct to the target at Castiglioni, north of Florence, the secondary target. Four steam engines at the head of trains were observed. Dropping down from 6,000ft to 1,000ft the railway yard was bombed north to south. Two bombs were direct hits on passenger coaches, destroying the railway line on which they stood and blowing six more coaches off the track. A five-floor building in the railway yard was partially demolished with two direct hits. Two strafing runs were made: Dennis claimed four coaches destroyed and two damaged. Weather 'was perfect, no cloud.' Bad weather throughout the 11 August curtailed operation flying, and it was not till 14 August that Dennis landed as Red 2 at Rosignoni.

OPERATION DRAGOON

PLANNED AS OPERATION Anvil in March 1944, this was to be a simultaneous landing in the South of France and Normandy. Churchill argued that the invading force would get marooned on the beach, much like what had occurred to General Mark Clark's 5th Army at Anzio during Operation Shingle, which ironically was an operation Churchill had vocally championed. Due to the need to supply the Allied beachhead at Anzio, Anvil was quietly dropped.

Despite Overlord's success in getting boots on the ground, the Allies were bottled up in the narrow lanes of Normandy. It had every chance of becoming a second Anzio debacle. Caen had not yet fallen. By July 1944 the landing in the south of France was reconsidered for three reasons: an attack was needed to divert German resources from Normandy, and secondly, as the clogged-up nature of the ports in Normandy demonstrated, the Allies did not have the capacity to adequately supply the Allied forces through Normandy alone. Thirdly, the High Command of the French Liberation Army pushed for a revival of the operation. Why? The French wanted to participate in the liberation of their homeland, and operation Anvil was to include large numbers of French troops. As a result, Anvil was reactivated, and Operation Dragoon was finally approved in late July to be executed in August. The planning was all top secret. Christopher Lee recalls:

> 'I remember before the invasion of Southern France, AC Pike sent for me and showed me all the maps for where the various air units had to go. I had dozens if not hundreds of maps: I was practically the only person who had them on the wing. When we crossed over to the west coast of Italy to near Livorno, on a given day and time, I had to call the squadron commanders in and some of the pilots and brief them about what was going to happen.'

The troops selected for the operation were the U.S. VI Army Corps and the French 'Army B', later the 1st Army, commanded by General Jean de Lattre de Tassigny. They were supported by some airborne units, numerous aircraft and a large naval armada. They were to face the German 19th Army, composed mostly of third-rate units, as most of the crack units had been withdrawn to stem the growing Allied pressure on the Normandy front. The German defences were nowhere near as strong as the Atlantic Wall in Northern France. The Allies landed 94,000 men on the morning of 15 August, and suffered just 395 casualties.

Dennis Varey:

'On 15 August 1944 we were ordered to provide top cover for the glider force invasion of the south of France. At the briefing, Chris told us that we were to draw off the enemy flak to protect the gliders. That meant flying at 6,000. Chris in a matter-of-fact fashion informed us that based on Headquarters best guess, that we should expect 50% casualties. That news went down like a lead balloon.

'Our flight of Mustangs was led by the Group Captain, and we were in the air by 0700. The job entailed a round trip of 4 hours, for which we carried long range tanks. In the event, it was not that bad a time. We arrived about 0700 and after patrolling the area from Les Adrets to Bagnols, skipper decided to head for home as the C-47s were late. Over Corsica heading back we met the C-47s (60 plus) with the gliders escorted by P47s. This was the formation we had been detailed to escort. So, we had no choice but to turn back and escorted them to the landing area and back to the coast. Fortunately, there did not appear to be much opposition and it turned out to be a successful operation. We were back at base by 1035.

'Because we had had to spend more time in the air, our big worry was petrol. I got back with about 3 gallons of petrol left in my tanks. I had a big twitch on. If the C-47 had not been late then we would have been fine. As it was, it was a close-run thing. Some of the fellas landed and left their kites on the runway as they had no petrol left to taxi into dispersal.

'We spent the rest of the day brewing up. A second flight went off just about half five. Squadron Leader Johns led. They encountered no flak and let 112 take over whilst the gliders landed. They got back before 9 o'clock. We then had a bit of a session. Even those who barely touched a drop indulged, thankful we had all made it. Thankfully we had the following day off ops to get over our hangovers.'

Despite early success, the German forces were able to conduct a fighting retreat in the Rhone valley, delaying the American advance. The First French Army quickly surrounded Marseille and Toulon. Both cities fell to the French on 28 August, a full month earlier than anticipated, thus capturing two large harbours, which were to play a significant part in supplying the Western Front. In mid-September, Allied units advanced from southern France and met with victorious units attacking from

Normandy, forming the Western Front. Four weeks of fighting cost the Allies about 25,000 casualties; the German army lost about 150,000 men, mostly prisoners. The operation was a resounding success. It opened up a new supply route for Eisenhower, expelled the Germans from southern France, and provided the French with an opportunity to participate in their own liberation. The conclusion of the operation was not the end of the debate surrounding it. In Churchill's post-war memoirs, he continued to ridicule the operation. Indeed, Churchill cited it as one of the reasons why Stalin was able to amass influence in the Balkans and Eastern Europe. Contradicting Churchill, Eisenhower, claimed that Dragoon was a vital tipping point in defeating Germany as it opened a new front.

Dennis again:

'On 18 August I was promoted from sergeant to flight sergeant. It meant more pay.

'We moved to Jesi in middle of August. on the coast near Ancona. The airstrip was reasonably long for a forward airstrip. We had the whole 239 Wing there under the command of Group Captain Eaton. He was a hard-bitten Aussie who needed all his toughness to look after his squadrons as we shared the place with a unit of American Thunderbolts. These oversized monsters dominated the place and as the Americans often did the air traffic control, they were almost always given priority with landing and take-off.

'The other obvious thing about the landing strip was just how congested it was. The whole place was packed with American Marauders. I don't ever remember seeing one fly. The place was really congested and it didn't help when USAAAF Liberators and Fortresses, both big four engine bombers, came in on the way home with problems, often needing fuel as they had got lost coming back from ops over Yugoslavia or further afield. Some of them came in with tails missing or smashed to pieces; wings would look more like colanders. You'd see them limping in, with one or two engines on, smoke all over the shop.'

The conversation stalled. The USAAF crews from the Fifth Airforce were bombing into Austria to attack German fighter production. RAF Bomber Command and Eighth Airforce's constant attacks into Germany had forced the Luftwaffe to relocate fighter production to Austria, now in reach of the Strategic Bomber force in Italy. If the pilots in 260 Squadron had a bad time with flak, the boys with the USAAF had it as bad, if not worse. Our conversation resumes:

'Once we moved to Jesi, our operations went further into enemy territory. Again, we were mostly to take out bridges and important buildings and we used thousand pounders quite often. This did make a bit more work for the armourers and ground crew as they were too heavy to lift by hand and had to be jacked into place with a hydraulic lift. As we had quite a good runway at Jesi, we found that they could get off (Just) with all tanks full, as well as two thousand pounds of bombs and two thousand rounds of 0.50cal ammo. There were snags with this.

'These snags caused us all a lot of "Twitching."

'The bomb racks on the Mustang had words painted on it in a red stencil "The Load On This Rack Should Not Exceed Two Hundred and Fifty Pounds." It was clear therefore that a thousand pounder overloaded the things rather a lot. Unsurprisingly, this gave us a lot of trouble as every so often the rack would refuse to release its bomb, a "Hang Up." If this happened on both sides, the pilot could probably carry on and shake the things off somewhere when all was OK. But if they would not release, the alternative was to fly over the sea, call up the Air-Sea Rescue service and when they were in position, bale out and get picked up. Some pilots were braver than others and landed with both bombs on, which was rather nerve fraying, or as we called it "Twitchy". I had a fair few Twitchy moments with hang ups I can tell you. I think we all did. If only one bomb kept on, it threw the balance of the Mustang off badly, and you had a devil's own job keeping it level, as its inclination was to dive over to the overloaded wing. You landed as gently as possible, one false move and bang, your number would be up.'

Hang Ups were a serious issue; Shep Sheppard relates the following story when the squadron was experimenting with 1,000lb bombs at Cutella back in Spring about Australian pilot Bruce Page:

'An Australian Pilot almost had a calamity when one of his bombs got hung up on the wing. The airfield controller called the mess where I was having a cup of tea and so I went down to the control – a small tent with a hand radio – very modern – to endeavour to talk Page through the various manoeuvres that would shake the bomb off. As the airstrip was at the beach, it was very easy to do it all over the sea. We tried everything, diving, half rolls, tight turns, keeping the bomb release full out all the time, but no joy. The damn thing simply would not come off. Some bright spark then suggested Page baled out, but we could not afford to lose an aircraft, so I killed that off right away.

'I was determined to get Page and the aircraft down somehow and in one piece. As a number of pilots had used this plane for the test, I knew that his fuel would now be getting very low. With this in mind, I decided to bring him down. Out came the blood wagon, and the fire engine, the armourers and fitters, all geared up to get to the aircraft as soon as it landed.

'In came Page, very carefully I must say, and as he landed, I told him on the R/T to keep his tail up as long as possible and to keep going to the end of the runway. By the time he was halfway along the landing strip, we were in motion with all the accident vehicles chasing the aircraft and, as it slowed, down came the tail and it stopped. Everyone rushed to it, the armourers to make sure the bomb was safe, myself up on the wing to the cockpit to get Bruce Page out. He was not there! Then it dawned on me that I had seen someone streak past as I got out of the flight truck and realised it was Page; he must have done 50 yards in about three seconds.

'All's well that ends well and the bomb was safely taken off. Page was safe and the aircraft was still in one piece. Everyone relaxed and I sent someone to taxi the aircraft into dispersal.'

The overloading of the bomb racks was a known problem, yet 'the high ups' never seemed to have worked on a solution. Other than dealing with hang ups, I asked Dennis what else 260 Squadron did:

'The other alternative job which the squadron did once we were at Yesi was long range escort, or bomb run into Yugoslavia, which entailed fitting drop tanks on the bomb racks. I think they held about 75 Imperial gallons and gave the plane over five hours endurance. We came back from some of these with about enough petrol left to fill a fag lighter and no ammo left as we always had a target to strafe on the way home. That gave us a big twitch.'

The conversation came to a natural end. 'Off duty, what prevented total boredom?' I ask:

'At Cutella in the end of the Nissan hut was a bar, we had a gramophone, radio and some chairs and tables that had been knocked off from Italian Airmen's accommodation at Foggia. The boys would obtain records off the Yanks.

'We had a chess set, and other games. We got hold of crosswords and other puzzles from the NAAFI. The Cinema was popular when we had access to it. We'd always gather in the mess after the last op had flown.

'Ever since I had arrived at Cutella our rations were not too good. Shep encouraged us to supplement them where we could. Mervyn and

I went around on the "egg run" in a knocked off American van. We bought from local farms who were always very pleased to supply us with anything that they had. We had a whip-round to pay for the stuff, or more often we would exchange our rations and NAFFI purchases, or Merve would knock stuff off the cookhouse wagon.

'We were well used to having the odd drink or two, cheap red wine made locally. Supplies of British type booze was hard to come by. We could get some lager off the Yanks, but it was not the same as the bitter we had in Yorkshire. Shep told us that in the desert they used the captured HE 111 to import beer: the 260 lads had obtained a cartload of Stella, and filled up the reserve tanks on the Heinkel. When they landed and served it out of the wing, the comment was the Stella would have tasted better if the tanks still had petrol in.

'We had a monthly ration of four cans of beer and one bottle of whisky, plus a free issue of fifty cigarettes and a bar of chocolate, the last three items were in prime demand with the farmers with whom we dealt to obtain our extra rations. The Americans, who were never far away, no matter which landing ground we were at, would sell their souls for a bottle of scotch whisky. I guess that's how Mervyn got the Ford light van we went around in. A "blind eye" was turned to these nefarious dealings. Real eggs were better than the powdered variety, like with milk, and being able to serve up chicken, tomatoes, apples, in fact anything we could get hold of, was a real boost to moral.

'Ted Duck was one of the great figures of 260. He always looked after the NAAFI. We always collected our NAAFI on a specific day in the first week of each month, which day it was I can't remember. Ted had been a bus driver before the war.

'Each month he drove down to the NAAFI stores and brought back our allocation. On getting back to us, he would prepare a list of issue for that month, which was typed by one of the orderly clerks. We had our NAAFI after pay parade, and most of us drew what we needed for the NAAFI, saving the rest.'

A NAAFI list in Dennis's collection records:

6 4oz packets of tea
5 2lb bags sugar
8 tins condensed milk
6 boxes of matches
1 bottle South African beer
2 oranges

2 tins South African peaches
2 tins of Australian pears
1 tinned New Zealand fruit cake
4 packets of biscuits
1 jar fish paste
3 bars soap
5 razor blades
3 sachets shampoo
1 stick of shaving soap
£4 2s 4d

Clearly, judging from the documents Dennis kept, the NAAFI ration changed, or his needs did. In a second list we find a list reporting 2lbs tea, 6lbs sugar, 6 tins condensed milk, 2 packets of biscuits, 2 tins of fruit, 1 tinned fruit cake, 1 tin of sweets, 3 bottles of beer, 2 bottles lemonade, 50 cigarettes, 8 boxes of matches, 3 bars of soap, 1 shaving stick, 5 razor blades, 3 magazines, and lastly 4 handkerchiefs, all for £3 14s 2d. Dennis continues:

'Most of the NAAFI issue was used in our barter system with the locals. Pay parade was always before breakfast, and one thing we always did was to empty our water bottles into a knocked off Jerry petrol can. We saved what water we could so we could have a bath once a week if we were lucky. We had two pints of water, chlorinated, a day. Breakfast would be something awful, corned beef dipped in batter and fried in margarine, reconstituted dried egg, a few baked beans and slice of bread, most importantly a mug of tea 9/10 sugar. If we were lucky, we had bacon: but it was cut so thin it could barely come off the greased paper, so we had bits of bacon and paper served up with scrambled eggs which were more like eating sponge rubber with a hint of egg flavour than what we considered scrambled eggs. We loathed the dried eggs and milk powder. Its what drove us to do our "egg runs."

'Most evenings, if we did not spend it in the mess, was spent at the "Padre Club". It was an escape from reading, playing cards and smoking. In our mess we had a radio, knocked off from God knows where, probably from Foggia like the chairs, on which we could listen to Glenn Miller, AFN Naples and the such. We managed to get hold of a gramophone for the mess. At the club, we could meet with chums from other sections, drink tea, eat buns which were little better than the stale things the NAAFI served us, play draughts, chess. It afforded some normality. Christopher Lee was largely responsible for this effort. He obtained a cine projector, which he powered off a

15cwt truck battery, as well as a few cans of film off the yanks and a table cloth and we had our own cinema. If we were on 60-minute standby waiting for instructions, you were tense all day. You could not relax: you lost the day. You couldn't settle to read, wash kit, mend kit, always on edge. Some of the South African lads turned in a big way to booze. Having our own place to go to was much needed. I wonder if he remembers? Nearly all the pilots in 260 smoked pipes rather than the fags we were issued.

'An intermittent luxury was mobile bath units: it meant we could get a hot shower rather than having to do the best we could.

'The Aussies in 3 Squadron always seemed to have a game of soft ball most evenings, or cricket. We had a cricket team, and spent hours playing cards, dominoes, whist, you name it. We had inter-squadron cricket and soccer teams, and between pilots and ground crew. It stopped us going off our rocker. Anything to forget that our number could be up on the next trip.'

Pilot Officer Gordon Brown was appreciative of Gus and Mervyns far from legitimate business operation:

'Food was mainly of the dried type – powdered egg, milk, even dried meat, plus tins of all kinds. The squadron used to organise "yaffle runs" consisting of two pilots, a driver and a cook. Latterly we had an Italian civilian cook who also helped with the language problem. We used to barter some of our stores for fresh food. The locals were desperate for salt, tins of sardines and the odd gallon of petrol for their tractors; also, cigarettes. We obtained a beautiful goose, a calf, eggs, potatoes, vegetables etc. One of the finest meals I had at this period was a brew up on a petrol fire consisting of tins of M and V and baked beans all mixed together.'

Quite how Dennis and Mervyn got a calf back to the squadron in a 15cwt lorry is lost to history. However, adhoc farming was well within 260's tradition. The obvious question is, how did no one notice the calf? Saying that 260 smuggled a pig from North Africa to Malta and on to Sicily, so anything was possible really!

It was not all fun and games though. At Yesi, Dennis remembers:

'I watched one of 112 's planes fall away on coming in to land, the engine cut and it dived straight into a petrol bowser which was refuelling a pair of Marauders. It exploded almost instantly. It transpired in the report afterwards, that a nut had found its way into the petrol feed pipe, and the carburettor was chocked of fuel.

The Mustang had a Bendix Stromberg carburettor, which was fully pressurized and Diaphragm operated with four main chambers. From 350ft he tried to regain the runway but his engine cut. He was extricated from the wreckage but died a few hours later in No.1 Canadian General Hospital.'

Sergeant Pountain remembers that the ground crews became very efficient in servicing the aircraft, but it could be murderously hardly work. He remember 'on famous day 260 Squadron flew ten, twelve aircraft sorties. That's a total of one hundred and twenty aircraft sorties. Two bombs per aircraft. So, on that day 260 Squadron armourers loaded TWO HUNDRED AND FORTY 1000lb bombs. In addition, they re-armed their aircraft TEN times. That is a very hard days work indeed.'

It was not just the pilots who engaged in supplementing their rations, as Pountain explains:

'We lived rather well in Italy, however, the Sgts mess, all ground crew of course, decided to pay a subscription for extra messing. I think we paid one pound per month each. Despite the shortage of food in the towns, there was plenty of food in the countryside. [...] We soon learned that the Italian farmers would not even consider the Lira notes issued by Allied authorities. So, we paid the money into the mess and purchased goods for barter [...] we exchanged these goodies for fresh eggs, dressed chickens, hams and joints of pork. Bartering for a fine ham with Persil, soap, candles and cigarettes was a pretty difficult job. Italian farmers, or, more correctly, Italian farmers wives, were very skilful at the bartering game.'

We are left to wonder just how many men 260 Squadron sent out on a daily or weekly basis on 'egg runs'? Clearly Dennis and Merve were not unique on the squadron, and I dare say other squadrons did the same. With millions starving and displaced across Italy by summer 1944, one feels the bartering may have brought some luxury to the farmers and their families.

15

FLAK HAPPY

SQUADRON LEADER JOHNS led A Flight up at 0745 on 21 August to attack a target at Lake Comacchio. Red Section was detailed to attack a bridge.

Dennis was flying as Black 1, Mervyn Talbot was Black 2 as part of an armed attack on a rail bridge in the Bologna area. The bridge was not destroyed, but the railway lines were cut. Two bombs made direct hits on the south approach to the bridge, one bomb overshot and destroyed a house in the town flanking the bridge. No strafing run was carried out as following a recce at 2,000ft no targets were seen. Whilst heading to the target, and over the target, a barrage of intense 20mm and 88mm ack-ack was encountered. Johns led Blue Section to Venice Lagoon where an 'F' Boat 'was well and truly clobbered and a 500' steamer severely damaged' reports 239 Wing Operations Record Book. An 'F' boat was a German specialised landing craft, which was heavily armed with anti-aircraft guns which included 88mm, 37mm and 20mm four-barrelled flak guns. All landed at 0955.

The following day, Dennis, as an experienced pilot on the squadron, was asked to air test the Mustang Mk II. He noted it could make 350mph in straight and level flight at 10,000ft flat out, with the blower at 16,000. The Mk II, rather than having the excellent Merlin, had a new Allison V-1710-81, and was armed with only four .50 guns in the wings rather than six. The new Allison, in theory, resolved some of the issues with the previous engine in power drop off and lack of boost. Despite the best efforts of the 'boffins' Dennis considered it 'a step backwards' and opined that 'I feared they were going to give us those bloody awful Kittyhawks again due to shortages of spares for the Mk 3.'

The conversation again stalled. Dennis refilled his pipe. I interjected, 'You mentioned that you were wounded?' He puts a hand in his right hip pocket of his jacket and brings out a handful of shrapnel and a complete 20mm cannon round:

> 'This is what the dug out of my arm and shoulder. We were on a sortie to bomb a position north-east of Bologna on a stretch of road that was entrenched with heavy German guns. I felt the aircraft being hit and buffeted around by flak. There was a big bang under the engine, and I climbed away quickly. Another huge bang... splinters

from a 20mm cannon exploded through the armour plate behind my seat and carried on through my shoulder, taking out the front of the canopy and instrument panel. More shrapnel bounced around the cockpit [Dennis goes silent at this point] I remember waking up in hospital and being told I'd be all right. They sent a telegram to my mam saying I'd been wounded; she was convinced I was dead.'

The squadron diary tells us that on 23 August Squadron Leader Johns took off at 1815 with a flight of six Mustangs, flying to Bologna at 7500ft. The target was a group of three motor transports. Encountering heavy 88mm flak and ground fire from machine guns, as well as 40mm and 20mm anti-aircraft fire, Mustang FB292 HS-H was hit, with control surfaces compromised. Shrapnel had entered Dennis's left arm and shoulder. Still able to fly, the squadron log prepared by Pilot Officer Lee tells us, Dennis managed to drop his bombs, and he was escorted back to by Flight Sergeant Corcoran in Mustang FB295. Severely wounded, Dennis was taken to hospital by ambulance to 22nd Field Hospital and thence 51st General Hospital. Dennis, in his logbook, describes his wound as CAT II, like that of his Mustang, serious but repairable.

Dennis was 'patched up' at 51st General and was released on 12 September with instructions for six weeks complete rest. He flew down to Capo de Chino the same day and was sent to RAF Convalescent Home Sorrento, arriving that evening. This was a specialist fifty-two bed hospital for treating psycho neurosis with tranquilisers and sleep.

The human *psyche* can only tolerate a certain degree of stress and anxiety until something snaps. When this happens, it is called a *psychosis*. The stress of flying day after day through skies black with flak was too much for those suffering from PTSD – whether officers or enlisted men, especially pilots and other aircrew recovering from serious injury. Flashbacks reliving the trauma were frequently reported. Regrettably compared to the USAAF as Dr Mark K. Wells has written about, the RAF were slow off the mark to remove stigma to PTSD and combat stress. Indeed, the USAAF had a more rigorous screening programme for pilots than the RAF, which allowed for psychological assessment of the potential pilots. By late 1944, the RAF had caught up to the USAAF in treatment of Combat Related Stress.

The impact of stress on pilots resulted in some airmen complaining of debilitating ailments while flying, including chronic cases of headaches, dizziness, nausea, involuntary shaking or apoxia (altitude sickness). The squadrons medical staff might easily diagnose these common conditions; yet often they had a psychological rather than physical cause. The pilots and bomber crews had their own terms for them. 'Flak happy' was one, as were 'Focke-Wulf jitters,' 'shell shock' and 'battle fatigue.' Ron Cundy remembers in late 1942:

'We had the odd fellow on the squadron from time to time who would get to that point of being pretty scared and would make any excuse to turn back. But there was one fellow I should talk about. A young Canadian came to us and he was sort of…you might even say, wet behind the ears. He looked as though he had just come off his mother's apron strings. He kept very much to himself, and he became a bit of a worry, and by this time I had been promoted and become a flight commander. One morning just before daylight and we were to go out on this daylight dive-bombing mission and he was on. The CO had the map down on the ground and he was explaining to us where we would cross into enemy territory, where we were to bomb and where we were to exit from enemy territory. This young Canadian tried to ask him a question, but he couldn't get the words out. I noticed that his hands were shaking and his knees were shaking. When the briefing was over, he walked around behind the operations tent and I followed him and there he was throwing his heart up. I said, "I'll pull you off. You're not feeling well. I'll pull you off. I'll get somebody to take your place." And he said, "Please don't do that." So, he went with us.

'He participated just as strongly as any of us and was right into it. But it was very obvious that his nerves were shot, but he wouldn't give in. He just would not. Anyhow, to cut a long story short we had to post him off the squadron because we felt it could affect the morale of the other pilots…I think perhaps he was the bravest man I ever met.'

A number of pilots developed phantom mechanical problems with their airplanes to avoid flak and combat. A new pilot with 112 Squadron, on his first operation, when coming under 88mm fire, dropped out of formation and landed at Capo di Chini airport in Naples, as veteran pilot with 112, Bert Horden, remembers:

'This turned out to be our new boy who said his engine was running rough […] he seemed very nervous so I told him to wait while I checked the engine of his Kitty. The engine ran up all right on the ground so I took it for a test flight […] I had a long talk with our new boy and eventually he broke down in tears admitting that he was just plain scared. I told him I was too. I sent him back to Cutella in his Kitty while I got a lift back in a B-17 […] The CO posted him away immediately as suffering from LMF (Lacking Moral Fibre – ed).'

Even experienced pilots could 'go to pieces.' Battle of Britain pilot Kenneth 'Hawkeye' Lee, who joined 260 Squadron in summer 1942 from a tour of operations in the battle and then a second tour with 112 Squadron before joining 260, was not a well man as Shep Sheppard remembers:

'I believe Hawkeye was already tour expired when he joined 260 Squadron and he eventually went "round the bend". He had a chicken, or so he thought, on his shoulder which he took everywhere. It was really sad to watch him, and he should have been taken off "ops" which indeed he was shortly afterwards.'

Bobby Gibbes, Commanding Officer of 3 Squadron (RAAF) concisely described his innermost fears about operations, the proximity of death faced day-in and day-out. He writes that following an operation:

'You then collect the remnants of your squadron, count them hastily, then the fires burning below. The feeling is a strange one. Some of those fires down below contain the mutilated bodies of your friends, but as you look down, you have no real feeling other than, I hate to confess, probably terrific relief that it is them and not you. It must be the animal in us really, I suppose, and the strong spirit of self-survival which has become uppermost. Man becomes animal when he thinks he is about to die.

'As you fly back to your base, now safe at last, a feeling of light-hearted exuberance comes over you. It is wonderful to still be alive and it is, I think, merely the after-effect of violent, terrible fear. I am not afraid to confess to being frightened. I was almost always terrified. On landing back, you look for your squadron aeroplanes at the dispersal sites, and if your friends' aeroplanes are there, your heart fills with gladness for you have become a caring human being again.

'Then, there is the anxious wait for other aircraft. Sometimes, after you have given up all hope, an aircraft comes into the circuit area. You look eagerly for its identifying letters, hoping against hope that it is one of the missing, returning. If it is, you feel terrific gladness and relief. Then again, you might wait for days to learn the fate of missing people. Sometimes they have been taken prisoner, sometimes word comes through that they were killed. If you had seen the aircraft go down, you have a good idea as to its fate, but you can never be certain.'

Facing such emotional strain, is it little wonder some pilots were unable to cope? Recognized today as post-traumatic stress disorder or PTSD, during the Second World War, some made light of the condition or viewed it as a sign of weakness. Mervyn Talbot:

'Flak was our worst enemy, that and ground fire.
'We had no choice, we had to fly through flak.

'We could not get above it due to the payload: but never out of reach of the 88s. Often we had Spits over the top for air defence from German fighters, whilst we plugged along at 10,000ft or less. Sometimes the Spits above us were hit by 88s. Coming into bomb, we had to keep on target, which made us vulnerable to mobile 20mm anti-aircraft in the back of a lorry or from ground fire from German troops. It was scary because you knew the flak was there and you knew you had to fly through it. And the Germans knew we were going to fly through it, too. The Germans knew we weren't going to change air speed, especially if we had started the bombing run, you just had to fly through it. I think we would all have rather taken our chances as fighter pilots rather than fly into flak day after day. My aircraft was damaged by anti-aircraft fire twice in two days, which necessitated repair. Dennis was our first casualty for a while. At the mess all you had was an empty chair, out of sight out of mind…you quickly forgot. Dennis was the only pilot who got back after being intercepted by flak… It was a real reminder of the damage flak could do not just to our kite, but to us physically and no one really thought of being wounded, losing an arm or a leg. It was easier to cope with an empty chair, out of sight out of mind, than knowing your chum is in a hospital bed. It reminded us that the clock ticking to our doom was still ticking and tough luck chum, your alarm may sound tomorrow. It was easier if pilots were reported missing. That gave us hope they were alive. Seeing friends blown to bits when their kite was demolished by flak unnerved us. Better to go west than be maimed in body and mind. We were all under intense mental strain. It was easier if men were reported missing: their beds were cleared away, and that was if, as if they had never been with us. Being wounded was a physical reminder of what could happen,

'We got listless. We either went up on pre-ordered armed recce's, at any point we could be radioed to a target, or we would be sitting in our chairs trying not to think, mending kit and we would be told to scramble and head to a certain grid ref to take out an obstacle for the infantry.'

'Not long after we lost Dennis, at the end of August Sergeant McGarry was strafing a train. He was low, 500ft straight and level with his guns going. He made an easy target for ground fire. He just disappeared in a flash: the lads on the same run said the flak was bad, 20mm stuff that was deadly accurate. He never bailed out. The kite just went into the deck in a ball of flame. I guess his tank was hit, and wallop.'

Sergeant Constantine McGarry, died on 30 August 1944, aged twenty. He was a native of Abbots Langley, Hertfordshire, and forever lies at Bologna War Cemetery.

Many pilots claimed it could not happen to them and referred derisively to the rest homes where exhausted aircrews were sent for time away from the battle as 'flak houses.' In Italy, Aircrew Rest Camps and Houses were available, which gave the pilots time away from the stress of flying. Aware of the psychological impact of trauma and stress, the RAF created what were termed Convalescent Homes, where inmates received rudimentary treatment for PSTD.

CHAPTER
16

OPERATION OLIVE

ANYONE WHO HAS ever been to Italy or seen a map will know that Italian rivers run to the sea from the central mountain spine; this meant that the Allies, as they moved up the country from the south, found that each river had a ridge behind it, while behind that ridge lurked another river. Superior Allied air power put pressure on German lines of communication as the advance slowly progressed, but German skill at moving troops by night and repairing damaged roads, railways and bridges meant that this was never decisive. A stalemate of sorts had been reached.

Since Kesselring had been forced back from the Arno line, the Allies had to formulate a new strategy to take on the Gothic Line, this became known as Operation Olive. The plan called for the Eighth Army to attack up the Adriatic coast toward Pesaro and Rimini and draw in the German reserves from the centre of the country. Clark's Fifth Army would then attack in the weakened central Apennines north of Florence toward Bologna with British XIII Corps on the right wing of the attack fanning toward the coast to create a pincer with the Eighth Army advance. This meant that, as a preparatory move, the bulk of the Eighth Army had to be transferred from the centre of Italy to the Adriatic coast, taking two valuable weeks.

For Mervyn Talbot, despite the loss of a cherished friend, it was 'back to the day job', there was no time for sentimentality. On 24 August, his steed was Mustang FB246. He was airborne at 1100, the flight of six planes led by Flight Sergeant Daveine, the target was a railway bridge. Despite very bad weather, all twelve 1,000lb bombs were dropped, one making a direct hit on the target.

The British Eighth Army crossed the Metauro river and launched its attack against the Gothic Line outposts the following day. As Polish II Corps on the coast, and I Canadian Corps on the coastal plain on the Poles' left advanced towards Pesaro, the coastal plain narrowed and it was planned that the Polish Corps, weakened by losses and lack of replacements, would go into Army reserve and the front on the coastal plain would become the responsibility of the Canadian Corps alone. The day the battle began, Prime Minister Winston Churchill paid 239 Wing a visit at Iesi. Preventing German troop movements was the principal activity of the squadron over the coming days.

By 30 August, the Canadian and British Corps had reached the main German defensive positions running along the ridges on the far side of the Foglia river. The Battle of Gemmano took place between 4 and 15 September 1944. The battle occurred in the area of the Gothic Line, near the Apennine Mountains in northern Italy, which would soon turn out to be the last line of defence for the Axis Powers in Italy. The village of Gemmano was eventually captured on 9 September 1944, and became known as the Cassino of the Adriatic. As a part of this action, 260 Squadron bombed the village of Monteuro on 1 September, demolishing houses and the church, which had become a strong point and German Observation Post early in the morning. The bombing run was immediately in advance of Allied infantry taking position in the southern part of the village, 260 Squadron, with 3 Squadron in support, were then radioed to bomb the northern part, the German defenders then being driven out.

As well as operating with the infantry, 260 Squadron was also taking out German artillery. Mervyn had been airborne at 0825, the flight of six being led by Flight Sergeant Davoine, on an armed attack against a previously identified German strong point. The target was a group of ten gun pits which had been recently evacuated. The target was bombed to prevent its future use, and the flight landed at 0925. Mervyn was in the air again at 1345, Davoine again in the lead on a Cab Rank patrol. The target was a crossroads, the flight then strafed two motor cycles with side cars, destroying both and killing the five occupants. The wing Operations Record Book reports:

> From a Lt Col in a Forward Observation post. 1 Sept. 1944.
> 'I watched the bombing today; the accuracy was quite unbelievable. The casualties and damage caused was devastating.'

> From the Brigadier, General Staff, Eighth Army: 'The Army is thoroughly grateful and has tremendous confidence in the bombing.'

239 Wing and 260 Squadron, were carving out an enviable reputation for its close support operations for the Army, as it tenaciously moved slowly and surely forward ever more into north Italy: advances were counted in meters and not miles, but glacier like, was unstoppable.

Amidst the carnage, the squadron diary tells us on 1 September that a rest house was established at Senegallia, where two senior NCO's and eight airmen were to be allowed forty-eight hours flak leave. A cook, junior NCO and two labourers were sent to oversee the house 'and to give every comfort possible to the men who would be sent down every forty-eight hours.' The house was located close to the beach, allowing the men to swim. Nearby was an Army canteen. Pilots now – in theory – did a shift of forty-eight hours on, and forty-eight hours off. The Wing lost three pilots on 2 September: Lieutenant Dickson of 5 Squadron (SAAF), Sergeant Greenaway 112 Squadron and Sergeant Docherty of 250 Squadron.

Both Brown and Talbot were sent after gun positions on 3 September, despite heavy rain, and knocked out two pillboxes. On 4 September a bridge was the target: on both operations intense 40mm and 20mm flak and ground fire was encountered. In thanks for the support given by the Wing to the Army, the following dispatch was received:

> The support given by DAF in the last three day's operations has been invaluable. Please convey my sincerest thanks to all concerned on behalf of the First Canadian Corps. Major General Vokes, Commanding First Canadian Division, in particular forwards warmest congratulations.

On the following day, 239 Operations Record Book reports:

> 260 Squadron (F/Lt Bagshawe and Capt R.T. Rogers) did an outstandingly successful recce in the UDINE area reported Wing Operations Record Book. The outcome of the recce was 'damaging 12 aircraft on RIVOLTO and VILLAORBO LGs, completely destroying a locomotive and 20 plus oil tankers, damaging another locomotive and probably destroying a 120/150' MV.

Mervyn and Brown were airborne on 6 September at 1020 to target shipping in the Adriatic, the flight of twelve, all of A flights available pilots and machines, led by Squadron Leader Johns. The Germans threw up 88mm flak and small arms fire, the squadron leader's Mustang being damaged by 20mm fire, but still operable. Four strafing runs followed against the marshalling yard adjacent to the harbour. With 0.50cal guns hammering the Mustangs swooped over the target out of low cloud, several motor transports were destroyed, one steam engine erupted in a sheet of steam. All landed safe at 1300. The 'bag' for the Wing that day included five locomotives destroyed and one badly damaged, as well as nine light tanks, an ME 109, four JU 87, one FW 190 and three Italian aircraft damaged on the ground.

The squadron dairy reports a request was made for volunteers to form a concert party in the wake of a successful Wing concert given by a 24-piece orchestra. The orchestra was provided by the New Zealand Concert Party at 450 Squadron, to which 260 Squadron had been invited. One feels there was some inter squadron rivalry going on.

The Gothic line was the target for 7 September, and Venice was the target for the following day. The commander of 239 Wing, Group Captain Eaton, led twelve Mustangs into the air at 0635. The objective was to destroy ammunition dumps. Flying at 9,000ft the flight headed to Lake Morano, the flight turned to head north-east. The ammunition dump was a series of twenty or more concrete sheds with blast walls around them. The Mustangs were directed on the bombing run, one of which was Meryn Talbot aboard FB946. Five bombs made direct hits destroying two sheds. The two remaining pilots were detailed to bomb a nearby ball bearing factory. Two bombs failed to explode, but the two that did devastated two factory buildings. Group Captain Eaton directed Red Section to strafe a train with six wagons: the engine exploded in a cloud of steam. The railway lines were destroyed. Blue Section had turned away to Campo Formido Landing Ground at Udine, catching the Luftwaffe on the ground. The Mustangs zoomed down from 6,000ft to 1,000ft or less, guns hammering: three FW190s and a JU87 were damaged. Two more JU87 were observed at dispersal and again strafed, along with a JU 52. The raiders were not going to be allowed to get away unscathed by the Germans: 88mm flak damaged FB288 flown by Sergeant T. Fergusson, and with an escort provided by Flight Lieutenant Bishop, left the fight and headed back to Jesi.

One of the attacked JU 87s was a wooden mock up: the Germans used decoys to draw the RAF to bomb phantom landing grounds, in the hope that the real thing would be left unscathed. On turning back to base, a train of one locomotive and ten plus wagons was strafed, again the engine exploded in sheets of scalding steam and flying shrapnel as the boiler and firebox distributed its remains across the landscape. All the time, 40mm and 20mm anti-aircraft fire came up, not one pilot was hit. The operation had achieved its objective: the Luftwaffe had been caught 'with their pants down' and four airplanes were damaged, four steam engines had been destroyed, railway lines cut and the ammunition dump damaged.

Once back, the squadron diary tells us the airmen had the opportunity to attend a South African Airforce concert party or a repeat screening of the film '*Mr Lucky.*'

Venice was again the target on 10 September, with twenty-one Mustangs going out in two flights, the first of ten was led by Flight Lieutenant Bagshawe, airborne at 0620, the second led by Captain R.T. Rogers, heading out at 1230. Mervyn was flying FB948 in this second wave of ground attack. The Germans were expecting them this time and threw up intense 88mm flak. The target was a marshalling yard, holding forty wagons, which was bombed from west to east. Four bombs overshot, one hit a fuel tanker which exploded with a blinding flash and a plume of black smoke. The bombing run claimed five wagons destroyed. Three strafing runs shot up the area, claiming a motor transport. Smoke was still seen rising from the mornings attack at the neighbouring marshalling yard: the bombs fell into the station area, destroying the locomotive and detonating the fuel tankers, which demolished the station buildings 'the whole yard was enveloped with flames, smoke rising to 3,000ft' reported the squadron log entry. The ten Mustangs then turned to again attack Campo Formido Landing Ground. Again, the Luftwaffe were caught on the ground. The Mustangs dropped down from 6,000ft the 0.50cal guns hammering. Six ME 109 under camouflage netting were shot up and rendered unserviceable: 260 Squadron 'bagged' eight 109's that day as damaged. On the way back to base, a Kubel wagon was strafed, its occupants killed and the vehicle destroyed. Another target of opportunity, a barge in the neighbouring canal, shot to pieces. As the ten

Mustangs headed home, a cloud of smoke half a mile long hung over the railway station, 'the whole station appearing to be on fire.' Mervyn landed at 1500hrs. 239 Wing Operations Record Book reports:

> 260 Squadron, in an early morning mission created havoc in CASARSA M.Yards. Three large fires were started among the goods trucks, later merged into one terrific blazer with oily black smoke to 5000' stretching a distance of one to two miles. (six hours later this cloud of oily black smoke lay like a cloud 20 miles long and 20-40 miles from the target where it had been blown by the N.W. wind) On the same mission, 260 Squadron had good results strafing M/T on the ground.

'No rest for the wicked' was true of 260 Squadron in those hectic September days. During the evening of 12 September, the following message was received from Air Officer Commanding DAF:

> Congratulate all squadrons in spending effort they are making and in the accuracy of their bombing. Much depends on 239 Wing and it is living up to its reputation.

Airborne on 13 September at 1000hrs, Mervyn was a on a Cab Rank patrol led by Pilot Officer A.L. Davoine. Rover Control ordered them to attack a series of German trenches, followed by a strafing run. The following day was another Cab Rank patrol. In the air at 1445 the targets were German pillboxes in the Gothic Line. The following message was sent by V Army to Wing Headquarters 'forward troops report your morning Cab Ranks wonderful.' The squadron diary reports that a second call for performers for the 260 Squadron concert party was made, the Padre Club was showing the film *Demi-Paradise*; moreover, the football team, fresh from facing 14th Light Ack-Ack, were to play 5 South African Airforce Squadron. The squadron had flown forty-two sorties that day in support of Eighth Army, reporting direct hits on gun pits.

The German landing ground at Aviano was attacked on 15 September. Five SM79s were caught in the open in front of the hangers and damaged. Climbing to gain height again, half mile north-east of the runway, Red Leader observed a dispersed group of German aircraft under trees, some in pens being refuelled. Ordering a strafing run, the six Mustangs came in at 500ft, the 0.50cal guns hammering, destroying a JU87 and a JU52, both of which exploded into flames. 239 Wing recorded:

> Today's efforts were mostly directed against strongpoints, gun positions etc., but there were two successful armed recces, including an outstanding one by 260 Squadron. F/LT Bagshawe led this with

F/O E.M. Hollinshead leading top section when they split up over VENICE lagoon. Red Section attended to rolling stock, shipping and aircrafts at AVIANO LG while, Blue Section attended exclusively to the railway.

Tragedy once more struck 260 Squadron, on 16 September. Taking off at 0630, Captain 'Roy' Rogers led a flight of six on an armed recce of Bolonga-Ostiglia-Ferrar sector. Once over target heavy flak claimed the life of Sergeant Hughes. The Germans had concealed their anti-aircraft guns in hay stacks, one such gun opening fire when Hughes was at 200ft, so almost point-blank range. The 20mm shells crippled Mustang FB287 during Hughes second strafing run. The 20mm cannon shells ripped apart the engine: billowing white smoke told its own story of a glycol fire. Rogers radioed Hughes to gain height to evade the flak and anti-aircraft fire. Whilst gaining height, Hughes was ordered back to base, escorted by Rogers, intense ack-ack meant Rogers could not accompany Hughes as he had to take evasive action of his own, or be shot down. Hughes and his burning Mustang were never seen again. He was reported missing, presumed killed.

The flight landed at 0830 one man short. Mervyn Talbot would learn of this on landing from his own operation at 0900. He had been in the air at 0730 on an armed attack against a German strongpoint comprising three buildings that had been converted into block houses. Forced to fly at 3,000ft, below the thick cloud base, a bombing run was made, all bombs were dropped on target with no observable results. On operation again at 1205, Mervyn's flight, led by Flying Officer Doug England, was directed against German gun emplacements. Douglas Walter Charles England was on his second tour with 260 Squadron and was awarded the DFC in February 1945, by then promoted to Flight Lieutenant. He had served with 260 From June 1942 to March 1943 as a flight sergeant, claiming two 109's shot down in December 1942. About operations, Mervyn remembers:

'By September we were all getting tired. The main targets became enemy transports moving up to the front. These targets were often heavily defended by light flak, which, although it was no stranger to us, was now seen in much greater concentrations than previously experienced. Because the small calibre weapons had a high rate of fire, the guns were often mounted as multiple units, and as we were attacking down to very low-levels, the odds of being hit were quite high. Worse, was when the guns were concealed in ruined houses, shooting through windows, or concealed in hay ricks. When these guns were stationary, we could see the crews, so we knew we were in for a rough time. Concealment was a real blow for us mentally.

'There was also another psychological factor which came into play since most of these guns used tracer ammunition. It was rather unnerving to be diving at a target from which streams of red or white ping pong balls were floating up at you, seemingly right at you. Usually, these would arc down before reaching you, having been fired out of range. Other times they would have the range but not the line and the pyrotechnics would sail by on either side. Not very comforting, knowing that just one of those things hitting your Achilles heel, the radiator, or fuel tank and your flying days would be over. By now, Sorento seemed a lifetime ago.

'As we were based along the Po, we were now plagued by Mosquitos and were given instructions to take precautions against Malaria. Mepacrine tablets and jabs were administered. We had to wear trousers and long sleeves morning and evening and concoct a degree of Mosquito netting around our beds. We were all shown a film on the danger of SDT's. We watched in good humour with a lot of barracking of "hard luck son" when some of the images came on screen with their prick swollen the size of a marrow or covered in sores. It was meant to be serious, but all a little too late.

'By now, the Germans knew they had lost. Paris had been taken in mid-August; I have a clipping from the *Union Jack* which gives the details. Whoever was running their war seemed intent on letting Italy and Germany be totally ground into the dust before giving in. It meant the slogging match carried on. We were all pretty browned off with this unending merry-go-round.'

On 17 September, the operations were centred on destroying two German block houses connected by a communication trench. The Wing Operations Record Book tells us that the Wing was employed 'softening up' a strongly held position at Fortunato, which was blocking the Allied advance on Rimini. Defended houses, trench systems and gun pits were all attacked. Gun positions were also attacked later that day, led by Roy Rogers, knocking out anti-aircraft batteries at Rimini Landing Ground. The squadron diary tells us Yesi Opera House was showing the film "*Eye on Leave*" and at the Cinema "*Northern Pursuit*." All ranks were cautioned of eating ice-cream: it was the reported cause of an outbreak of dysentery. 239 Wing Operations Record Book reports that on 18 September:

Twenty-seven missions, all of them close support on the Adriatic sector today flown by four squadrons. The first six were to attack enemy positions on the SAN FORTUNATO ridge […] 260 Squadron reported hits on trench systems and target houses […] the remaining missions were 'Cab Ranks' when opportunity targets of mortars, anti-tank guns and artillery positions and strongpoints were given […] 260 Squadron reported our troops cheering as a/c flew over to attack and scored direct hits on trench systems in front of them. 260 Squadron reported explosions followed by fire and black smoke from defended positions attacked.

Operation Timothy

With Kesselring now occupying the Gothic Line, as the Eighth Army edged towards Rimini, it was held up at the Fortunata Ridge. DAF was requested to fly close support as aerial artillery. Operation Timothy began at 1000hrs on 19 September, with 239 and 244 Wings beginning a 40-minute aerial blitz on the German lines. A bomb line was dropped by artillery, leaving white blobs of white smoke for the pilots to bomb onto in front of the forward troops of the Eighth Army. The bomb line crept forward every fifteen minutes, the attacking DAF being co-ordinated by Rover David. 244 Wing strafed the forward positions whilst 239 Wing dropped fragmentation bombs on enemy gun positions on the rear slope.

The morning that Operation Timothy began; Pilot Officer Brown was promoted to Flight Lieutenant. Five operations were flown that day, and the same number on the following day, but cloud prevented any operational flying on 21 September. During 22 September an Armed Recco of the battle area was conducted, with bridges, strong houses and any German transport attacked. German trenches were also bombed and strafed, with pilots flying along the German lines shooting up anything that moved. Twelve Mustangs attacked a marshalling yard in Treviso. Six steam locomotives were destroyed and twelve damaged. In the town itself, two staff cars and a bus were destroyed along with two lorries. Ground fire damaged two Mustangs CAT II. No. 260 Squadron also demolished the bridge over the Reno River; in the first attack, three bombs blew large craters in the bridge, on the second attack the entire centre span was destroyed.

Squadron Leader Johns left 260 on leave, Captain R.T. Rogers taking up command.

The following day was 'more of the same.' Treviso was again the target. Over 200 railway wagons and box cars and fifteen steam locomotives were bombed and strafed. 239 Wing Operations Record Book reports:

> Today's play opened with an armed recce by 12 Mustangs of 260 Squadron, led by Group Captain B.A. Eaton DSC DFC. Rolling stock on the TREVISIO-PADOVA railway was the main objective, pilots knocking up a tidy score of:
>
> 2 locomotives destroyed. 2 locomotives probably destroyed.
> 2 locomotives damaged. 2 rail trucks destroyed.
> And many trucks damaged.

A level crossing, railway lines and gun positions were the targets for 24 September, 239 Wing recording: '260 Squadron report cuts in rail tracks at two of the targets, but armed recces were in all cases disappointing, little or no movement seen.' At the close of the day, the following dispatch was sent to 260 from General Lease commanding the Eighth Army:

> 'Please convey to all ranks of DAF the gratitude and appreciation of the 8th Army for their magnificent support throughout our recent operations. The relentless pressures exerted by DAF on enemy defences, gun positions and communications has powerfully aided us in every phase of our advance. Our forward troops have entire confidence in the accuracy of the close support bombing and expressed their greatest admiration for the dash and gallantry of your pilots. In the more open fighting now ahead I know that you and your forces will seize every opportunity to harass the enemy and batter his columns. My thanks and best wishes to all.'

This was echoed by the commander of the 1st Canadian Infantry Division:

> 'I would like to express my appreciation and that of all ranks of the 1st Canadian Infantry Division on the excellent support again provided for us by DAF during recent shows. Any request for support was quickly and effectively provided. The help of the DAF was a large factor in allowing us to reach our objective.'

Operations were not yet over. The same day as the thanks was received, Mervyn was in the autumnal Italian skies at 0720. The flight of six was led by Flight Lieutenant Lowell. Flying to target at 8,000ft, the target was against a level crossing near Ravenna. Bombing at 500ft, the flight came under 88mm and 20mm fire, scoring six very near misses on the railway, four bombs destroyed the flanking road. Turning south, the flight headed along the road strafing a staff car and blowing up a motor transport. Landing at 0910, Mervyn was back up at 1150, an armed attack against concealed German artillery. Lowell led the flight with Flying Officer Brown as his No. 2. Three concealed German guns were bombed, and then despite intense 20mm anti-aircraft fire, the flight zoomed down to deck level to shoot the place up. No claims were made.

The 'Angel of Death' struck 260 Squadron once more on 25 September. Pilot Officer Lowell led six Mustangs into the air at 1400hrs, Mervyn was aboard FB948, with Gordon Brown as his No. 2. Climbing to 9,000ft, the flight headed out to sea, swinging north towards the target, a road bridge at St Carlo. All bombs fell on target, cratering the road, but leaving the bridge standing. Searching for targets to strafe, Lowel was hit by 40mm anti-aircraft fire, so too Sergeant Barnes. Escorted by

Lieutenant Cunliffe, Barnes headed back to base, his Mustang streaming petrol and glycol. Flames soon blossomed from the stricken aircraft and Barnes bailed out, parachuting into the sea. Cunliffe radioed in Barnes' position and reported Barnes had climbed safely onboard his inflatable rescue dinghy. Sadly, Air-Sea Rescue failed to find the dinghy, and it was reported on 12 December that his body was washed ashore on 29 September at Mondolfa Marota and buried under special license. Sergeant Ronald Hanson Barnes was from Colwyn Bay in North Wales. He was just 21-years-old when died. He lies in Ancona War Cemetery.

Despite Barnes' death, and the known risks of attacking the same target twice, on the same day, the bridge had to be destroyed. 239 Wing reports:

> 260 Squadron, led by F/O D.W. England, blew 100' out of the ST CARLO road bridge (confirmed by photo). Later in the day, the same squadron led by F/O E.M. Hollinshead knocked out a 30' gap in the MONTEGELLI road bridge.

Away from the stress of flying, pilots from 239 Wing could attend the Padre Club cinema which was showing '*Mutiny on the Bounty*' for the second time, or visit the Opera House at Jesi showing '*Stars in battle dress.*' Alternatively, pilots and ground crew could attend Iesi cinema which was showing '*Navy Blues*' starring Ann Sheridan and Martha Raye; these films offered a break from the routine of combat operations and a chance of the normality of home life: but having experience the horror of war, none of the men in 260 Squadron or any who served in the Second World War would ever be the same again.

Talbot and Brown were airborne at 0800 on 26 September; the objective was suspected German gun pits. After bombing the position with no observable results, the flight turned to strafe anything that could be found: halftracks and lorries were attacked, but no claims were made. A goods train was the next target which was again shot up, but no claims made despite 88mm flak. Landing at 1000, Talbot and Brown were again flying to a new target at 1145, again led by Lowell. A German block house was bombed and, again, anything that moved was strafed. All returned safe and sound at 1306, the pair were ordered back into the air fifteen minutes later, climbing into recently prepared Mustangs. The attack was against a reported tank concentration. No tanks were observed, but the target was bombed.

Mervyn was on the ground throughout the twenty-seventh, whilst Brown went on two operations destroying steam engines and wagons in a marshalling yard at Corvignano. The target had been bombed earlier that day by 112 Squadron, who claimed nineteen steam engines destroyed. 260 Squadron claimed two engines destroyed and one damaged, four railway wagons, two rail born ammunition wagons destroyed, plus one lorry and a halftrack damaged. No operational flying was conducted on 28-29 September: the heavy rain and low cloud allowed the pilots the first rest period that month.

During this down time, Mervyn had completed 195 hours on 28 September. For him, the war was over, as he remembers:

'The policy in fighter squadrons was to consider a tour completed by about 200 hours on operations before being sent off for a rest. By the end of September, I had flown 193 hours, so I began to think about the possibility of surviving and not going down in a sheet of flames or ending up in a hospital bed for weeks on end like Shep and Gus. It was 50/50 to finish a tour: we knew that all too well from bitter experience. Policy on squadron was for the skipper to end a pilot's tour on approaching 200 hours, rather than make them loose concentration, knowing it was their last op. I did my lost two operations on 26 September. As I got back, Johns, our skipper, called me to his office "that's about it Merve. You are now due for a rest" or similar words. The relief flowed through me when I got back to my bivvy. You never showed your excitement and emotion in the mess, as it would be unfair on those who had a lot more to do. So, I packed my things and was sent on my way in the back of a lorry to Naples and comparative safety.'

AUTUMN TO WINTER '44

AS SEPTEMBER CAME to an end, for those on operation flying on 260 Squadron, six 'Rhubarbs' were flown on 30 September, which were remarkably successful. With the Mustang, 260 had the ideal tool for the job. Fast, agile, able to carry a 2,000lb payload, these 'Rhubarbs' allowed the pilots the freedom to operate free from the constraints of Cab Rank. Lieutenant Stone (SAAF) was in the air at 1010: he caught a German train heading north consisting of a locomotive and over thirty flatcars carrying lorries and other vehicles. The steam engine was destroyed and the train strafed five times. It had been partially concealed with tree branches. A lone engine was strafed and destroyed. Stone's Mustang, FB277, was hit twice by ground fire, considered CAT II damaged.

Duke Kent and Pilot Officer Maddison were up at 1015 heading to a marshalling yard at Venice. A steam engine was destroyed at the head of a train consisting of thirty flatcars carrying lorries and halftracks. Two staff cars were also attacked and five anti-aircraft guns. Similar Rhubarbs in pairs were flown by Lovell and Lie, England and Walker, and Cunliffe and Dufton. Cunliffe was hit by flak, a CAT II situation, but he coaxed the Mustang back to Yesi. Pilot Officer Hollinshead was airborne at 1000. He claimed on his Rhubarb, one steam engine destroyed at Mestre, a German motor transport and its soldiers, at Aviano, three ME 109s were caught on the ground, one claimed as damaged. At Campo Formido Landing Ground, eight 109s were caught at dispersal and strafed, four being claimed as destroyed: a remarkable solo operation.

However, during a twelve strong armed recce over Treviso and Venice, Flying Officer Hollinshead and Sergeant Cheeseborough were hit by flak. It was a reminder of the dangers that pilots faced every day. Hollinshead's Mustang was last seen pouring black smoke and loosing height rapidly. It was believed he crash-landed: no explosion was observed. On returning to Yesi, it was Christopher Lee's task to instigate an investigation to determine what had happened. Lee reported Hollinshead missing presumed killed. No investigation was needed for the second casualty of that op. Cheesborough's Mustang was likewise hit by 20mm fire, starting a glycol fire. With white smoke engulfing the Mustang, Cheeseborough coaxed the stricken airplane to 6,000ft, no doubt hoping and praying that the smoke remained white and the petrol in his tanks did not erupt. Bailing out, deploying his parachute, he landed safely and was seen waving to the circling Mustangs and running to a house. He was reported safe, presumed POW.

As Autumn began at Yesi, Flying Officer Brown recalls:

> 'All this time we had lived in tents, but on about 1 October we moved into a villa for winter quarters. We were at Jesi, swimming parties were organized to the nearest Adriatic beach – no swimming costumes, just all boys together.'

Memory is a fickle thing, as the squadron diary says on 8 October the adjutant reported it had been impossible to find billets for the winter, all ranks were to be under canvas. Eventually, by 10 October, pilots were housed in the village of Yesi, ground crew remaining under canvas in an increasingly wet and muddy Autumn. Yesi was also increasingly congested with the arrival of 79th Fighter Group USAAF with fifty-two P-47 Thunderbolts on 4 October. The landing ground also had fifty-two DC-3 as well as 'several fortresses and Liberators.' Given the number of aircraft operating from the base 'flying control had an anxious time' reported 239 Wing Operations Record Book noting: 'On one or two occasions aircraft were hurtling down the runway in opposite directions' but thankfully 'there were no crashes, though at least one Liberator bogged itself' when it came off the end of the runway.

As a break from operations, sometime on 5 October, 260 Squadron played football against lads from 239 Wing headquarters. On 7 October, 260 was sent out 'bridge busting.' Thunderbolts from 79th Group claimed to have destroyed two bridges in the Savio region, however the squadron adjutant pithily recorded:

> Our two sections of 260 Squadron reported that they both appeared undamaged so that the Americans either indulged in wishful thinking or attacked the wrong targets.

260 Squadron duly demolished both. The 239 Wing Operations Record Book commented that bad weather meant no flying on 8 October. During this lull in operations, Sergeant 'Sandy' Street, who had joined 260 with Mervyn, Dennis and Kent, was tour expired and was posted to Naples on 16 October with a commission in General Duties.

The Gothic line had been breached in September: all attention was now focused on capturing Bologna. On 11 October, 123 Martin B-26 Marauder bombers of the 12th Air Force dropped 700 bombs on an ammunition depot located inside the city. Operation Pancake was launched the following day when a massive bomber force mustering 698 B-17, B-24 and B-26 bombers of the 12th and 15th Air Forces, took off from the Foggia airfields to blitz the German lines. They were escorted by 160 Lockheed P-38 Lightning and Republic P-47 Thunderbolt fighters.

The bombers dropped 1,294 tons of bombs on the enemy positions. During 12 October, 3 Squadron (RAAF) and 260 Squadron 'collected a "bag" of seventeen locomotives, two passenger coaches and two rail tankers destroyed, two locos, four rail trucks and one M/T destroyed' reported 239 Wing.

During 13-14 October, the Germans fell back on the River Savio. DAF was again to the fore, and by 15 October 239 Wing had destroyed all the bridges on the Savio. Despite bad weather, DAF claimed fifty-seven steam locomotives, fifty-two boats or barges and another 166 vessels. For most of these operations, 260 Squadron was operating Cab Rank Rover Paddy, hitting strongpoints, bridges, troop movements: anything that moved was to be destroyed. From the middle weeks of October, operations were now focused in the Venice area despite almost continuous rain.

The Operations book for the Wing makes sobering reading about the rapidly worsening weather: torrential mud and rain almost 'stopped play'. On 23 October, the weather was so bad, rather than twelve missions, just one was flown: a long-range armed recce by 260 Squadron, during which a German F Boat was damaged, eight steam locomotives were destroyed and a single motor transport. Squadron Leader Johns held a full squadron meeting in the mess at 1830 at which he thanked the squadron for their hard work despite the bad weather and poor living conditions for most of the personnel, the majority living under canvas. Johns also began planning for the Christmas party.

By the second half of October, it was becoming increasingly clear to Alexander that despite the dogged fighting in the waterlogged plain of Romagna and the mountains of the central Apennines, combined with exhaustion and combat losses increasingly affecting his forces' capabilities, no breakthrough was going to occur before the winter weather returned.

RTU

RTU is short hand for Return to Unit.

On 17 October, Dennis flew from what is now Naples International Airport to a landing ground at Littoria aboard DC3 555. Littoria is South of Rome. According to 239 Wing records this was for a psychological assessment. During 19 October he flew from Rome to Ancona as a passenger with Mediterranean Air Transport Service, the flight departing at 0840. He was back with 260 Squadron on 20 October, passed as fit to fly.

On returning to unit, Dennis flew two air tests, pointedly recording in his logbook '21 October 1944: Aircraft OK. Pilot Ropey.' Not all was well it would seem. He noted on 23 October 'Aircraft, OK.'

After close to six weeks rest, Dennis flew his first operational trip on 24 October. Airborne at 1400, Squadron Leader Johns led ten Mustangs on an Armed Attack. Dennis flew as Blue 2 to Captain Rogers. The target was three lock gates: two bombs were direct hits on a pair of gates, two more bombs destroyed a group of moored barges in the canal. Due to engine trouble Pilot Officer Green, escorted by Flight Lieutenant Ruiter, returned to base. Red Section then broke and strafed a steam locomotive and ten coaches at Morselise, and then attacked the railway station, strafing four steam engines: due to gun problems, the attack was halted and no claims made. Owing to this and heavy ack-ack, Red Section landed at 1614. Blue Section also found itself a steam train to attack, dropping down to 500ft the engine and two wagons were destroyed. This was followed up by three strafing runs against stationary locomotives. The flight landed close behind Red Section. On this run Dennis claimed one engine destroyed, five damaged, noting Mustang HB938 HS-D, an inferior MK 2 with which 260 Squadron were issued due to lack of spares for the MK 3 before the MK 4 arrived, was damaged CAT I by 20mm fire. Dennis comments about the tactics used when attacking a train:

> 'With no Luftwaffe to worry about, we could concentrate on the job at hand. A railway train or line was a fairly easy target to attack. If we had to stop such and such train on such a such line, the details given to us in the briefing, the job entailed attacking the line in front and behind the train. We would fly to the target in close six formation. Two pilots would break and fly low and fast along the line, passing in front of the train each would drop their two 1,000lb bombs. As long as the bombs fell close to the railway line, the debris kicked up would put a stop to the train going forward, often derailing the engine. The other pilot would bomb behind the train. Having trapped the train, the other four of us would bomb the engine, carriages and other wagons and then turn and shoot it up. The Germans were very good at repairing the railway lines though. Often, we would be sent back three or four days later to cut the same piece of line. The Jerries simply pushed the wrecked engine and wagons off the line and put in new rails.
>
> 'PO Davoine got very skilled at tunnel busting. He would fly in fast, low and level to the tunnel mouth, release his bombs about 200yards in front of the tunnel and then he would turn and climb as hard as he could. The bomb would continue its flight into the tunnel and explode 100 yards inside. When we went tunnel busting, the bombs would have long delay fuses.'

Airborne again as wingman to 'Roy' Rogers, again Blue 2, Dennis was in the air at 0915 on the following day. The operation was an armed attack on a road bridge. Climbing to 7,000ft, dense cloud forced the flight of twelve Mustangs down to 5,000ft. On dropping out of the cloud, the three span bridge was bombed south-west to north-east. The bridge was badly damaged and the road blocked. All landed at 1045. Dennis recorded, '1 direct hit on bridge. No AA. Weather Duff.'

During 27 October, 1.7inches of rain had fallen between midnight and 0700, and due to the waterlogged nature of the ground, no flying was possible that day or the following one. Seven missions were flown involving forty-seven aircraft on 29 October. 260 Squadron attacked lock gates at Cavanella 'and followed it up with an armed recce destroying eleven and damaging three locomotives. Two attacks were made on an SS Headquarters' reports 239 Wing.

Flight Lieutenant Lovell led five Mustangs up at 1015 on 30 October, on an armed attack on a Bailey bridge: a single direct hit on the bridge was made. Dennis flew on this operation as Yellow 2. The flight encountered some light ack-ack, 20mm from the target area, and 40mm from the north of Forni, resulting in CAT II damage to Dennis' kite, MK 2 Mustang HS-D. This was the eleventh time Dennis had written flak damage into his logbook. 'Twichy' Dennis was taken off operations for rest.

With troop movements at a standstill in Italy, interdiction of supply routes in Yugoslavia and into Northern Italy took priority.

Arriving with 260 Squadron as October came to an end was Australian Flight Sergeant Lyall Fricker. He flew his familiarisation trip in a Mustang on 30 October. He remembers:

'So, I went by train from Naples to Perugia, which is very close to Assisi and there they had a unit which was just a refresher flying unit, and we put in about five hours at this refresher unit where people just checked on the quality of our flying. We had a South African lieutenant who was a very hard task master. Well, he liked to think he was a "gung-ho" tough guy. He was saying, "You know you have got to do this and this."

'One of the things you had to do was to land, have your wheels touch down on an area the size of that carpet there. And he would be sitting there alongside the runway just watching as you came in and he had a stopwatch for some reason, I can't remember why. I mean I had no trouble with that, I don't think any of us did because we had been flying Kittyhawks in Egypt and so forth.

'We did about five hours there, and we did strafing attacks on Lake Trasimeno just to make sure we could still fire the guns accurately. We had an Australian flight lieutenant who took us on a formation flight around the sky in which we just had to follow him and he did all sorts of aerobatics, slow rolls and this sort of thing and we just had to follow. Basically, we didn't know what we were doing, I was number two to him, so what I had to make sure was that I stayed twenty or thirty yards behind him and he didn't get away, so whatever he did I did as well. And without seeing the ground or horizon you didn't know what was happening. You were conscious of the fact that you were pushing hard on the stick on some occasions or pulling hard back on others or had heavy G forces, anyway when we got back, somebody said, "Oh yes, you did a couple of slow rolls." "Oh, did we?" Didn't know.

'So that when I actually joined the squadron, I was quite fresh. I mean I had been flying the day before. Joined the squadron, went onto the Mustang the next day.'

Fricker was born on 25 April 1923, in Adelaide, Australia, and joined up in 1942 aged eighteen. Training in England and Abu Sueir, training on the Tiger Moth, Harvard and Wirraway. The relaxed atmosphere of 260 Squadron that had been cultivated in North Africa remained, as Fricker recalls:

'It was a good squadron, everybody got on well with everybody else. And they also had on that squadron an institution which was rare in the RAF, a Pilots' Mess. They didn't have officers and others; you had a Pilot's Mess. It didn't matter if you were the squadron commander, the squadron leader, or a sergeant, you were all in the same mess and that made for a very good team spirit between all of the pilots.'

It was that team spirit that drew pilots back for a second or third tour with the squadron. About Squadron Leader Johns, Fricker continues:

'He was on his third tour of operations because he was one of those that joined the RAF as an apprentice back in the 1930s and had become a pilot and he had gone through, I am not sure whether he was in the Battle of Britain or not, maybe he came in towards the end of it. Then he had done another tour of operations in North Africa and he was on his third one. And he was very calm, lethargic. Of course he seemed like an old man, he was about thirty I suppose. And it was old, our flight commander was a South African, Captain Roy Rogers, he seemed like an old man to most of us and he was twenty-two. I mean when you look back on it, we were just boys really.'

Squadron Leader Johns led a flight of six Mustangs to Sarajevo at 1240 on All Saints Day 1944. Johns bombed the railway line at Derventa, two steam engines were attack, one destroyed close by, along with a train loaded with staff cars and other vehicles: two flatcars were destroyed halting the train. Zagreb was attacked the same day, again destroying bridges, level crossings, railway lines and trains. 239 Wing Operations Record Book tells us:

1 Nov. For the first time for many months the Wing once more operated over Yugoslavia putting 5 missions of 30 sorties in and destroying 37 locomotives with another 7 damaged.

A message of congratulations from Air Vice-Marshal W.F. Dickson commanding DAF copied into 260 Squadron's Operations Record Book read:

'My congratulations to 260 on their very successful long-range mission to Yugoslavia today. The manner in which this task was carried out reflects much credit to the squadron. Well Done.'

Dennis returned to operations on 3 November, when he headed out a long-range run to Yugoslavia, to attack positions in the Zagreb and Maribor area. Squadron Leader Johns led the flight of six, Dennis flying as Red 2, wingman to Johns. All were in the air at 0640, the Mustangs fitted with long-range paper mâché drop tanks. John's flight arrived half an hour after the same target had been bombed by A Flight from 260 Squadron. Smoke rose 2,000ft and constant explosions were witnessed as the petrol tankers and ammunition trucks exploded. It meant the Germans were waiting for them. Despite heavy flak, a train and its wagons attacked in the earlier attack, was strafed: two of the lorries on the flatbed trucks were destroyed in flames. A steam engine moving five flat wagons again loaded with vehicles was attacked, the engine erupting in a sheet of scalding steam, and flames. Two steam engines shunting in the marshalling yard were strafed, one blowing up. Dennis reported in the attack six steam engines were destroyed and two damaged. His Mustang was holed by shrapnel from an exploding steam engine, considered CAT II. Clearly, he had gotten a little close to his target to ensure it was destroyed.

Yugoslavia was again the target for the following day, attacking Rebnich village. Squadron Leader Johns led up all of A Flight at 1430. Second Lieutenant Veitch (SAAF) flew as Red 2, Jack Green, now promoted to Pilot Officer, flew as Yellow 1, Dennis flew as White 1 with Sergeant Dufton as his wingman. The flight climbed to 9,000ft, flying direct to target. Dennis records; 'all bombs in target area. Plenty of destruction and confusion. No AA.'

Dennis was again back over Zagreb, bombing and strafing railway sidings. Johns led a flight of nine Mustangs into the air at 0745 on 5 November. Dennis again as White 1 in Red Section. Climbing to 9,000ft in good weather, the flight proceeded to Zagreb. Dennis had Flight Sergeant Fricker as his wingman on his first operation. About his baptism of fire, Fricker recalls some sixty years later:

'My plane was hit by flak six times and I got shot down twice. The first trip I did, for example, I didn't realise that I had been hit, but when I landed my ground crew checked over the plane and they were sticking their finger up through the holes and so on, and one of them was just behind where the chair is, had gone up just behind me. And people said, "Wow, if that had been six inches over you would be dead." And my answer was, "Yeah, but it didn't, it missed me by six inches." So, there was nothing to worry about [...] I didn't ever think of it that way. And similarly, when there would be discussions about the more trips that you did the nearer you got to the time that you would be killed – and that of course is true if you do two hundred trips without injury, then there is a greater chance of being hurt in the next hundred trips than there was when you first started, but it doesn't work on a trip by trip basis because the odds at the beginning of each trip are exactly the same as the one before and the one before that. And so, I would say, "Well this trip is no more dangerous than the last one."'

Returning to the events of 5 November 1944, Captain 'Roy' Rogers led Blue Section, Susskind was his wingman, and Lieutenant Cooper and Nelson as Green 1 and 2. Johns, Red 1, Pilot Officer Green and Sergeant Dufton, Yellow 1 and 2, left the operation early due to engine trouble and or fuel issues. Dennis flew White 1 with Fricker as White 2. The first target was a marshalling yard with ten engines: four were in steam. Diving down, bombs were released at 900ft, all six bombs dropping amongst the engines. The squadron diary tells us three strafing runs were carried out, five locomotives probably being destroyed, one damaged and two wagons written off, covered in flames. Intense flak was put up: Lieutenant Cooper and Sergeant Ficker's Mustangs were hit, classed as CAT I and CAT II, they peeled off back to base trailing smoke. This left Rogers, Dennis, Susskind and Nelson, which Johns led on an armed recce of the immediate area. Four locomotives were strafed in a station along with a train coming into the station; two steam engines were claimed as destroyed. As the Mustangs dropped into their strafing run, intense 20mm fire was put up. Suskind's Mustang was hit, white glycol smoke was observed pouring from the stricken airplane. He was ordered to gain height and once back at 6,000ft he bailed out. Landing, he was seen by 260 Squadron pilots removing his parachute and hiding it under some bushes. He was presumed POW. Johns now turned the flight to head home: during the flight back to the Adriatic coast, a target of opportunity was attacked. A goods train was strafed 'medium intense accurate 20mm fire came from the trucks in the station yard and Flight Sergeant Varey's aircraft was hit in the petrol tank' reported the Squadron Operations Record Book. For the twelfth, and what would be the final time, Dennis logged CAT II damage. It had been a costly day in men and aircraft as 239 Wing Operations Record Book reports:

Eleven missions and ninety-six sorties were carried out. Railway strafing in YUGOSLAVIA was evidently causing the Hun some considerable headaches for today it was noticed that every train included at least one flak truck, and for a total of thirty-seven locomotives, fourteen rail trucks, two passenger coaches and a petrol tanker, two aircraft at CAT III, two aircraft CAT II and one aircraft CAT I. 2/Lt Susskind and Lt Van Der Merwe, both No. 260 Squadron RAF were seen to bale out and land safely.

About the operation Dennis remembered:

'The trips to Jugland were dodgy. The flak was the worse we ever had. There should have been a sign "Abandon all hope all ye who enter." Some wag joked we could get out and walk the flak was so heavy. The Jerries had put flak guns on the trains. This made our train busting ops dodgy. We all had a big twitch on once we found out about the flak guns on the trains.

'On my last trip over, four of the kites got pranged out of the nine of us. I'd been hit on a previous run, and was already twitchy before we set off. I felt a sudden bang under my kite, looking round, a hole the size of my fist was in the port wing. My petrol gauge told me a tank had been holed.

'After the fear of fire, the biggest was getting back. We were all vey twitchy on these jobs as they were right on the limit of what we could do without drop tanks. We had tanks on a previous run that lasted over three hours, but under that, the high-ups said no tanks. We'd used half our petrol to get here, deep inside Yugoslavia, breathing down the neck of Hungary, and we had to get back to Italy. With a tank holed, my chances of making it back were slim.

'Once out of flak and heading home, I had two choices, pancake on the deck before we crossed the coast and take my chances with the Germans or partizans, or take a risk and hope like hell I had enough petrol to cross the Adriatic. I told Roy, who was flight skipper, that I thought I had enough to get back. I was never so glad to see Italy come into view. Once over the coast, it was a matter of praying I had enough fumes to land at Yesi. The motor gave some alarming coughs as the landing ground came into view. Switches off, throttled the motor back. Touched down. Never been so grateful as to get back on terra ferma. As I got out, and walked to the back of the kite to meet the ground crew, I noticed oil was dripping out by the back wheel. The engine had sounded very rough, I must have crossed the Adriatic with little to no oil in it all. A bullet had nicked the oil sump. An inch either way and the engine would have been a write off. It could have seized at any moment.

'All the lads on that run were very twitchy when we got back. Two lads had bailed out, which meant two empty chairs in the mess.'

Sixty years later Fricker recalled about the trip:

'Flew over to Zagreb and strafed and bombed a railway marshalling yard there. I was really concentrating on getting my bead on this train, the marshalling yard and making sure there was no slips or skids. Anyway, I fired my burst and I hit the engine, I could see the tracer bullets going into it and I went up into the cloud. So, I had a great sense of satisfaction. I pulled away and all around me there are puffs of white smoke you see. And I am looking at this with interest and all of a sudden, I realised that's flak, and so then of course I started skidding and diving all over the sky to get away from it. But on that first run through there was six of us did the attack and my recollection was four of us were hit. One of them came down immediately, within a few miles of Zagreb.

'Another one got further out towards the Adriatic and I am not sure whether he came down on the coast or whether he actually got out to sea a bit, but the leader then said, "Well, that's enough, we're off home now." So, four of us got back to base and two stayed where they were. Both of them, one was killed. The first one that went down was killed, and the second one was picked up by the partisans who looked after him and he got back to base about a fortnight later. He was another South African. And so that was a fairly rude awakening.'

It had been a costly operation with seventy-five per cent of aircraft which participated on the attack either damaged or lost. For Dennis, all was not well: the following day the 239 Wing medical officer recommended that he was to be taken off operational flying and rested. About losses Fricker continues:

'I can't tell you exactly, but my recollection was that of the people that joined the squadron, about fifty per cent would be there at the end of it, the army blokes couldn't believe it. They said, "If we had losses like this we just couldn't go on. It's no good at all." [...] some people did think about it and they used to get quite concerned and have breakdowns and so on. I had a fairly cavalier attitude towards it [...] There were blokes that had done a lot of trips and they were a great source of comfort. "There is so and so there, he has done sixty trips." So, you know that he is reliable and steady and it is good to fly with him because he comes back each time. I think that if one of those blokes was killed, then the attitude would be then of course, you have got to expect it, he had done so many trips it was only a matter of time before it caught up with him. So, you rationalised both ways.'

Despite the losses, Johns was back in the air at 1300, heading to Zagreb railway station. Encountering heavy flak Second Lieutenant Van Der Merwe's Mustang was hit. Pouring petrol and white smoke from a glycol fire, he bailed out and landed safely. The following morning, Johns led a flight back to Zagreb, destroying a 150ft long railway bridge. This was to be his last operation: his fourth tour expired, with 749 operational hours.

I asked Dennis about what he could remember about this period. 'Your logbook shows you flew C-47s. When did you train on twin engine types?' I asked:

> 'I had experience coming back from Abu Suer as co-pilot. On returning to 260, rather than Ops, Johns, our squadron skipper, had me doing lots of odd jobs. Yesi had a lot of types on it. As well as our single-seat fighters, it had a lot of twin-engine bombers and the like. We did a lot of unofficial flying, or at least some of us. We could hitch a ride on days off, pretty much where we wanted to go. It was like thumbing a lift for a taxi. When we were based near Rome, we were alongside the Italian Airforce. I got matey with some of them. I managed to get a flight in a three-engine bomber. It was all good fun.'

Going for unofficial flights was 'par for the course' as Christopher Lee remembers:

> 'I got involved quite wrongly in having to fly a DC3 with some of the ENSA people on board getting down to Naples, a communications flight just for a few days leave. We went up into the crater of Vesuvius. Two or three days later, it erupted! I went back to the squadron in an American Air Force B25 Mitchell light bomber. In those days you hitched a ride whichever way you could get it..'

Dennis spoke of Lee with fondness, always calling him Chris. Of Course, in DAF rank and names did not really matter:

> 'Chris was a white Russian. He'd fought the Russians in the Finnish Army, and said he'd lived with some Russian prince or similar who was a cousin. He had the air of being a duke or prince, but was always very affable. That kind of thing did not matter. We had a job to do. The C-47, DC3, normally has four, pilot, co-pilot, navigator and radio. I'd already got thirteen hours on the type as co-pilot, so, there I was on this twin-engine type, fetching and carrying all sorts for the squadron on my first solo. Taking lads on leave, ferrying stores up to the ground crew, bringing in food, mail, booze. We used it as the squadron hack. Basically, I was an odd job man for a time. Someone would come up and say go fetch X Y Z, and off I'd go. I think I did

jobs for other units on the wing. When not on this, I was helping the adjutant and Chris in the Ops lorry.

'When we were over the Po, Chris disappeared one evening. He left me to do the following days briefing. When he got back Chris said he had gone on a night-time bombing run on the Po. Now, in theory Chris was grounded, and not allowed to fly, of course that never stopped him and he went on unauthorised trips. All off the books. To the best of my knowledge, we never did night flying or solo runs, so what he did baffled me. I know we used to drop supplies to the Itie partisans, which was all hush hush. Either way he dropped me in it, so he could spend the night on the Po [laughing] can you imagine the telegram, "I'm sorry your son has died on the Po."'

Into November

On 7 November, Flight Lieutenant England and Sergeant Lloyd's aircraft was CAT II damaged by flak. A German HQ centre was destroyed on the following day, and on 10 November a German train at Motta station was destroyed, the Mustangs flying through rain clouds. As the five Mustangs from 260 Squadron pulled out of their bombing run, American B-24 Liberators unloaded their cargo of bombs on the same target. Aware that moral was starting to drop due to spending winter under canvas, 239 Wing realised:

In an attempt to alleviate the strain imposed on personnel by a long period of sustained, intensive operations and to maintain high moral during the winter, the problem of leave facilities was tackled in earnest.

A hotel in Florence, 'considered to be a well-nigh ideal place', was requisitioned, despite the fact 'the hotel restraint had been disused for some considerable period' the Rest Centre was up and running by 8 November. One pilot who used the rest house was Flight Sergeant Fricker:

'I also had a couple of spells of leave in Italy and one was to go to Florence and there was three of us, another Australian, myself and an Englishman and we had a week in Florence. And the RAAF had taken over a hotel on the banks of the Arno just near the Ponte Vecchio [...] we had a very good time in Florence.

'Florence was another open city. Nevertheless, the Germans, before they had retreated, had done an enormous amount of damage, they had blown up every bridge across the Arno except the Ponte Vecchio. And with the Ponte Vecchio they left the bridge there, but they blew up all of the approaches on both sides. So that when we were there, we had bay bridges, the army bridges, across the Arno where the old bridges had been. And of course, you had to pick your way around through the rubble to go around through the Ponte Vecchio and so forth.'

Despite the lure of Florence, the squadron was still under canvas in the Italian winter: to endeavour to resolve the issue, a Wing meeting was held on 9 November to try and organise better accommodation for the wing.

The same day, the squadron commanding officer ordered that if personnel were found wearing USAAF clothing and equipment, it would be a court martial offence. Clearly local shortages and the cold forced officers and men from 260 Squadron to use whatever clothing they could obtain. Dennis remembers:

'Although we shared the airfield with the Yanks, we did not see a lot of them, it was as if the runway acted as an invisible barrier between us and them; they kept to their side and us to ours. On the few occasions that we did cross the runway we did become envious. They had better kit, and it was not unheard of for us to swop a bottle of Scotch for a Yank flying jacket and boots. I remember my mate Larry Johnson, a South African, exchanged a bottle of Scotch for a Jeep and kept it for the whole of the time he was on the squadron. Nearly all this bartering took place in the local bars. The Yanks accommodation and food was very much superior: Unlike us living off powdered or tinned food, the Yank's rations included tinned ham and chicken, ice cream, doughnuts – you name it, they had it. They had larger tents, each man with a decent camp bed, ablution blocks all under cover and it wouldn't have surprised me if there wasn't hot and cold water laid on as well. Our ablutions consisted of a Jerry can of water and a strip wash in all weathers outside the tent. Larry, Duke and I managed to rig up a bath by cutting an oil drum in half, I think when we were at Falerium. I was volunteered to test it out. I could barely sit in the oil drum, but I did give it ago despite having my knees up by my chin and toes over the edge...Good job it was a warm day. We got up to all sorts of escapades. We fitted out our mess with "liberated" easy chairs and other furniture to make it as comfortable as possible. Old couches, soft chairs, you name it, we borrowed it. We all had a chair in the mess.

'Our latrines comprised about six buckets with wooden seats located well away from the tented area in a field with a length of Hessian stretched on poles to the rear with no protection overhead and nothing to the front. My god the smell was something awful in the summer. The "shit house orderly" had to shovel quick lime on top religiously to keep the smell down. We hoarded old newspapers and old magazines; well, you can work out for yourself what they were for.'

Lieutenant K.W. Johnson (SAAF) of Johannesburg, South Africa, or 'Larry' to the squadron, had become tour expired on 9 September 1944, with 196 hours. He had joined 260 Squadron on 6 November 1943. Despite officer status, Larry, Duke Kent and Dennis messed together and shared a bivvy, along with Mervyn Talbot. I wonder what happened to the Jeep?

The squadron began preparations to move to a new base, Fano, on the 16 November, which was close to the east coast, the first party arriving on the seventeenth. The same day, six Mustangs escorted a flight of eighteen B-25 Mitchell bombers over Zaprisio. This was in support of Operation Bingo and the fighting for Forli by the Eighth Army. Eighteen Baltimore's were escorted the following day. 260 Squadron arrived at Fano – or as the Pilots seemed to have called it 'Fanny' – on 19 November at lunch time. After partaking in 'tiffin', the squadron diary reports:

> Action was immediately taken to allocate billets to all sections of the unit, as every effort is being made to avoid having personnel under canvas again this winter.

The following signal has been received from the AOC Desert Air Force:

> 'On this third anniversary of your operations in support of the Eighth Army, I congratulate all ranks of 260 Squadron on their fine record of service. Over a long period of time, the squadron consistently has maintained a high standard of efficiency, has earned a far-reaching reputation for its great work and aggressiveness. Please convey to all ranks my gratitude and pride in 260 Squadron. The Best of Luck to you all.'

About improvised accommodation at Fano, Bill Barwick from 112 Squadron remembers:

> 'Slowly the front moved up the leg of Italy and as we got to the later months of 1944 we were warned of another move. This time to Fano (18 Nov 1944). Right on the Adriatic coast. The runway starting inland and ending almost in the sea. It lay very low and some of the advance party who camped in the 'drome in tents had a very wet and uncomfortable time. In the main party we went into billets which were just old derelict houses. I landed in a very small room with Paddy Woods and Bill Bailey. They were good blokes, but really untidy. From my bed I could look up and see the sky, but although we were there for the winter and it actually snowed. I never got wet. There were two doors as it was a right of way to another room and one small window. Which had no glass. Not luxury, but

better than a tent in a muddy field. We were in a slum area near the wrecked railway station [...] There was no let up with the flying until the weather clamped down. Work went on just the same. I felt at home on the squadron and we were almost sure we would be in Fano for the winter so we could make ourselves as comfortable as we could. We built a fireplace out of an old oil can and stole timber from wrecked buildings.'

At 'Fanny', Dennis again found himself filling in as Intelligence Officer rather than being on operational flying. With Christopher Lee being posted off squadron, Dennis and other officers took it in turns to do the briefing and liaise with Wing HQ and intelligence. On 21 November, Flight Sergeant Fricker crash-landed, recalling in later years that following flak damage as he returned to base:

'The engine cut out and I was too low to bail out [...] there was the tremendous shrieking of tearing metal, the banging and thumping, and then all was silent. Now I probably was knocked out for a while, I don't know. Because after the tearing of the metal and the spinning around, both wings were torn off and the fuselage was broken in half and the plane spun around as it went across the ground. And the next thing that I heard was a sort of crackling sound. Suddenly I thought fire! Once again, the brain was very clear indeed and I went to eject the hood off the plane but it got twisted in the crash and wouldn't budge. So, then I realised that the Perspex had been broken anyway, so I could get out through the framework of the hood.'

He had a lucky escape. Bad weather, mud and extreme cold reduced operations during the darkening November days. Despite the cold, Flight Sergeant Fricker remembers:

'Most of the big bases had a camp cinema where they would show pictures maybe every night. When we were on the squadron there used to be concert parties, for example when we were in Parma at the local theatre, they had several, one was a concert party of Italian ex-opera singers and so on who put on *Madame Butterfly*. And this was very good, they really were very competent, they had retired but they really had beautiful voices and they knew the opera backwards and so on. And then there'd be an American concert party would come through with the big band style of thing.'

Despite the mud, life was a considerable improvement over the infantry in the front lines that winter.

CHAPTER
18

TO VICTORY

IN THE WINTER and spring of 1944-45, extensive partisan activity took place behind the German lines both in northern Italy and Yugoslavia. In north Italy the Germans had created a fascist puppet state, the Italian Social Republic (ISR). But many locals backed the Allies and the pro-Allied Italian government in Rome. As a result, the struggle took on the characteristics of a civil war. Allied special forces and commandos provided direction and arms to the partisans, sabotaging lines of supply and communication, and pinpointing targets for air strikes. But the Germans, along with Italian fascists, carried out many reprisals against civilians suspected of supporting the partisans and Allies. Partisans were to be crucial in returning shot down pilots.

260 Squadron was still employed on interdiction as well as bombing and strafing German infantry positions, and escorting the Tactical Airforce bomber campaign as part of Operation Bingo. The following dispatch arrived on 22 November:

> Commanding General MATAF send to all ranks of the Desert Air Force the following message by Air Commander in Chief; Begins: 'I have noted with the greatest pleasure the high volume of effort your Air Forces have thrown against the enemy on four successive days beginning with 842 fighter and fighter-bomber sorties and 263 medium bomber sorties on November 16th. Continuing with 800 fighter and fighter-bomber sorties and 294 medium bomber sorties on November 17th and with 953 fighter and fighter-bomber sorties on November 18th. Plus, a very strong number on November 15th. This demonstrates complete that your organisations is very strong on the administrative and maintenance sides, I wish you would particularly emphasise to your hard working engineering staff and maintenance crews how much we value and applaud their remarkable effort.'

On 24 November, Second Lieutenant Susskind, having been previously reported missing following bailing out over Yugoslavia returned to 260 Squadron. In a remarkable chain of circumstances, having evaded capture, with the help of partisans, he had crossed Yugoslavia and through the German lines. A remarkable achievement! Two days later, tragedy again struck 260 Squadron.

Flight Sergeant Charles Alexander Walker was shot down by flak. He was the son of William and Catherine Walker of Geddington, Northamptonshire. Just twenty-one when he died, he lies buried in Naples War Cemetery.

The squadron diary reports that nine days had been lost due to bad weather during the second half of the month, and operations had switched from close support of the Army at Treviso to interdiction action in Yugoslavia 'resulting in the score of locomotives and trucks being substantially increased [...] Railway bridges were also cut in the Brod-Zagreb area, and good results obtained on several occasions.' Indeed, the following message was received from Lieutenant General Oliver Leese, Commanding Officer of the Eighth Army, about 260 Squadron's operations:

> 'I want to send you and all ranks of DAF my warmest congratulations and grateful thanks for the splendid air support which 5th Corps and the Polish Corps have received during the hard fighting which has driven the enemy back from Forli over the Lamone River. I have myself seen many fighter-bomber attacks during these past few days and I and all commanders whom I have met have been very impressed with the accuracy of the bombing and strafing so close to our own troops and the magnificent way the attacks have been pressed home in difficult weather conditions. This splendid close support has been a decisive factor in our success.'

As December began, the squadron received news that Van Der Merwe, who had bailed out from his crippled Mustang on 5 November, was safe, and was expected back with 260 Squadron in the new year. He had been protected from the Germans by Yugoslavian Partisans and had managed to get back into Italy and into the Allied lines. Pilot Officer Hollinshead, who had bailed out at the end of September, was reported as POW. On 4 December, 260 'went rail cutting between Treviso and Casarsa, but were hampered by bad weather' reported 239 Wing.

Throughout December, when weather was favourable, the squadron was over Yugoslavia. On 16 December, the squadron celebrated a notable success: it destroyed twelve plus ME 109 and FW 190 caught at dispersal at Aviano. Tragedy befell 260 the following day when Sergeant Hooper was taking off on an operation. Eyewitnesses reported that during the take-off run, due to a slight cross wind, the Mustang swung to the right, almost off the edge of the runway, Hopper tried to correct the swing, and instead swung violently left; he became airborne, but with insufficient height to clear a row of parked

P-47 Thunderbolts. One of his 1,000lb bombs was dislodged from its rack and exploded, the force of the blast sending the Mustang tumbling into the Thunderbolts. The remaining bomb exploded shredding several P-47's and killing American ground crew in the blast or resulting fuel fire. Leslie Walter William Hooper was just 21-years-old when he died. He lies in Ancona War Cemetery.

On 19 December, Squadron Leader Johns was posted to No. 1 MORU as deputy sector controller, working with Christopher Lee. In his place, 'an old friend' returned to 260 Squadron. Peter Blomfield had left 260 in August when he was recommended for his DFC. He had been 'rested' at the Air Bombing and Gunnery School at Ballah, once again being rated as 'Exceptional' in Air Gunnery and on 20 December 1944 he returned to 260 Squadron.

About life on the squadron that winter, Flight Sergeant Fricker recalls:

'The winter in Italy was really ghastly, I mean cold and wet and the mud was unbelievable. People really did lose their gum boots in the mud; they would sink down to knee level and when they were pulled out their boots were still in the mud and they just had to stay there for the rest of the year. But then in the evenings there would be, not quite fun and games, just the sort of fellowship that goes on with a bunch of people together. There would be people playing cards. We always had some kind of a bar, and about the only stuff we could buy was vermouth, the local brew; people would have the odd vermouth. The people who were flying the next day basically stayed off it, but the people who had completed their day's operation they would have a few drinks of vermouth.'

Christmas Day was of mixed emotions, whilst some sat down to Christmas dinner and bonhomie, their friends were raining down death as the squadron diary recorded:

Christmas dinner on the squadron was great a success as ever, the cooks having done a great job. Officers and pilots waited upon the tables and a good time was had by all. Unfortunately, all the pilots could not attend, as operational flying took place at the time. The squadron senior NCOs assumed most of the duties which had to be performed, in order that the squadron's operational activities could continue, and at the same time relieving ground personnel from their usual tasks [..] Bombing of Treviso marshalling yards by Marauders and escorted by aircraft of the squadron [...] bombs seemed well concentrated [...] four bursts of 40mm fire came from the mouth of Faivre river.

On Boxing Day, fourteen missions were flown, representing 101 individual sorties. On one operation 3 Squadron (RAAF) was 'jumped on' by a flight of three ME 109s, who shot down Pilot Officer Quin, although the 109 was reported damaged in the ensuing dog fight. Quin walked away from his pancaked Mustang. Christmas cheer was severely lacking in 1944. Leave to Florence for ten pilots and ground crew began on 29 December, yet as Blom's logbook reports, the war went on:

> 29 December: Bomb railway bridge – Piave River. Heavy 40mm. 2 hits. 1 span down.
>
> 15 January [1945]: Bomb rail bridge – Gemona: Cut bridge. Cratered Rail. Hit 1 loco.

During January, fifteen days were lost due to bad weather on operational flying. Despite this, the 'Bag' for 239 Wing was 177 missions flown, and 2,523 bombs had been dropped. 260 Squadron claimed a steam engine destroyed and fifteen damaged, twenty-four items of railway rolling stock damaged or destroyed, four lorries damaged and seven other vehicles 'written off.' Two pilots, Henderson and Susskind, were lost in action. Susskind died on 21 January 1945, aged just twenty. His engine failed on an operation over Ravenna, those flying alongside him thought that he ran out of petrol. With the engine stopped, Susskind endeavoured to 'pancake' onto the sea. Rather than bellying landing, he went in nose first and he was killed on impact. His body has never been recovered. He is commemorated in the Ravenna War Cemetery. Captain G.M. Henderson, came from Durban, South Africa, was twenty-seven when he was killed on 15 January. He lies at Udine War Cemetery.

Outside of the 'day job', weekly dances were held in the mess, and leave parties had been sent to Rome and Florence, the latter being not as popular as Rome, as the house was on the outskirts of the city and not the centre. On 4 February, Nick Nicholls, returned to 260 Squadron for his second tour of duty.

The day Nick returned, Fricker (now warrant officer) remembered:

> 'I had been strafing a convoy up near Travaglia in the Po Valley and there was fairly low cloud base, so after I had finished my run, I pulled up into the cloud thinking I was fairly safe there. Instead of doing my normal evasion tactic I just held it on a straight line and went up into the cloud. And in the cloud, there was suddenly a god-awful bang and I got thrown over on my back. Anyway, I righted the plane and flew up through the top of the cloud and rejoined the squadron. My oil pressure by this time had dropped down to zero, and the others called up and said, "You're trailing a lot of black smoke, are you okay?" and I said, "Yes, I am all right, I have lost

oil." I was then told to head back to base, so I slowed the engine down so that it was ticking over on fairly low revs and put it into a glide and headed out over the Adriatic. Came over the coast near Venice. And then continued trying to get as much distance as I could because our bomb line, that's the area between the Germans and ourselves, was just north of Ravenna, so the engine continued, I flew for about twenty minutes altogether without any oil pressure. And was able to glide down and land on this emergency strip on the beach just near Ravenna. And when I got out of the plane and counted the holes, there was about forty holes all along the leading edge of both wings and in the engine itself, so I was lucky that the engine held out for that length of time. They were a very good engine indeed.

'Then of course when about a week or so later they had repaired the wings, and whether they had put a new engine in it or not I don't know, but the plane was ready to fly again. So, I went up there in a truck to pick it up and it was a Spitfire squadron on the airfield, on that airstrip, and when I was ready for take-off, I thought I will do a bit of showing off here, in a Mustang. There was always a rivalry between the Mustangs and the Spitfires. So, I got onto the end of the runway and I held her on the brakes, got the engine up to full revs and then started screaming down the runway. Picked up the undercarriage but held it low so that I was picking up speed all of the time and the control tower eventually got a bit nervous and said, "Watch out for the trees." Anyway, when I got to the end of the runway, I selected ten degrees of flaps which gives you a lot more lift and pulled the stick back and went straight up like a lift, to about five thousand feet, thinking to myself, "I let the Spitfires know, see if they can copy that." And then having got up to the five thousand feet I rolled it over came back over the centre of the runway again and waggled my wings to say, "Thanks very much" and went on my way. So that was a bit of bravado. I didn't get any reaction from the Spitfire boys.'

About operations in the New Year of 1945, he adds:

'We had a range of jobs. The whole of our desert air force, the 1 Tactical Air Force, that was the correct name for it – 1st TAF. Tactical Air Force meant that they were in support of the army, so as the 8th Army advanced up through Italy the 1st TAF was there to support what they were doing. And there was a whole variety of mechanisms there. One was to do close support, so that we had an operation called 'cab rank' [...] there was another one, operation 'rover paddy', where you would do a roving patrol, you would go up and down looking for targets yourself instead of being directed, you would find your own targets and blast those. And for the longer-range ones we would go from the centre of Italy, we would either fly up north over the Alps and come back, but generally we would fly across the Adriatic to Yugoslavia, and we would have some targets identified to us from intelligence.

'And we would also look around ourselves for things like ammunition trains, anything that was moving transport. And we would fly across to the railway line joining say Belgrade, Maribor or Ljubljana, we would follow that railway line around into southern Austria: Klagenfurt, Villach and Viet and then we would climb back over the Alps down through northern Italy.'

At the end of February 260 Squadron was on the move, the first party moving out to Cervia on the twenty-third, Fano being taken over by 57th Bomber Wing USAAF three days later. One of the ground crew from 112 Squadron remembers:

'Up the coast again this time to Chervia. Which had been a fishing village converted into a holiday village with lots of small villas, which we took over. I, this time, decided to be on my own and found a small villa kitchen. There were no services in it and it had room only for one bed so I had a room to myself.

'Chervia had at some time had a small forest of pines, planted I presumed to hold the large area of sand together. Through this we had carved a runway and paved it with the boot scraper road of steel plates linked together. There were miles of sandy beach and some quite good swimming. If you could put up with small crabs nipping at your toes. It was at Chervia that 260 Squadron were equipped with rockets with sixty-pound warheads. Just along the beach from our dispersal was a great sheet of four-inch steel, so Groupy Eaton took up one of their Mustangs and fired some rockets at this. They went through it like it was butter. 260 Squadron soon found out that these rockets went so fast that if they were fired at a normal ship, they often went right through it and exploded in the sea. leaving a neat hole all the way through.

'It has been said by others elsewhere, that a salvo of all eight rockets represented a destructive force equivalent to a broadside from a destroyer. Whether or not this was actually true, the psychological effect of the rocket armament was considerable. We do admit that whilst being extremely powerful weapons, the rockets were notoriously difficult to aim.'

The squadron diary tells us that the fitting of rockets to Mustangs was top secret, and 'this step' notes the diary:

> '…is regarded as opening a new era in the history of the squadron, comparable to the previous major change such as equipping with Mustangs after Kittyhawks and the introduction of 1,000lb bombs. The keenness shown by personnel, now that 260 are once more in the spotlight, is marked.'

Cervia 'is most pleasant being located in pine woods bordering the Adriatic' continued the squadron diary, adding that eighty per cent of personnel were accommodated in holiday chalets on the coast, with the remaining twenty per cent still under canvas. Aircrew and personnel were reminded not to cut down the pine trees for firewood. Full blackout precautions had to be followed in case of an air raid. As March began, 260 Squadron remained on interdiction operations both in Italy and Yugoslavia, but now flying into Austria on 10 March, bombing targets at Klagenfurt on the eastern shore of Lake Wörthersee, the capital city of the southern Austrian province of Carinthia. 260 Squadron was part of a Wing operation over Split on 18/19 March. The raids were to prevent the Germans re-supplying their forces by air using JU 52s. These operations were in support of Yugoslavian partisans. In the air the squadron 'flew in groups of six, three pairs' remembers Warrant Officer Fricker, continuing:

> 'Rather like the pelican you see with a leader out here and the others out on the wings. And the leader, the only job he had to do in theory was to make sure that he was on the right track, map-reading and so on, and that he picked the right target and that sort of thing.
>
> 'His two number ones were there to search the sky ahead, the ground ahead and feed advice to him and essentially be a backup in case he was shot down and so on. The three number twos had to weave backwards and forwards all of the time watching, not only the sky ahead, but the sky above to one side and back, so that as you turned around this way you would be looking over here searching all of that sky, then you would swing back the other way and look at all of this bit back here. And you maintained your position by the width of the sweep, you didn't change your throttle setting at all, if you were getting too close to the one in front, you just took a wider sweep and come back again the other way and increased that difference. And basically, the number twos didn't look at the ground at all until they reached the targets. And then the instruction, "Target on port side," and so on and that's when you would start focussing on the ground, picking out your target and get ready to do the dive.

And you flew up alongside the target, there was no point having the target ahead of you because once you got reasonably close to the target it would be under the nose and the nose of course went out for six feet in front of you so you wouldn't see it. So, you flew alongside the target and when you were ready to attack, you peeled off, dived off that way and straightened up and opened fire and whipped off the other side.'

Operation Bowler

Operation Bowler was the only authorised bombing raid to be made on Venice throughout the war.

By early 1945, the rail and road networks of northern Italy had sustained severe damage, forcing the Germans to resort to shipping goods into Venice and then moving them from there along rivers and canals: DAF had opened an aerial blitz on anything that moved. For example, at the start of March, 239 Wing attacked over 800 railway vehicles in a marshalling yard at Conegliano: one steam engine and 129 items of rolling stock was destroyed. On operations in the Balkans the following day, 260 Squadron's Mustangs operating with rocket armed P-47s destroyed fifteen locomotives, 106 railway wagons and fifty road vehicles in a 24-hour period.

With such crippling losses, and the shift in emphasis of German logistics, an attack on the harbour at Venice was deemed necessary by Allied command, although the risk of damage to the city's architectural and artistic treasures was high, as it had been in other battles of the Italian campaign, such as the Battle of Monte Cassino. The operation was planned to be extremely precise to avoid any such damage and was named Operation Bowler by Air Vice-Marshal Robert Foster, as a reminder to those involved that they would be 'bowler hatted' (returned to civilian life) or worse should Venice itself be damaged.

260 Squadron flew a succession of weather recces to Venice from 0600 on 21 March to ensure good weather over the target area. The fourth operation of the day, landing at 1355, reported clear visibility and the ship in the harbour had steam up. With the target clear, Acting Wing Commander George Westlake led the attack in a Curtiss P-40 Warhawk from 250 Squadron. Flight Sergeant Walters of 450 Squadron recalls:

'This was my twenty-seventh bombing sortie; by far the biggest I flew on and the only time we operated as a wing with all five squadrons together. At briefing, the Boss told us that we had a special target and that no bombs must go astray under any circumstances. If we were unsure, we had to drop the bombs in the water. He also said that it had to be a complete success because there was no way we wanted to go back for a second attack with all the defences alerted. He then unrolled the map and we saw that the target was Venice, which came as a surprise, so we immediately understood why it was essential to be accurate. Each squadron was given a specific aiming point and our target was a 700-ton coaster but, if it was already hit as we dived down, we were free to select another target in the same area. Before taking off we studied a detailed map of the dock area and the layout of the docks was imprinted on our minds.

'We carried a single 1,000lb bomb on the fuselage pylon […] We were the second to attack and gave top cover to 250 Squadron as they dived down. Then it was our turn and we dived at sixty degrees, pulling out at 1,500ft. I was firing my six cannons all the way down as the flak was intense but you just had to ignore it. Firing away probably didn't do much damage but it was good for my morale and I had a good view of the target and released my bomb and then pulled hard as I turned away.'

Roy Rogers led just four Mustangs from 260 Squadron whilst 450 Squadron attacked. Warrant Officer Fricker from 260 again:

'Venice itself was an open city and not supposed to be used for military purposes at all. But the Germans had some ships in there which were carrying arms and ammunition for their forces in Italy. And so, it was decided to knock these ships out but you weren't allowed to touch Venice itself. And it was decided that the desert air force, and particularly our wing, should be given the job of doing this because we were supposed to have the precision dive-bombers et cetera. Now my squadron, 260 Squadron, had been equipped with rockets only about a fortnight before, we were the first to have them. And I had been able to get in about ten hours of practice with these rockets, using a cement head instead of a shell […] then they decided on this particular exercise and they said, "Oh, we have got a rocket firing squadron now so they can go in first and knock out all of the flak." We were dubious on it, so four of us, including myself, were detailed to go off and attack this island in the Venice lagoon which had all of the anti-aircraft guns mounted on it and our job was to keep them quiet. We did that. I was number two, my leader was the South African captain, Roy Rogers. As we came up towards Venice, which was on the port side, we got abreast of our target and by this time there was so much flak around that my leader disappeared entirely. Gone. There were just black clouds of anti-aircraft fire everywhere. And I thought, "Oh well, he has had it." And then the next minute he appeared out of the bottom of the cloud on his way down to the island and then I was in it and it was my turn to go down and follow him. [And all of this was very well.] But when we were being equipped with the rockets they had an accident with one of the armourers, when he slid the rocket onto the rail contact had already been made somewhere between the cockpit and that and as soon as he slid it on the rail the thing ignited and zoomed off the rail and the steel fin cut off his arm at the elbow.'

'So, in order to stop that happening again, they put a little master switch in the cockpit, and this was just a simple toggle switch and they just stuck it on the side of the cockpit with masking tape to do the job. So, when I started diving down on this island and once again concentrating like fury as I did, got to the right range, pressed the button, nothing happened. And I realised immediately I had forgotten the master switch, so I leaned forward flicked the master switch, pressed it again and away they went. But in that time, I had lost at least a thousand feet and the ground was coming up very fast indeed. So, I pulled back on the stick, as hard as I could and blacked out and so I held the stick in my stomach until such times as the speed started to wash off, at which time I knew I was coming out of the dive.

'I eased forward slightly so that the blood came back into my eyes and I could see where I was. And when my sight returned the first thing I saw was a high-tension cable looping across Venice lagoon. I somehow managed to get between these high-tension wires and the sea itself. Now had I hit the sea, or the wires of course, I would have been reported as having been killed in action, and I certainly would have been killed, [...] I was very lucky. Anyway, I headed up to rejoin the squadron and we came around and did our next run and by the time we did our fourth run there was virtually no opposition at all, we had knocked out all of the anti-aircraft guns and the operation itself was a great success. They sank the ships and the only damage I think was to one of the warehouses on the wharf itself and the city as such was untouched, so it was quite a triumph for the Tactical Air Force.'

The Operations Record Book of 250 Squadron reports:

Fine and sunny to-day for the long-awaited 'Bowler' operation which was carried out most successfully by 120 aircraft as an anti-shipping strike on Venice Harbour.

229

The Wing was led by Wing Commander G. Westlake, DFC and our twelve aircraft were led by Flight Lieutenant E.H. Strom, DFC.

Using 1000lb bombs and firing in dive our bombing was excellent, resulting in a possible direct hit and one direct hit on the stern of a 700-ton ship; direct hits on three warehouses; one direct hit on the marshalling yard and a very near miss on a 3500-ton ship.

Wide publicity was given subsequently to this well organised and most successfully carried out attack, nearly all co-operating aircraft recording excellent results.

The attack sank the German torpedo boat TA42 (ex-Italian Alabarda), two merchant ships as well as naval escorts and smaller vessels. It seriously damaged a large cargo ship and destroyed five warehouses, an Axis mine stockpile (blowing a 100-yard (91m) hole in the quayside) and other harbour infrastructure.

The following day, 260 Squadron was back on interdiction operations in Yugoslavia. A sugar refinery was destroyed, primarily through rocket fire, on 23 March. The following day, the operations were to take out German fuel dumps: the rockets igniting fuel stocks. No flying on the twenty-fourth, Anti-Shipping occupied the twenty-fifth. Bloms logbook takes up the story:

29 March: A./Recce. Zagreb – Celje – St. Vert. 9 locos, 3 trucks and 4 M./T. damaged. 1 loco. and 3 trucks destroyed. Hello Germany!

31 March: A./Recce. Klagenfurt – Lubltana. Caught 2 Ju. 88s over Klagenfurt. 4 trucks destroyed. 4 locos damaged. 2 Ju. 88s confirmed.

A Life on the ocean wave

During what would prove to be the last weeks of the war, one pilots adventures stood out from his comrades as Bill Barwick of 112 Squadron remembers:

'One of 260 Squadron's pilots got shot down in Venice harbour, bailed out and got into his dingy. He paddled away out to sea and the rest of the gang drove a German rescue boat back with threats. A converted Wellington flew over him and dropped a lifeboat, which he got into and drove off out to sea where a Royal Navy destroyer picked him and his boat up. A Catalina amphibian then collected him from the destroyer and he was home within a few minutes. This was regarded as something of a joke until he did the same thing the next day. They told us they sent him off to be an air-sea rescue instructor.'

Squadron Commander Blomfield adds more details about 2nd Lieutenant Raymond Veitch. Veitch was known on the squadron as Drongie: Drongie is Afrikaans for drunkard and Veitch was teetotal. Blomfield notes:

'Drongie was flying at the end of the war as my No. 2. In April '45 we were mostly involved in interdiction, rockets and strafing. Twice in the first week in April and again on the thirtieth he was hit by flak – a few feet ahead and it could have been me! He managed to make it to the north Adriatic coast and bailed out into a minefield near Trieste. Each time the RAF or Yank's air-sea rescue service dropped him an airborne lifeboat. As his CO and No. 1, I felt obliged to lead a section of Mustangs to cover the operations. I've never ceased to wonder why those prolonged and obvious rescue operations so close to the enemy shore went completely unopposed; but whether from lack of petrol or skin-saving now the that war was obviously nearly over, they never came to molest us.'

239 Wing Operations Record Book reports:

Lieutenant Veitch of 260 Squadron achieved the distinction of being the first pilot of the wing to be rescued by means of a Warwick dropped lifeboat. This occurred on 2 April, but on 5 April he must have needed to go and to it again, almost inside Trieste harbour. Once again, the Warwick came to the rescue, but on this occasion, Veitch had to spend one night at sea, as by last light he had not managed to get out of the very extensive minefields. However, all went well and he was back home by midday on the sixth. Constant fighter patrols from this and other wings covered him all day and at least four surface craft put out from Trieste to intercept him were sunk or discouraged. The enemy, on viewing the air effort put out on the rescue, may well have thought that the person in question must have been an Air Vice-Marshal at least. On the last day of the month, he went and did it again!

According to Blom, after the third time Veitch was downed, Air Officer Commanding DAF sent a memo 'Personal from Foster to Veitch, I have appointed you Honorary Commodore of Desert Air Force Yacht Club when it is formed.' Part of this message is recorded in the squadron diary.

Interdiction remained 260 Squadron's day job for early April. Tragedy came when Flying Officer McParland, who had flown with, become friends of, and gotten drunk with, Dennis and Mervyn, was killed on 16 April. His Mustang, KH560, 'pancaked' near Lugo following extensive damage by ack-ack. Bloomfield's logbook reports:

17 April: A./Recce. Celtje – Maribor – St. Viet. Clobbered a troop train. Seven locos damaged. Four trucks and two M./T. destroyed.

20 April: Anti-tank recce. N. Portomaggiore. One tank 'brewed'. Four M./T. damaged.

21 April: Attack ships – Parenzo. Both hit. One down by stern. Heavy 20 and 40mm.

As Blomfield's logbook notes, for much of March and April 260 Squadron attacked anything that moved on land and sea. Warrant Officer Fricker, when interviewed sixty years later, was very candid about his views when shooting up German lorries:

'The fact that there were human beings there didn't make a difference because we were getting a beating too and you would see the tracer coming up from the ground. They were trying to kill us […] the fact that you were killing people on the ground really wasn't a problem, it was a matter of, "If I don't kill him, he is going to kill me." And the other thing of course was that they weren't in their convoys in their trucks, they weren't sitting ducks. As soon as an aircraft was sighted, or as soon as the alert was given, they would pile out of the truck into slip trenches beside the road and the trucks would just be there. You could strafe them and they would burst into flames and in theory at least those trucks would be empty.

'Now on one occasion that I can remember there were about three trucks in a row and I was coming down to strafe them and a German soldier came out of a house over on the side of the road, raced across to get in his truck to drive it away. I thought at the time, he is a brave man. Having time just to think about it I pressed the trigger and his truck went up in flames and he was a dead man. But there was no sense of guilt or anything like that.'

One eyewitness to the aftermath of such an attack was Flight Sergeant Stan Watt of 450 Squadron, who encountered the wreckage of a German convoy destroyed the previous day:

'Bodies were hanging out of vehicles, or splayed like rag dolls across the ground. Wisps of smoke still drifted lazily from the burnt-out trucks. Flies were already buzzing, disturbing what would otherwise

have been an unearthly silence. One soldier appeared to have taken
a fighter's cannon-shot in the stomach, causing it to burst like a
watermelon.'

War is hell.

Victory

Since the end of 1944, the front had remained largely static. That changed on
9 April 1945, when British forces attacked in the east, followed five days later
by an American assault in the west. Cutting through enemy resistance, the attacks
converged on Bologna, which fell on 21 April. Four days later, the Allies crossed
the River Po, and Verona was captured on 26 April. Mussolini, who had earlier
been rescued from Italian captivity by German commandos, retreated north with
the Germans and their ISR allies. But he was captured by partisans and executed
on 28 April 1945. The following day, General Vietinghoff, commander of German
Army Group C, agreed to the unconditional surrender of all German forces in
Italy. British, US, and Soviet officers were present. The US 1st Armoured Division
reaches Lake Como. 239 Wing diary reports:

> The end of the month saw virtually the end of organised resistance
> in Italy and, as it broke, we created havoc among what little MT
> remained to him. In the last three days of the month over 50 MT
> were destroyed or damaged by the Wing in NE Italy so that, by the
> end of the month, the wheel had turned full circle with a slaughter of
> MT […] the month's final total of MT destroyed and damaged is the
> impressive figure of 1,139.

The 'bag' for 260 Squadron that month included four tanks, two 88mm, one
half-track, nine steam engines, nine railway wagons, three railway coaches, two
sloops and 138 MT destroyed. Sadly, with peace days away, two pilots were
lost, Lieutenant Gibbings, who was brought down by flak but bailed out, and
Warrant Officer Klinger, missing presumed killed. Gibbings had been posted from
450 Squadron on 2 October 1944. He was later reported safe. Albert Charles 'Bert'
Klinger, was flying KH 573 on 29 April 1945 as part of an armed recce into norther
Yugoslavia and southern Austria. In a statement by Flying Officer Masters, one of
the pilots in the formation, reported:

> 'I took off at 0615 hours on 29 April, flying as Blue 3, Klingner
> being number 2 (Blue 4). After about fifteen minutes, while
> flying across the Adriatic, the CO called Blue 4 and told him he

appeared to be losing petrol from the fuselage and to check his fuel cock.

'Blue 4 did not reply, and after being told twice more, still with no reply, I was detailed to escort him to base. Altitude at the time was about 4500ft. We turned and flew west and after about three minutes I suddenly saw KH 573 dive into the sea at about a 45 deg angle. I saw no parachute and although I searched the area for about fifteen minutes, before being joined by the rest of the squadron, who then searched, could see no sign of parachute or dinghy.'

A tragic waste of human life.

In Berlin, on 30 April, Adolf Hitler committed suicide in his bunker. Two days later, on 2 May the surrender signed by General Vietinghoff went into effect. The war in Italy was over and the 2nd New Zealand Division captured Trieste. Warrant Officer Fricker had finished his 200 hours on 28 April and:

'I was actually flying down from the squadron back to Egypt when the radio operator, we were in a DC3 and the radio operator came out and said, "The war is over. Hitler committed suicide; Admiral Doenitz has surrendered. The war is over." And all of the English-speaking people said, "Ahhh!" and I was sitting next to a Yugoslav partisan officer and he was looking puzzled, "What is all of this about?" So, I then said to him in English, "The war is over." He still didn't understand. So, I then said in German, "Das Krieg ist kaput." He still didn't understand so I said "Da warra is finita!" "Ahhh!" You know. So, we landed at Bari and everything was put on hold for twenty-four hours. There were none of the movements which should have gone on the next day.

'There was about six of us sitting in the transit mess in Bari […] and here was the six of us sitting there virtually crying into our Vermouth because we were all thinking about the blokes that had been killed; in my case, my particular mate Bert who came from Mackay was a married man with two small children, he had been killed only two days before.'

Victory in Europe Day was declared on 8 May. Blomfield noted in his Flying Logbook 'War Finito!', by which stage he had amassed a final tally of 228 operational sorties, totalling nearly 400 hours flying time. He was recommended for an immediate DSO. The original recommendation for an immediate award published in the *London Gazette* 13 July 1945. states:

Squadron Leader Blomfield has had command of his present squadron during a most difficult period. Almost coincident with his arrival the squadron converted from dive-bombers to rocket-projectiles, and it was almost entirely due to his outstanding enthusiasm and supervision that all pilots became speedily trained and very accurate with a completely new weapon which they wielded with great success for the final two months of the Italian campaign.

All types of targets were attacked, but chiefly road, rail and canal traffic, until the 'flare-up' on the Eighth Army's front when the squadron was diverted to gun positions, tanks and enemy occupied HQs, again with the same high degree of accuracy and success.

In all these attacks Squadron Leader Blomfield has proved himself to be an exceptional leader, his consistent accuracy both when using R/P and when strafing, regardless of personal safety in the face of intense A/A fire, had proved a splendid example to all his pilots, as proved by the following results obtained in the past two months of operations, when the squadron destroyed: 140 motor transport and damaged a further 236, as well as damaging 60 locomotives, tanks, barges, HQs and bridges.

After the Army's 'push' had started the squadron was again used in an anti-communication role, mostly around Northern Italy, Austria and North Yugoslavia, again creating havoc amongst the enemy's harassed columns. In this period Squadron Leader Blomfield destroyed one tank, five locomotives, twelve motor transport, and damaged six locomotives and twenty-three motor transport, and led the squadron on a final target when four ammunition dumps were completely destroyed, which coupled with his previous score of some forty-two locomotives destroyed or damaged, and forty-six motor transport destroyed or damaged with numerous trucks and H.D.V., proved a fitting end to this officer's share in the Italian campaign.

At all times cheerful, efficient and popular, this officer has been an asset both to his squadron and to the Wing under which he served and richly deserves an immediate D.S.O. for his exemplary service.

Blomfield and Nicholls had lasted two tours of operation with 260 Squadron. They had survived the lottery of life and death. DAF and 260 had won a hard-earned reputation for inter-service co-operation. DAF had tipped the balance for the allies after men and material had been shipped to Normandy or the beaches of southern France. 239 Operations Record Book states:

Churchill announced the surrender this afternoon and named tomorrow as Victory in Europe Day. Oddly enough celebrations were, generally speaking, far more mild than might have been expected. The odd rocket and a number of Very cartridges were let off, but the end of the War in Europe seems to have come as an anti-climax and many of us are now virtually out of a job [...] tho' there was considerable 'joy' at night. Units and groups held their own celebrations and there was many a hearty preparation of a heavy hangover.

Pilots and ground crew were exhausted. Many were simply glad to be alive. 260 Squadron was stood down in August 1945, gone but not forgotten. On the home front, Italy was all but forgotten as Jeane Cresswell remembers in 2002:

'VE Day, and the people of Wakefield celebrated in Wood Street outside the Town Hall. At school, we assembled at the usual time in the morning, but after assembly there was a ceremony when the flag was raised on the lawn and the whole school marched down to the Cathedral for a joint service of thanksgiving with the boys from QEGS, conducted by the Provost.

'That was alright as far as it went, but what of the War in Asia? I had a cousin, a captain on the staff at Bombay, and another somewhere in the jungle having gone through Burma with the Chindits. A cousin by marriage, Lister Simpson, a prisoner on the infamous Burma Railway, what of them and their war? Lister came back weighing less than six stone and Joyce could not see him for a year whilst he built his strength back. What of those who fought in Italy? My cousin Dennis had flown sorties over the Monastery of Monte Cassino. He was home in early '45, wounded, a changed man. He was never the same after the war. Those not at D-Day were branded 'D-Day Dodgers' by Lady Astor. Ever since, Dennis and my cousins Jim and Eric have been forgotten. War changes people: it defined my cousins lives as much as it did Daddy in the first war and all those at home on war work. Their sacrifice should not be forgotten.'

CHAPTER 19

SOME ENDINGS

BY EARLY 1944 it was estimated that a pilot had a 50/50 chance of serving their 200 hours tour of duty without being killed or made POW. Of that remaining fifty per cent, half would be wounded or maimed. So out of 100 pilots, twenty-five would complete a tour: 260 Squadron was no exception to this. Most of the pilots in 260 Squadron were aged twenty-three. Dennis, in his diary, called them boys. Instead of confiding in wives or lovers, Dennis, like many others, were writing letters to parents or family. It is a sobering statistic that almost all of those in 260 Squadron were too young to have seen the premieres of the movies of Fred Astaire and Ginger Rogers. As Shep Sheppard wrote when aged twenty-two in 1943, eighteen months service had made a boy into a man. This was true for all those who fought in the Second World War.

Fighter-bomber pilots were exposed to more stress and danger than the pilots of Lancasters and other heavy bombers. Bomber sorties averaged between five and seven hours, of which take off, forming up and getting to target would take up two-thirds of this time, leaving two hours or slightly more, in the 'critical zone' on the bombing run and over enemy territory. This made for seventy hours flying in the critical zone over thirty operations. For a fighter pilot, the average operation would be one hour twenty-five, one-third of which was in the critical zone, about sixty hours out of 200. In Italy, Shep Sheppard asserts:

> 'Landing grounds were closer to the front line and we found that invariably we were over the line in about ten to fifteen minutes and, therefore, time spent in the "critical zone" increased to something like sixty per cent of flying time. On this basis, added to the fact that one was being fired on nearly the whole of the time in the "critical zone" – heavy ack-ack, Breda, light ack-ack, machine gun and even rifle fire – the stress on these pilots was greatly increased and operational tours should have been between one hundred and one hundred and twenty hours.'

Fighter-Bomber pilots faced as much danger as bomber crews, yet their contribution to the war is often overlooked or ignored. He continues:

'One was being fired at nearly the whole of the time once crossing into German territory. In Italy we were fifteen minutes at most from crossing into occupied territory, thus flying time over occupied territory was much greater than in Africa. An operation over the German side would last an hour thirty, often two hours, which meant you were being shot at, often two or three times a day, for over an hour a time.

'Flight commanders, doctors, our intelligence officer and the adjutant all watched for signs of stress and fatigue because everyone is different in how they react under these trying circumstances. Experience to combat changed all the new pilots. They either became brash, willing to take risks and became trigger happy, or became calculating and daring, but more skilful. I always tried to weigh the risks before committing, and was mindful I had comrades to be mindful of.

'New pilots would fly one in six operations at first, increasing as they gained experienced. Flight and section leaders flew every operation, as would pairs leaders. The number 2s would be new pilots and only promoted to pair leader after fifty hours. The strain was colossal on the pair and flight leaders.'

Dennis's logbook shows he was made pair leader on 8 June 1944. Being pair leader was an increase in responsibility and participation in flying combat operations.

Fighter-bomber squadrons and Cab Rank paved the way for the development of close support air operations, which are commonplace today, with drones replacing pilots. The human cost in perfecting Cab Rank to allow the Allied Airforce's to be as successful as they were during Overlord, was significant. It is time to acknowledge the crucial role of the fighter-bomber pilot as much as bomber crews and fighter pilots.

The Italian campaign has come to be seen by the Allies as a massive holding attack. It had forced the Germans to keep a high proportion of their strength in the Mediterranean theatre and make the task of Allied forces elsewhere easier.

This strategy was controversial from the day it was agreed.

Indeed, it can equally be argued that the Germans were tying down Allied forces, which might have been better employed elsewhere. The same argument is used to state Operation Dragoon was likewise a failure, lengthened the war and made the Cold War inevitable.

Yet, the facts of the matter are, that for most of the last fourteen months of the war, the Germans deployed more divisions in Italy than the Allies. The fighting drew in German units that would otherwise have been deployed in northern or eastern Europe. As a diversion, the Italian campaign helped win the war. German casualties for the Italian campaign were around 336,000, while those of the Allies totalled

313,000. Italy also offered an ideal launch pad to send out heavy bombers to destroy oil production in the Balkans and destroy factories making aircraft for the Luftwaffe, which had been moved into Austria to avoid heavy bombing by the USAAF and Bomber Command from England. Crippling German manufacturing capacity was as important as drawing German troops away from the D-Day beaches. Wars are won through a combination of resource depletion – men, machines, equipment and the systems for training and production – as much as by great battles between armies. The Italian campaign was vital in the outcome of the war.

What of the pilots we followed in 260 Squadron?

Sparky Black died aged sixty-six in 1984: he left the RAF, and became ultimately a Judge.

Rick Rattle finished his tour in the Mediterranean on 8 March 1944 and was posted to 59 OTU at Crosby-on-Eden, in Cumberland. On expiry of his tour and the coming of peace, he returned to Ontario, Canada, where he married and had a family.

Shep Sheppard, seriously wounded, was sent back to England for further hospital treatment, with a broken back. Out of hospital by October 1944 he was grounded, having flown forty-four operations with 260 during 1944, taking his tally to 189. He had flown eighteen different types of aircraft ranging from the Tiger Moth, Spitfire, Hurricanes 'and the best fighter of the 39-45 war, the Mustang III (P51-C), [...] it had been a pretty hectic three years, crowded with excitement and activity and, on reflection I would not have missed any of it.' He died in 2005 at his home in Newport, South Wales.

Sergeant Mervyn Talbot had finished his tour of duty on 28 September 1944, and was posted on 16 October 44 to 3 Base Personal Depot close to Naples:

> 'I was lucky to survive 119 operations with the squadron, (of which I have details), with a total of 195 hours, this being the normal span for a tour of operations. We had used seven airfields in Italy, starting at Cutella and ending up at Iesi near Ancona. I had planned to stay on till Gus had finished his tour. Unfortunately, Gus was unable to leave at the same time as he was in hospital as a result of a shrapnel wound in his shoulder.
>
> 'He was in a bad way, but we did meet up again later.
>
> 'The day before I left, I was chewed out for the "egg runs" we ran, being told it was strictly forbidden to sell on issued fags and NAAFI items. All good things come to an end. After the dressing down, John's shook my hand, thanking me for the efforts we had gone to, to keep moral up. I guess he had to chew me out as it breached Kings Regs. Next stop for me was England and a "rest" tour as an instructor on operational procedures at OTUs at Rednal when I met up with Gus again. From Rednal, it was off to Montford Bridge and

finally Keevil in Wiltshire, all equipped with Mustangs, although we also converted to Spitfires because the Mustangs were shortly to be disposed of, due to lack of spare parts. The conversion procedure to a different aircraft is simplicity itself "There she is in dispersal, read the pilot's notes, hop in and take it up, fly it around for a while and bring it back!" This was the Vb mark and I thoroughly enjoyed a 55-minute trip to be able to put it through its paces and compare it to the Mustang. I also flew the Vc and finally the mark XVI.

'Two last bits of excitement. Firstly, I was asked to carry out a flight test on a Mustang and the engine cut out at about 600ft., there being a large wood directly ahead. Fortunately, as I lowered the nose to maintain flying speed the engine spluttered and picked up, but only briefly. I made a quick circuit on a stop/start basis and was glad to hand the aircraft back to the maintenance team.

'Soon after this I married, on 15 September 1945, with Dennis as my best man. My wife and I were able to live out at Westbury, from where I cycled the seven miles to Keevil on most days, until I was demobilized on 2 March 1946, having completed six years' service in the RAF and having logged 651 flying hours on six different types of aircraft.'

Mervyn died during 2007.

Armistice Day 1944, Flying Officer Lee was posted away from the squadron with the rank of Flight Lieutenant. The squadron diary reports:

Lee has been with the squadron since the latter part of the African campaign, and was greatly responsible for the smooth running of operations and the moves to Malta and Sicily when the invasion took part last year.

He was posted to fill a vacancy with the Mobile Operations Room Unit, MORU for short. On 21 December, Lee was posted as intelligence officer with 232 Wing. After the war, he went on to become an international film star. He died in 2015.

Another November leaver was Dennis Varey. The squadron diary reports:

25.11.44 Flight Sergeant Varey, who was wounded by flak on 23 August 1944, has been recommended by the Commanding Officer for employment on non-operational flying as he has suffered from general ill health since returning from hospital.

Squadron Leader Johns, recognised that Dennis did not lack courage or moral fibre, but his operational flying days were over due to stress trauma, and he needed to fly in relative safety away from flak. Dennis writes in his logbook 'Tour EXPIRED!!!!'. He was posted on 27 November to 38 Personnel Transit Camp at Semigallia, where he arrived on 5 December. It takes an incredibly brave person to cope with intense flak, coming close to being shot down a dozen times, seeing friends killed and ultimately being shot down and wounded yourself and to then go back to combat operations. It is impossible that Dennis or any other pilot in this situation was not affected psychologically. Following a severe traumatic brain injury, I was diagnosed with PTSD and have been in constant psychological care ever since due to being 'a poor coper' with adverse stress reaction. I fully empathise with my uncle when he notes in his logbook 'twitchy' or 'pilot ropy' when trying to carry on as normal and one's stress reaction is so overpowering as to make one not want to undertake the task at hand. We all react differently to stress. Flashbacks are one aspect of PTSD: I have those for my brain injury, and I'm sure pilots who were shot down, or seriously wounded, suffered flashbacks as much as I do. To face down these demons and keep flying shows Dennis's bravery in being able to return to duty and be shot at again by flak before being withdrawn from the front line.

Dennis's logbook records he had flown 129 operational hours on eighty sorties, totalling 439 hours flying experience since joining 22 EFTS. He arrived at Sorrento and 3 Base Personnel Depot on 7 December and remained till 21 December, before returning to where his operation tour of Italy began at Portici a year earlier.

After spending Christmas in Naples, Dennis sailed home on HMT *Scythia* on 27 December, arriving back in England on 6 January. On return he was granted a month's leave:

'A "rest" tour as an instructor with 61 OTU followed, arriving at Rednal on 5 February 1945, and then Montford Bridge in March flying Mustangs, Harvard's and at long last Spits. They were not as good as the Mustang. The Mustang was more robust and was more versatile. The Spitfires we had in Italy kept breaking down, and could not do the same types of operations as a Mustang. It's a ballet shoe compared to a boot, and we needed boots in Italy.

'I was posted in April to RAF Holme on Spalding Moor, flying Hurricanes. I was teaching night fighter pilots how to defend bombing wings. Not as fast on the level as the Mustang, the Hurricane performed well in the role assigned for them. I was here for most of April, and in May, it was off to 1660 Operational Conversion Unit, at Swinderby until October '45. Again, we had Spits and Hurricanes. I was given this ancient Hurricane to fly, but once I was up it had a total electrics failure and I had a prang, pancaking onto the Lincolnshire farm land.

'I was trained on the twin-engine Oxford, getting in a few hours solo, in preparation for my next move. I had flown a twin-engine Dakota in Italy as our squadron hack.

'Having flown both the Mk 2 Hurricane and Mk 5 Spitfires, the Hurricane was a better gun platform: it was more stable, and packed a bigger punch when armed with cannons. It could take damage the Spitfire could not. With legs out landing gear the Hurricane was much easier to land, rather than legs in on the Spitfire which gave it a much narrower tread. Until we put cannons on our kites, we had nothing to answer the 109. The Spit could turn tighter and faster than both the Hurricane and Mustang, but it lost power. In the Mustang you came out of the loop at the same speed you went in.

'In terms of the cockpit space, the Mustang was really more luxurious than anything we designed ourselves. The Mustang was a bloody good aircraft. When pushed, it could really shift. It had the same Rolls-Royce power plant as the Spit, but somehow, the Yanks got more speed and power from it. Wing design I think mattered here. The .50cal guns in the Mustang showed what the .303 in the Hurricane and Spit really were, pea shooters at a gun fight.

'I found myself sent to fighter command HQ in the middle weeks of October. I was there a month before returning to 61 OHU at Keevil, in Wiltshire, on Spitfires and Harvard's again, but also the wooden wonder, the Mosquito. It really was a marvellous plane to fly. I met up with Merve again.

'I spent much of November seconded to Rolls-Royce at Derby, learning how Merlin and Griffin engines were made. On leave that winter, I married Mary just before Christmas '45. I was able to occupy married quarters and cycle to work every day. Merve and his wife lived a few doors away.

'From then on, my task was training the pilots of the future. We were flying Mosquitos. It was from Keevil where I was discharged in July 46.'

Dennis died in February 2007. His colleague, Peter Blomfield, who commanded the squadron in the last months of the war was posted to No. 3 Squadron at Tangmere in July 1945. Here Blomfield gained experience on Tempests and, following brief service as Commanding Officer of No. 112 Squadron, ended his career at No. 104 Personnel Despatch Centre, Hednesford, in December of the same year. He died in 1995.

Ron Cundy earned the DFC and the DFM for gallantry when flying fighter-bomber sorties over Tobruk. His DFM citation reads: 'In the course of numerous operational sorties over enemy territory, Flt Lt Cundy has shown fine qualities of leadership, keenness and determination.' After leaving 260 Squadron, he then served with 452 Squadron RAAF and, from 1943, participated in the defence of Darwin. The squadron operated Spitfires for the entire conflict, first over Britain and then transferring to Australia to help defend the nation's northern towns from vicious Japanese air attacks. As the Allies pushed back the Japanese, the squadron also sortied over the Dutch East Indies. Ron passed away aged ninety-seven in July 2019.

Lyall Peterie Fricker left 260 Squadron on 8 May 1945 and was posted to 67 Squadron. On leaving the forces, he was appointed to the Commonwealth Office of Education in 1955 and held a variety of positions within the Commonwealth Department until 1970. Committed to education, he became South Australian Deputy Director General of the Department of Further Education in 1981 and in 1982 was appointed South Australian Director General of Technical and Further Education, a position he held until his retirement in 1988. He died in 2007

Stocky Edwards, after helping to form and instruct at the Middle East Central Gunnery School in El Ballah, Egypt, in December 1943, was posted to RCAF No. 417 Squadron in Italy, flying Spitfires, then was transferred to No. 92 East India Squadron in Italy. In February 1944 he shot down four enemy aircraft in twenty-six sorties over the Anzio beachhead, south of Rome. Edwards was then promoted to Squadron Leader with command of No. 274 RAF Squadron. In April, his squadron was posted to England with two other Spitfire squadrons flying support for operations that included D-Day, 6 June 1944. Through June and July, his squadron escorted bombers over Europe. He completed his second tour and was awarded a Bar to his DFC. In February 1945, at age twenty-three, he was promoted to Wing Commander of RCAF No. 127 Wing, heading four RCAF Spitfire squadrons over Europe. On 3 May 1945, Stocky flew his 373 and final sortie of the war, shooting down a JU 88. He was the last surviving veteran of 260 Squadron, and died approaching his 101st birthday in May 2022. With his passing, 260 Squadron slipped from memory to history.

This book is in their memory and all those Lady Astor called 'D-Day Dodgers'. Their war was as bitter as any faced in Normandy. Mythos has us believe no Allied soldiers were in Europe from Dunkirk to D-Day. This does all those men who lived and died in North Africa and the Italian campaign a disservice. Their war needs to be recognised. The Cab Rank and Aerial Artillery developed by 260 Squadron was vital in the outcome of the war. In 1940, during the campaign for France, the French asked Churchill for fighters to attack German armour and ground troops. Churchill replied fighters were for intercepting fighters and not for the role for which the French requested them for. By summer 1944, most types of fighter had become adapted for ground attack as fighter-bombers. The understanding of what airpower could achieve as tactical support was transformed by squadrons like 260. German General Vietinghoff, Commander of the German Army Group C in northern Italy, noted that the fighter-bombers were the most destructive weapon in the Allies arsenal, which:

'Hindered practically all essential movement at the local points. Even tanks could not move during the day because of the employment of fighter-bombers. The effectiveness of fighter-bombers lay in that their presence alone over the battlefield paralysed every movement.'

Air Chief Marshal Slessor of the RAF summed up the importance of DAF to the Italian campaign when he said, had it not been for the air force, the German army would have made the invasion impossible. In a small way, I hope the service and sacrifice of the boys in 260 Squadron and their comrades in arms across the squadrons of 239 Wing has told the story of the important part they and other fighter-bomber pilots played in the Allied victory in 1945.

BIBLIOGRAPHY

Archive Sources

Imperial War Museum
Documents 14379 Personnel Papers Chief Technician Pountain

The National Archives, Kew

AIR 26/315 No. 239 Wing: Operations Record Book 01 April 1942 – 31 December 1944

AIR 26/316 No. 239 Wing: Operations Record Book 01 January 1945 – 01 January 1947

AIR 26/317 No. 239 Wing: Operations Record Book 01 April 1942 – 31 July 1944. Appendices

AIR 26/318 No. 239 Wing: Operations Record Book 01 August 1944 – 31 December 1944 Appendices

AIR 26/319 No. 239 Wing: Operations Record Book 01 January 1945 – 31 May 1945. Appendices

AIR 27/1537 No. 260 Squadron: Operations Record Book 01 November 1940 – 31 December 1943

AIR 27/1538 No. 260 Squadron: Operations Record Book 01 January 1944 – 31 August 1945

AIR 49/126 No. 239 Wing: medical reports Oct. 1942 – June 1945

AIR 49/246 No. 250 (Sudan) Squadron, R.A.F: reports

WO 208/3319/1853 Escape/Evasion Reports Gordon George Rattle, Flying Officer, J. 17653, 260 Squadron

Digital Sources

https://www.3sqnraafasn.net/indexpages/story.htm
http://raf-112-squadron.org/billbarwick.html
http://www.450squadronraaf.org.au/home.html
https://griffonmerlin.com/wwii-interview/christopher-lee/

https://australiansatwarfilmarchive.unsw.edu.au/archive/165
https://australiansatwarfilmarchive.unsw.edu.au/archive/1354

Printed Sources

Richard Townshend Bickers, *The Desert Air War 1939-1945*. Leo Cooper: London, 1991

Ron Cundy, *A Gremlin on My Shoulder. The Story of an Australian Fighter Pilot*. AMHP: Loftus, 2001

Bryan Evans, *The Decisive Campaigns of the Desert Air Force 1942-1945*. Pen & Sword: Barnsley, 2014

Vic Flintham, *Close Call: RAF Close Air Support in the Mediterranean. Volume I Defeat in France to el Hamma 1939-1943*. Crecy: Manchester, 2021

Vic Flintham, *Close Call: RAF Close Air Support in the Mediterranean. Volume II Sicily to Victory in Italy 1943-1945*. Crecy: Manchester, 2022

James Holland, *Together We Stand: North Africa 1942-1943, Turning the Tide in the West*. London: Harper Collins, 2005

James Holland, *Sicily '43: The First Assault on Fortress Europe*. London: Bantam Press, 2020

James Holland, *The Savage Storm: The Battle for Italy 1943*. London: Bantam Press, 2023

James Holland, *Cassino '44: The Brutal Battle for Rome*. London: Bantam Press, 2024

Bert Horden, *Shark Squadron Pilot*. Independent Books: Bromley, 2002

Jeremy Lammi, *Canadians and War Volume 1*. Lammi Publishing: Alberta, 2016

Michael Lavigne and James F. Edwards, *Kittyhawk Pilot*. Turner-Warwick: Battleford, 1983

Robin Rhoderick-Jones, Pedro: *The Life and Death of a Fighter Ace*. Grub Street: London, 2010

Lionel J. Sheppard, *Some of our Victories*. Compaid Graphics: Warrington, 1994

Christopher Shores, et al *A History of the Mediterranean Air War 1940-1945*. Volume 3. Grub Street: London, 2016

Christopher Shores, et al *A History of the Mediterranean Air War 1940-1945*. Volume 4. Grub Street: London, 2018

Christopher Shores, et al *A History of the Mediterranean Air War 1940-1945*. Volume 5. Grub Street: London, 2021

Nick Thomas, *Kenneth 'Hawkeye' Lee DFC. Battle of Britain & Desert Air Force Fighter Ace*. Pen & Sword: Barnsley, 2011

Mark K. Wells, *Courage and Air Warfare: The Allied Aircrew Experience in the Second World War*. Frank Cass: London, 2014